PAULO FREIRE

A critical encounter

Edited by Peter McLaren and Peter Leonard

London and New York

The editors wish to give special thanks to Chris Rojek
for his encouragement and advice throughout this project.

First published in 1993
by Routledge
11 New Fetter Lane, London EC4P 4EE

Simultaneously published in the USA and Canada
by Routledge
a division of Routledge, Chapman and Hall, Inc.
29 West 35th Street, New York, NY 10001

Typeset in 10/12 pt Times by J&L Composition Ltd, Filey, North Yorkshire
Printed in Great Britain by
Mackays of Chatham PLC, Chatham, Kent

British Library Cataloguing in Publication Data
A catalogue record for this book is available from the British Library.

Library of Congress Cataloging in Publication Data
McLaren, Peter, 1948–
Paulo Freire: a critical encounter/edited by Peter McLaren and Peter Leonard.
p.   cm.
Foreword by Paulo Freire, translated from Portuguese.
Includes bibliographical references and index.
1. Education–Philosophy. 2. Educational sociology. [1. Freire, Paulo,
1921–   .] I. Leonard, Peter.
LB880.F732M35 1992
370′.1–dc20
92–9965
CIP
ISBN 0–415–03895–2 (hbk)
ISBN 0–415–08792–9 (pbk)

CONTENTS

NOTES ON THE
CONTRIBUTORS

Stanley Aronowitz is a former trade union activist and steelworker. He is a Professor of Sociology and Director of the Cultural Studies Program at the Graduate Center, City University of New York. His most recent book is *The Politics of Identity: Class, Culture and Social Movements*.

Henry A. Giroux holds the Waterbury Chair Professorship at Pennsylvania State University. His most recent book is *Border Crossings: Cultural Workers and the Politics of Education*.

bell hooks is the author of *Talking Back: Thinking Feminist, Thinking Black, Yearning: Race, Gender, and Cultural Politics* and, with Cornel West, *Breaking Bread: Insurgent Black Intellectual Life*. She is Professor of English and Women's Studies at Oberlin College.

Colin Lankshear is an educational consultant and writer based in Palmerston North, New Zealand. He has had a continuing involvement in research and small-scale developing projects in Nicaragua since 1984. Formerly with the Education Department at Auckland University, his books include *Literacy, Schooling and Revolution* and *Critical Literacy: Politics, Praxis and the Postmodern* (with Peter McLaren).

Peter Leonard is Professor of Social Work at McGill University, Montreal; formerly Professor of Applied Social Studies at the University of Warwick, UK. He is author of *Personality and Ideology* and other books and papers, and General Editor of *Critical Texts in Social Work and the Welfare State*. He is currently President of the Canadian Association of Schools of Social Work.

Donaldo Macedo is Professor of English and Director of the Bilingual Education and ESL Programs at the University of Massachusetts. He has co-authored, with Paulo Freire, *Literacy: Reading the Word and the World*.

Peter McLaren is Renowned Scholar in Residence and Director of the Center for Education and Cultural Studies at Miami University, Ohio. He is also Associate Professor in the Department of Educational Leadership.

He is the author of *Schooling as a Ritual Performance, Life in Schools* and is the co-editor with Henry A. Giroux of *Critical Pedagogy, the State, and Cultural Struggle*. Professor McLaren is on the international advisory board of the Paulo Freire Institute, São Paulo, Brazil.

Ira Shor is Professor of English at the Graduate Center of the City University of New York. With Paulo Freire, he co-authored *A Pedagogy for Liberation*. His other books are *Critical Teaching and Everyday Life*, *Empowering Education* and *Culture Wars: School and Society in the Conservative Restoration, 1969–1991*.

Tomaz Tadeu da Silva is Professor of Theory of Curriculum in the Department of Teaching and Curriculum at the Federal University of Rio Grande do Sul, Brazil. He also teaches Sociology of Education in the Graduate Program of Education at the same university. His writings on curriculum and the sociology of education have been published in several Brazilian journals of education. He is the editor of *Teoria & Educação*, and has recently finished writing *What Produces and What Reproduces in Education*, which is being published in Brazil.

Carlos Alberto Torres is an Assistant Professor in the Graduate School of Education at the University of California at Los Angeles. Widely published in Spanish, Portuguese and English, he is the author of *The Politics of Nonformal Education in Latin America* (also published in Portuguese); with Daniel Morales-Goméz, *The State, Corporatist Politics, and Educational Policy-making in Mexico*; and, most recently, *The Church, Society and Hegemony, A Critical Sociology of Religion in Latin America* (translated by Richard A. Young).

Cornel West is the author of *Prophetic Fragments, The American Evasion of Philosophy* and, with bell hooks, *Breaking Bread: Insurgent Black Intellectual Life*. He is Professor of Religion and Director of the Afro-American Studies Program at Princeton University.

FOREWORD

Paulo Freire

Translated by Donaldo Macedo

In this impressive volume, Peter McLaren and Peter Leonard have attempted to bring together a group of international scholars and educators in order to reflect upon my work as it has been taken up in various educational and political contexts in England, Africa, New Zealand, Latin America, and the United States. More than a testament to my work alone, however, this volume attempts to grapple with a number of pivotal issues currently engaged by critical scholars who have set out to refine and develop a critical pedagogy attentive to the changing face of social, cultural, gender, and global relations. These issues include, but are no means limited to, the manner in which subjectivity is constituted in language; the relationship among discourse, social action, and historical memory; the connection between interpretation and historical practice; and how forms of authority may be addressed and justified in the context of feminist pedagogy and practice. In short, this volume represents a foundational inquiry into the relationship between power and pedagogy.

I do not wish to direct attention to each of the chapters in turn, but rather to affirm some of the central principles of my work which are reflected therein, and in so doing attempt to clarify some issues which have been raised about my position on the politics of liberation.

Over the years, educators such as Henry Giroux, Peter McLaren, Ira Shor, Carlos Alberto Torres, Donaldo Macedo, and bell hooks, among others, have tried to reinvent my writings and research on literacy and pedagogy so that they may be applied to North American struggles for liberation in schools, the workplace, the home, and universities and colleges. In my view, this has been exceedingly productive work. A number of these authors have attempted to bring my work into conversation with European thinkers who represent what has come to be called 'modernist' and 'postmodernist' strains of thought.

Although my own work does not specifically address many of the issues contained in the work of those thinkers who are currently assessing the merits of postmodern critical thought, I nevertheless appreciate how much has been accomplished by what Giroux describes as 'critical postmodernist thought.' For example, Giroux's chapter in this volume, and those by McLaren, da Silva, and hooks, have, in their own respective ways, tried to illustrate the ways in which my understanding of subjectivity, experience, and power bear some resemblance to certain strains of poststructuralist thought. In addition, they attempt to reveal how some aspects of my work can be appropriated into and extended by critical postmodern educational practice, without sacrificing some of modernity's most laudable goals. I agree with Giroux and McLaren when they caution educators that excursions into the discourse of postmodern social theory are often purchased at the price of sacrificing narratives of freedom underwritten by an ethical imagination. I share their concern that current epistemological and ontological shifts taking place in social theory must be firmly grounded in human narratives of emancipation and social justice.

I also appreciate the attempts by feminist critics and educators to rethink my work through their own specific struggles. Since the 1970s I have learned much from feminism and have come to define my work as feminist, seeing feminism closely connected to the process of self-reflexivity and political action for human freedom. As the chapters in this volume attest, it is important to appreciate the multiplicity of modes of oppression suffered by women and people of color in the United States and elsewhere across the globe; it is as equally important to discount claims to a unitary experience of oppression not only among women, but with respect to all oppressed peoples. I have always challenged the essentialism reflected in claims of a unitary experience of class and gender, inasmuch as it is assumed that suffering is a seamless web always cut from the same cloth. Oppression must always be understood in its multiple and contradictory instances, just as liberation must be grounded in the particularity of suffering and struggle in concrete, historical experiences, without resorting to transcendental guarantees. This is why, as many of the authors in the book remind us, it is always important to foreground the particularity of oppression against a background of multiple possibilities. That is, it is important to redress and transform particular instances of suffering and oppression while at the same time recognizing the consequences for liberation not simply at the level of the nation state, but also in relation to emergent social movements, cultural forms, institutional practices, and the formation of critical modes of subjectivity.

While I have not undertaken deliberate discussions of the role of men in the development and practice of feminism, I have always maintained that a pedagogy of liberation must be structured as a partnership among groups of women and men devoid of hierarchical control and free of patriarchal assumptions. To this end, it is important, as the chapters in this volume make clear, that a critical pedagogy works best when it is coalitional and attentive to the role of power in experience. Such attentiveness, the authors maintain, is not undertaken to defend an already given social order but rather to participate in the construction of new social formations dependent upon divergent cultural and gendered practices, discourses, and identities.

One of the main messages of this book is that we must not lose sight of the need to recognize multiple constructions of power and authority in a society riven by inequalities of power and exclusionary divisions of privilege and how these are implicated in the constitution of subjectivity differentiated by race, class, and sexual preference. We produce history in our thinking, and in our dialogue and actions with others and as this book makes clear, there are many paths which we may take in our own development as historical actors and in the propagation of communities and societies in which we can struggle toward a better local and global future.

Another important position stressed in this volume is that as many new groups – both reformist and revolutionary – enter the field of action for liberation, there must be a growing recognition of new forms of subjectivity and new strategies of emancipatory praxis which are derived from non-Western settings or beyond the borders of so-called developed nations. Narratives of refusal and struggle which will lead to new forms of political culture and structures of radical democracy are not only emerging from Eastern Europe but from struggles in Latin America. Narratives of liberation must not ignore the cultural particularism of their roots, yet at the same time they must not abandon the opportunity to co-ordinate themselves on a global basis. The chapters in this volume also suggest that the hope which sustains stuggles for liberation arise with the experiences and the suffering of the oppressed, a hope which refuses at all costs to exercise a totalizing closure on their future.

It is clear from the messages contained in this book that the struggle for democracy is the centerpiece for the struggle for liberation. Yet it is also clear that democracy has different meanings for different peoples through-out the world. For some, it is synonymous with capitalism, the propagation of acquisitiveness and greed, the barbaric practices of colonialism, and conceptually opposed to socialism. For others, it is a process of achieving equality of social justice for all peoples through popular sovereignty. This book confronts the reader with the overarching question: What accounts for the passionate struggles which the idea of democracy has created in countries across the globe? But more significantly, what accounts for the fact that some countries have greater opportunities for realizing the dream of democracy while others cling only to its shadow which has been cast from the more industrialized and postindustrial nations? And why is it that when democracy is claimed to be victorious, such a victory can almost invariably be traced to the exploitation of the colonized other, to those who inhabit the vortex of imperialism and oppression – to those who live at the periphery of the global state known as the Third World? These are questions with which the authors in the McLaren and Leonard volume attempt to grapple.

The chapters in this volume offer no smooth consensus as to what, in effect, the consequences of democracy might be for the future. Yet they do point to directions which discourses of liberation might take, those which are purposeful, rational, dialectical, yet non-totalizing and open to the particular and specific needs of the oppressed. This, I believe, is a way to avoid both the totalizing Eurocentric and androcentric logic with its Hegelian roots, and the pessimism that comes from a critical theory solely trapped within a philosophy of non-identity. Narratives of liberation are always tied to people's stories, and what stories we choose to tell, and the way in which we decide to tell them, form the provisional basis of what a critical pedagogy of the future might mean. Such a pedagogy recognizes that identity is always personal and social and that while we cannot predict the path of historical action or name human agency in advance, we can never give up the struggle for self-formation and self-definition such that domination and suffering in this society are always minimized. To invent new identities as active, cultural agents for social change means to refuse to allow our personal and collective narratives of identity to be depoliticized at the level of everyday life. Postmodern theorists have begun to make it clear in their writings that what must contingently ground identity in a postmodern world in which subjectivity has become unmoored from its former narratives of social justice is a postcolonial politics of ethics and compassion.

What makes this volume so compelling is that the chapters offer more than simply a critique of prevailing structures of oppression which serve to reproduce privileged pathways to power, but also, to borrow a term from my friend and colleague Henry Giroux, a 'language of possibility.' That is, taken together these chapters constitute a search for an immanent transformation of schools, bureaucracies, and other sites of social and cultural possibility. The authors explore with an admirable insight the Utopian possibilities and practices constitutive of liberatory pedagogy: that is, the type of praxis required for people to become active participants in shaping the economic, social, cultural, and subjective formations that affect their lives and the lives of others. This means waging a cultural politics that seeks to make presently unassailable and impenetrable cultural borders indeterminate, that encourages new forms of political redress, a remapping of the boundaries of culture, and the creation of new self-formative practices and cultures of resistance that are capable of establishing new grounds of enfranchisement for all peoples.

PREFACE

Cornel West

Paulo Freire is the exemplary organic intellectual of our time. If Antonio Gramsci had not coined this term, we would have to invent it to describe the revolutionary character and moral content of the work and life of Paulo Freire. It is safe to say that his classic work, *Pedagogy of the Oppressed*, was a world-historical event for counter-hegemonic theorists and activists in search of new ways of linking social theory to narratives of human freedom. This complex lineage led Freire to put a premium on dialogue, the construction of new subjects of history and the creation of new social possibilities in history. In contrast to Hans-Georg Gadamer's call for dialogical hermeneutics and Richard Rorty's charge for edifying conservation, Freire's project of democratic dialogue is attuned to the concrete operations of power (in and out of the classroom) and grounded in the painful yet empowering process of conscientization. This process embraces a critical demystifying moment in which structures of domination are laid bare and political engagement is imperative. This unique fusion of social theory, moral outrage and political praxis constitutes a kind of pedagogical politics of conversion in which objects of history constitute themselves as active subjects of history ready to make a fundamental difference in the quality of the lives they individually and collectively live. Freire's genius is to explicate in this text and exemplify in his life the dynamics of this process of how ordinary people can and do make history in how they think, feel, act and love. Freire has the distinctive talent of being a profound theorist who remains 'on the ground' and a passionate activist who gets us 'off the ground' – that is, he makes what is abstract concrete without sacrificing subtlety, and he infuses this concrete way of being-in-the-world with a fire that fans and fuels our will to be free.

In this way, he adds new meaning to Marx's famous eleventh thesis on Feuerbach, 'the philosophers have only interpreted the world in various ways; the point, however, is to change it'. This new meaning consists of recasting philosophical reflection among subaltern peoples in their every-day life-settings and of reconceiving change as the creation of new

xiii

collective identities and social possibilities in history over against vicious forces of dehumanization. Paulo Freire dares to tread where even Marx refused to walk – on the terrain where the revolutionary *love* of struggling human beings sustains their faith in each other and keeps hope alive within themselves and in history.

EDITORS' INTRODUCTION
Absent discourses: Paulo Freire and the dangerous memories of liberation

This volume of chapters on the work of Paulo Freire is an intellectual contribution to the central political project of our time: how to struggle for the social transformation of our postmodern and postcolonial world in the interests of the liberation of subordinate populations and cultures from the structures and ideologies which dominate them. It is a domination which is in part traditional and in part the degrading consequence of the process of modernization, of the development of new forces and relations of production which negates for most of the world the potential for human freedom and physical well-being which the Western Enlightenment project has made its goal.

This is a book which centers on the work of Paulo Freire not primarily to celebrate him, but as its sub-title suggests, to engage in a critical encounter with a philosopher and revolutionary educator of pivotal significance to the project of liberation and social transformation. To participate in a productive dialogue with Freire is to become involved in a cultural politics which is committed to a belief in the transformative possibilities of willed human action, both individual and collective. The authors of this book, whatever the sources of their critiques or the varying interests they express, stand on the same side of the political struggle as that occupied by Paulo Freire. Even disagreement with Freire on any particular issue shows us that, in the words of Carlos Alberto Torres, 'we can stay with Freire or against Freire, but not without Freire.'

Many authors in this book refer to the biographical details of Freire's life and work. This is because he is a revolutionary activist whose concrete practice is the basis of his educational philosophy: his critical praxis demands attention. Over the last two decades in fact, few individuals have made such an innovative and far-reaching impact on educational practice throughout the world. As a Professor at the University of Recife in the early 1960s, Freire worked with peasants in the Brazilian Northeast during the country's national literacy campaign. At this time, he evolved a theory of literacy based on conviction that every human being is capable of critically engaging the world in a dialogical encounter with others. In 1964

1

Freire was arrested and later sent into exile after the military seized control of Brazil's government. He returned in June 1980, only after an amnesty was declared in 1979.

A respected and popular figure among advocates of radical educational and social change, Freire's work has been employed in literacy programs in dozens of countries spanning four continents. For example, his work has been instrumental in the literacy campaigns of Nicaragua, Cuba, Portugal, Chile, Angola, Tanzania, and Guinea-Bissau. Today, Freire's influence extends far beyond the area of literacy and includes developments in social work education, economics, sociology, liberation theology, participatory research, and critical pedagogy, developments of concern to a number of the authors of this book.

That Paulo Freire's work is making a leading contribution to central issues of contemporary political struggle, and the theory with which it is linked is evidenced throughout this volume. Most important for the reader to consider, is how Freire's theory and practice are situated in the context of crises which have currently a particular impact on us. Perhaps of deepest significance is the so-called 'failure of socialism' seen in the collapsing regime of the Soviet Union, the apparent stampede towards capitalist economic and social relations which characterizes the former socialist countries of Eastern Europe and the exclusionary and separatist politics of particularism, bringing with it new waves of nationalism but also xenophobic and anti-democratic social identities and new racist formations. The fact that these socialist experiments failed in part because they were not also democratic and emancipatory offers limited comfort, but Freire's work shows us that liberation and democracy cannot be *opposed* to socialism. These 'failures' are reflected in different forms in continuing struggles in Latin America, and all in the context of the growing hegemonic power of the United States in establishing a new capitalist eschatology and 'new world order' reflecting its own interest and in no way tied to the liberation of oppressed Third World peoples to which Freire has devoted his life.

At a quite different and related level is the crisis, or some would say, challenge, presented by postmodern social theory to which several authors give attention, including Freire in his Foreword. Postmodernist thought can be used in a critical, liberatory way, but in its most conservative form shows a lack of political will, in part mystified by its proliferation of new and difficult languages. However, as a critique of the failure of Marxism as a totalizing theory and practice of emancipation, postmodernist thought deconstructs the problems of grand theory and its relationship to 'techno-capitalism' in a valuable way and stands alongside feminism's critique of grand theory not only because grand theory has historically ignored or marginalized gender but because of its totalitarian and objectifying tendencies, a critique which we can see expressed throughout Freire's work.

2

Freire's philosophy also confronts the essentially Eurocentric nature of dominant traditional social and political thought – white man's theory. In his argument for the deconstruction of the category of 'the oppressed' and the acknowledgement of diversity, Freire, like the feminists, provides a rationale for the development of alternative forms of 'progressive' social and political thought, including an Afrocentric conception of the social world, of knowledge and of culture, related both to Africa itself and to the African Diaspora, populating both Latin America and North America. The same could be said of the possibilities of new social theory emerging from the 'Fourth World' of aboriginal peoples suffering from the colonization of their land and their cultures: the five hundred years of oppression and exploitation since the European invasions and settlement of the Americas and later of Australia.

In the current crisis of social theory and revolutionary possibilities, Freire stands, like Habermas, as a modernist, though not, we would argue against postmodernist critics, to be seen as a 'disappearing species' within a 'dying class.' Although his philosophy is rightly given substantial attention in this book, for Freire the politics of liberation is essentially about *doing* on the basis of a language of hope. His humanist philosophy, echoing the humanist Marx, centers on the ontological vocation of humans to become more fully human. To become more fully human involves discursive struggle over meaning: human subjects are, as in Marx, rooted in historical struggle. It is Freire's positive 'Utopianism' which is, perhaps, most attractive today in a climate of apolitical pessimism, for it refuses to be rendered powerless in the face of oppression; it emphasizes the need for courage and hope, and so helps us to continually renew our optimism through, as Giroux puts it, a 'language of possibility.' Freire's is a humanist project, *par excellence*.

In his Foreword to this volume, Paulo Freire identifies a number of issues dealt with by the authors which in his view are central. These include the relationship between his work and postmodernist thought and particularly the connection between language and subjectivity; the feminist critique and rethinking of his pedagogy; the constitution of subjectivity, its differentiation by class, race, and gender, and its relation to different forms and contexts of struggles for liberation. All of the authors address these major concerns to differing degrees from their own particular contexts, interests, and perspectives.

Paulo Freire's thought and work is revolutionary, but continuously in danger of being domesticated, as many authors suggest, by the 'progressives' in Western cultures into mere methodology. Stanley Aronowitz, in his essay on 'Paulo Freire's radical democratic humanism,' places considerable emphasis on this danger of incorporation and argues strongly for the revolutionary soundness of Freire's current emphasis on the struggle for a 'radical democracy' on the grounds that in the present

3

historical circumstances it is not realistic to put socialism on the immediate agenda. His is an interesting argument concerning the different forms that liberation can take in a postmodern era and is bound to raise many issues for debate. Equally interesting, perhaps, is Aronowitz's interpretation of Freire's analysis of the subordinancy of the subject to the social structure, an understanding of the ensemble of social relations which constitute the subject being based upon the use of psychoanalytic theory, especially Freud's theory of sado-masochism.

Ira Shor's chapter, 'Education is politics: Paulo Friere's critical pedagogy', shows how the essence of Freire's work lies in a focus on problem-posing as the basis of dialogical education, how resistance to this process may be overcome, and how the questioning of power and knowledge is a central expression of the development of critical consciousness.

In the debate on revolutionary practice in the context of a postmodern and postcolonial world, it is important to reassess theories of modernity, of which the most important is that of Critical Theory. Given the 'failure of socialism' in many countries and its connection with the 'failure' of Marxism as a theory of emancipation, what are the grounds for hope? Surely it is a hope which requires that the division between pedagogy and theory be broken, so that 'grand theories,' such as Critical Theory, can be reformulated in a way which develops concrete practices. Enter Paulo Freire!

But if revolutionary practice must interrogate and challenge grand theory, it must also, Freire insists, be based upon experience. The theory and practice promulgated by banking education is that which domesticates the student, whilst dialogical education is based on the process of praxis in which the cultural experience of the student seeks to define the social world and to challenge theory from the perspective of her/his oppression. The chapter entitled 'Knowledge under siege' by Tomaz Tadeu da Silva and Peter McLaren considers a major challenge to Freire's politics of praxis as posed by Dermeval Saviani, who has attempted to build an alternative to Freire's pedagogy. At the heart of Saviani's challenge is a disagreement over Freire's understanding of the relationship between discourse and experience. Da Silva and McLaren give extended attention and rebuttal to Saviani's criticisms and alternatives. The chapter by Peter McLaren and Tomaz Tadeu da Silva, 'Decentering pedagogy: critical literacy, resistance and the politics of memory', also directs attention to the possibilities and problems of experience in a pedagogy of liberation. They develop an analysis of 'historical remembrance' which, given the ambiguous role of stories and memories that may exclude social reality as well as connect to it, becomes in the postmodern situation of multiple subjectivities the act of redemptive remembering. McLaren and da Silva also discuss the critiques of Freire's work from postmodernist and postcolonialist perspectives.

4

Perhaps the theme most readily identified with Freire's work is that of literacy. What is quite evident if we examine literacy programmes world-wide is that they can be either mildly reformist or revolutionary in their intention and effects. In Colin Lankshear's words, they can be 'domesticating' or 'liberatory,' a distinction he uses to evaluate the notion of functional literacy in his chapter on 'Functional literacy from a Freirean point of view'. An exposition of Freire's humanist philosophy is used as a powerful critique of the Adult Functional Competency model as being narrowly instrumental and utilitarian and thus essentially reproducing oppressive relationships. He suggests that a humanizing model of functional literacy is possible, one which furthers the ontological historical vocation of humans to become more human, rather than reinforcing their subordinancy.

Whilst Freire's pedagogy originated in Third World countries, its connection to First World countries and to different historical circumstances raises significant issues in this volume. In a chapter on the Latin American and African political backgrounds to Freire's educational programs, Carlos Alberto Torres in 'From the *Pedagogy of the Oppressed* to *A Luta Continua*: the political pedagogy of Paulo Freire' raises important political questions about Freire's work. This neo-Marxist and specifically Gramscian interrogation about the kinds of struggles within which Freire's pedagogy has a place centers on whether it is a pre- or post-revolutionary pedagogy, and whether the development of critical consciousness might be thought of as the process of building a counter-hegemony. Questions about the political purposes to which 'progressive' pedagogy is put are especially important when a wealthy First World country develops programs to assist Third World countries to achieve certain social goals. How are we to judge such programs?

Described by bell hooks (Gloria Watkins) as a 'playful dialogue with myself,' 'bell hooks speaking about Paulo Freire – the man, his work' evokes the poignant memory of her first meeting with Freire and describes the ongoing dialogue she has had with his writings throughout the course of her own development as a radical intellectual and political activist. Defending her indebtedness to Freire's work in the face of challenges from (predominantly) white feminists, she places the sexism of Freire's language and his phallocentric concept of liberation within an historical perspective while at the same time stresses the importance of his ideas and his work for people of color and other peripheralized and oppressed groups in the United States.

This may be seen as a challenge to the revolutionary political commitment of the Western authors contributing to this book. Are we seeking transformation or reform? The possibilities, problems, and challenges of using Freirean philosophy and pedagogy in Western countries other than the United States are illustrated in Peter Leonard's chapter. Leonard's account of attempts to develop a critical social work education and practice in Britain is outlined in his chapter 'Critical pedagogy and state welfare: intellectual encounters with Freire and Gramsci, 1974–86', Leonard argues the critical importance of Freirean perspectives in social work education and shares with readers his personal struggle with the problems involved in recreating these perspectves in different cultural and historical conditions.

In an interview with Freire by Donaldo Macedo entitled 'A dialogue with Paulo Freire', Freire attempts to answer some of the issues raised by various authors in this volume, choosing to concentrate on the concept of gender and oppression. Macedo poses several challenging questions to Freire in this regard, drawing attention to the situatedness and location of oppression within specific historical moments and cultural sites. This affords Freire the opportunity not only to speak to the criticism leveled by feminists against *Pedagogy of the Oppressed* but also to clarify his political project which is decidedly feminist. The final essay by Henry Giroux, 'Paulo Freire and the politics of postcolonialism', situates Freire's work within a postcolonial discourse and raises serious questions surrounding the appropriation of Freire's work by Western metropolitan intellectuals. It also raises important theoretical and political concerns with respect to Freire's own work, especially with respect to his current location as a Brazilian intellectual. Giroux sounds a profound caution to First World theorists that they do not unwittingly incorporate Freire's work from a colonialist or neocolonialist perspective.

In our Introduction to this volume we, the editors, have focused our comments on Freire's praxis as a revolutionary educator and on the implications of this praxis for the emancipatory political struggles to which we are committed. We have done so with the intention of allowing Freire's work to be reinvented within the decolonizing spaces of new social and political discourses. But we have also been producers and readers of texts, Freire's and others, and so there are perhaps some critical reflections which we as readers and writers might give to the texts collected here. Freire is essentially concerned in his pedagogy with the culture of daily life, with *its* language, because this culture and language is, he believes, the base from which radical change can spring. Given the negative lesson of much of postmodern writing – its inaccessibility – we need to ask whether *our* language is accessible to those in, or near, the front line of struggle. What will the school teachers, social activists, social workers, or community organizers make of the texts we have written? We know that as an intellectual stratum we are continuously seduced into obscurity of language by the very nature of 'academic work' and the structure of university discourses – a dilemma agitating all intellectual labor at this current moment.

But we are also aware that the discourse of textual production goes beyond the issue of accessibility, and brushes up against the current assault today on the efficacy of theory in the process of political struggle. There are occasions, we believe, when new social conditions invite and some-times demand new and difficult vocabularies of meaning. Whilst as academics we are aware of the dangers associated with an uncritical allegiance to grand theories and master narratives, we also feel that critical social theory can enable the specificity of human suffering to be addressed in both global and local contexts in important ways.

In a recent interview with one of the editors,[1] Freire maintained that when presented with a difficult theoretical language, students always have the right to ask their teachers to translate their ideas. In responding to such a request, teachers have the obligation to strive to be simple, but never to be simplistic. We believe this distinction to be an important one. To be simple is to find ways to give words relevance and concreteness in the everyday world of the student without falsifying the meaning of the theoretical ideas being expressed. To be simplistic is to abuse the act of translation by reducing the theoretical ideas being expressed to a shadow of their original meaning in the misguided belief that students are incapable of grasping the central concepts underlying the theoretical formulations being discussed. The latter act of translation, notes Freire, is one of élitism. In striving to be simple but not simplistic, Freire is able to rupture the conditions for locating the academic theorist simply as an 'other' who is obsessed with either scholarly pedigree or pristine objectivity; similarly, Freire is able to disrupt the idea that more activist forms of social critique possess some kind of radical purity and authenticity that diminishes the emancipatory possibilities of the 'organic' or 'specific' intellectual. The answer is in translating theory, not retreating from it.

We hope that as the chapters in this volume are translated and discussed by readers, or groups of readers, their ideas may be made more simple but never simplistic. The readers of this book will take away from the texts what they wish, but for the writers their texts are not 'thrown to the wind,' nor hopefully are they produced within the narrowly defined reading formations of academics and educationalists, but are part also of a wider context, the emancipatory struggles in which many groups, populations, classes, and cultures are involved.

Peter McLaren, Cincinnati, Ohio
Peter Leonard, Montreal, Quebec

NOTE

1 Response by Paulo Freire to an essay by McLaren that was presented at a conference of invited scholars at Lesley College in Boston, 26 July 1991.

1

PAULO FREIRE'S RADICAL DEMOCRATIC HUMANISM

Stanley Aronowitz

THE FETISH OF METHOD

The name of Paulo Freire has reached near iconic proportions in the United States, Latin America and, indeed, in many parts of Europe. Like the cover comment by Jonathan Kozol on the US edition of Freire's major statement *Pedagogy of the Oppressed* (1990), his work has been typically received as a 'brilliant methodology of a highly charged political character.' Freire's ideas have been assimilated to the prevailing obsession of North American education, following a tendency in all the human and social sciences, with *methods* – of verifying knowledge and, in schools, of teaching, that is, transmitting knowledge to otherwise unprepared students. Within the United States it is not uncommon for teachers and administrators to say that they are 'using' the Freirean method in class-rooms. What they mean by this is indeterminate. Sometimes it merely connotes that teachers try to be 'interactive' with students; sometimes it signifies an attempt to structure classtime as, in part, a dialogue between the teacher and students; some even mean to 'empower' students by permitting them to talk in class without being ritualistically corrected as to the accuracy of their information, their grammar, or their formal mode of presentation. Or to be punished for dissenting knowledge. All of these are commendable practices, but they hardly require Freire as a cover.

Consequently, Freire is named a master teacher, a kind of Brazilian progressive educator with a unique way of helping students, especially those from impoverished families and communities. The term he employs to summarize his approach to education, 'pedagogy,' is often interpreted as a 'teaching' method rather than a philosophy or a social theory. Few who invoke his name make the distinction. To be sure, neither does the Oxford dictionary.[1] Yet, a careful reading of Freire's work combined with familiarity with the social and historical context within which it functions, obliges the distinction: nothing can be further from Freire's intention than to conflate his use of the term pedagogy with the traditional notion of teaching. For, he means to offer a system in which the locus of the learning

8

process is shifted from the teacher to the student. And this shift overtly signifies an altered *power* relationship, not only in the classroom but in the broader social canvas as well.

This type of extrapolation is fairly typical of the US reception of European philosophy and cultural criticism. For example, after more than a decade during which many in the humanities, especially literature, made a career out of working with the concept 'deconstruction' as formulated by Jacques Derrida, treating the French philosopher as a methodologist of literary criticism, one or two books finally appeared that reminded the American audience that Derrida is, after all, a philosopher and that his categories constituted an alternative to the collective systems of Western thought.[2] Some writers have even begun to grasp that Derrida may be considered as an ethicist. Similarly, another philosopher, Jurgen Habermas, has been taken up by sociology as well as a small fraction of younger philosophers and literary theorists and read in terms of their respective disciplines. What escapes many who have appropriated Habermas's categories is his project: to reconstruct historical materialism in a manner that takes into account the problem of communication and especially the non-revolutionary prospect of the contemporary world (Habermas 1979). Whether one agrees or disagrees with this judgement, the *political* configuration of his theoretical intervention ought to be inescapable, except for those bound by professional contexts.

None of these appropriations should be especially surprising. We are prone to metonymic readings, carving out our subjects to suit our own needs. In all of these cases, including that of Freire, there are elective affinities that make plausible the ways in which these philosophers and critics are read. For example, with the progressive education tradition, Freire rejects the 'banking' approach to pedagogy according to which teachers, working within the limits imposed by their academic discipline and training, open students' heads to the treasures of civilized knowledge. He insists that no genuine learning can occur unless students are actively involved, through *praxis* in controlling their own education (here 'praxis' is understood in the sense employed by several strains of Marxism – political practices informed by reflection). He is firmly on the side of a pedagogy that begins with helping students achieve a grasp of the concrete conditions of their daily lives, of the limits imposed by their situation on their ability to acquire what is sometimes called 'literacy', of the meaning of the truism 'knowledge is power.' Freire emphasizes 'reflection,' in which the student assimilates knowledge in accordance with his/her own needs, rather than rote learning and is dedicated, like some elements of the progressive tradition to helping the learner become a subject of his/her own education rather than an object of the system's educational agenda. Like many progressives, Freire assails education that focuses on individual mobility chances while eschewing collective self-transformation.[3]

There are enough resemblances here to validate the reduction of Freire to the Latin John Dewey. Accordingly, if one adopts this analogy, his frequent allusions to revolutionary left-wing politics can be explained as a local phenomenon connected to the events of the 1960s and early 1970s, especially the advent in Brazil of the military dictatorship in 1964, the resistance to it, and the powerful popular social movements, particularly in Chile, with which he worked. Presumably, given a more thoroughly democratic context such as that which marks the political systems of North America and Western Europe, the core of Freire's teaching, the Method, would become apparent.

Similarly, while Dewey wrote on science, ethics, logic, and politics among a host of other topics, outside the tiny band of Dewey specialists within schools of education, educational theory and practice routinely ignores the relationship between his general philosophical position and his education writings. And, until very recently he was virtually unread by professional philosophers. Once at the center of American philosophy, his ideas have been deployed (in the military sense) by an insistent minority in full-scale revolt against the prevailing analytic school. Needless to say, just as Freire's revolutionary politics are all but dismissed in the countries where he has been elevated to a teacher/saint, Dewey's engaged political liberalism is generally viewed as a (surpassed) expression of the outmoded stance of public intellectuals at the turn of the century until the immediate postwar period. What can professional Dewey scholars say about his role in the founding of the American Federation of Teachers in 1916, or his role as chair of the commission that investigated the murder of Leon Trotsky?

Since American education has been thoroughly integrated into the middle-class cultural ideal that holds out the promise of individual mobility to those who acquiesce to the curriculum, engaged intellectuals like Dewey and Freire remain 'relevant' to the extent that they can be portrayed within the dominant paradigms of the social sciences upon which educational theory rests. It is not surprising that Kozol can refer to Freire's 'methodology' given the depoliticization of educational theory and practice in the United States, that is, the relative isolation of education issues, at least until recently, from the wider economic, political, and cultural scenes. Seen this way his characterization of Freire as a 'highly charged politically provocative character' seems almost an afterthought, or more to the point, a personal tribute not crucially intertwined with the 'brilliant methodology.'

Ivan Illich's statement on the same cover that Freire's 'is a truly revolutionary pedagogy' comes closer to capturing what is at stake in his writing. The modifier 'revolutionary' rather than 'progressive' signifies an intention that is carefully elided by many of Freire's followers and admirers in schools. Or, the term must be instrumentalized to mean that the pedagogy itself, as a methodological protocol, represents a radical departure from banking or rote methods of instruction. Therefore, it is possible, if not legitimate, to intepret the significance of Freire's work not in the broader connotation of a pedagogy for life, but as a series of tools of effective teaching, techniques that the democratic and humanist teacher may employ to motivate students to imbibe the curriculum with enthusiasm instead of turning their backs on schooling.

True, Freire speaks of 'method', especially in Chapter 2 of *Pedagogy of the Oppressed*. In the early pages of this chapter, Freire seems to focus, in the narrow sense, on the 'teacher–pupil' relationship as if to valorize the tendency of much educational theory toward microanalysis. For example, he provides a detailed 'list' of characteristics of the banking method. Aside from obvious choices such as who speaks and who listens, Freire makes his central point: 'the teacher confuses the authority of knowledge with his own professional authority, which he sets in opposition to the freedom of the student.' From this and the other specifications issues the conclusion that in the banking method 'the teacher is the Subject of the learning process, while the pupils are the mere objects' (Freire 1990: 59).

To this 'method' Freire counterposes 'problem-posing education' where 'men [sic] develop their power to perceive critically *the way they exist* in the world with which and in which they find themselves; they come to see the world not as a static reality but as a reality in the process of transformation' (Freire 1990: 71). This is where most American educators stop. Taken alone, the tacit thesis according to which Freire, notwithstanding his political provocation, is essentially a phenomenological progressive who uses language not too distant from that of psychologists working in this tradition such as, say, Rollo May seems to be justifiable. There is reference here to see life not as a static state of being but as a process of *becoming*. This spiritually laced education talk might be found as well in the writing of George Leonard and other American educators. American educators influenced by phenomenology are, typically, concerned with saving individuals from the dehumanizing effects of what they perceive to be an alienating culture. With few exceptions, they have adopted the implicit pessimism of most of their forebears which, despairing of fundamental social transformation, focuses on individual salvation.

But I want to argue that the task of this revolutionary pedagogy is not to foster critical self-consciousness in order to improve cognitive learning, the student's self-esteem, or even to assist in 'his' aspiration to fulfill his human 'potential.' Rather, according to Freire,

Problem posing education is revolutionary futurity. Hence it is prophetic. . . . Hence it corresponds to the historical nature of man. Hence it affirms men as beings who transcend themselves. . . . Hence it identifies with the movement which engages men as beings aware

11

of their incompletion – an historical movement which has its point of departure, its subjects and its objective.

(Freire 1990: 72)

It is to the liberation of the oppressed as historical subjects within the framework of revolutionary objectives that Freire's pedagogy is directed. The 'method' is developed within a praxis, meaning here the link between knowledge and power through self-directed action. And contrary to the narrow, specialized methodologically oriented practices of most American education, Freire's pedagogy is grounded in a fully developed philosophical anthropology, that is, a theory of human nature, one might say a secular liberation theology, containing its own categories that are irreducible to virtually any other philosophy. What follows is an account of this philosophical intervention and its educational implications.

FREIRE'S HUMANISM

To speak of a philosophical anthropology in the era of the postmodern condition, and a poststructuralism which condemns any discourse that betrays even a hint of essentialism seems anachronistic. Indeed, any superficial reading of Freire's work can easily dismiss its theoretical scaffolding as quaint, however much it may be sincere. For example, we read:

The Pedagogy of the oppressed animated by authentic humanism (and not humanitarian) generosity presents itself as a pedagogy of man. Pedagogy which begins with the egoistic interests of the oppressors (an egoism cloaked in the false generosity of paternalism) and makes of the oppressed the objects of its humanitarianism, itself maintains and embodies oppression. It is an instrument of dehumanization.

(Freire 1990: 39)

Now, we have already learned about the 'fallacy of humanism' from the structuralists, especially Althusser and Lévi-Strauss. In Althusser's critique, humanism defines the object of knowledge 'man' as an essential being, subject to, but not constituted by, the multiplicity of relations of a given social formation (Althusser 1970). In adopting the language of humanism, Freire's debt to the early Marx and to Sartre is all too evident. He relies heavily on Marx, the Feuerbachian, whose materialism is severely tempered and reconfigured by a heavy dose of philosophical idealism. Recall Feuerbach's critique of religion in which human suffering is displaced to God's will (Feuerbach 1964). Feuerbach argues that religion is made by humans and the problems to which it refers can only be addressed here, on earth. As if to underscore his own formation by this

12

'flawed' tradition, Freire goes on to argue that the pedagogy he advocates addresses the problem of the authentication of humans by means of their self-transformation into a universal species:

> The truth is . . . that the oppressed are not 'marginals', are not men living 'outside' society. They have always been 'inside' – inside the structure that made them 'beings for others'. The solution is not to 'integrate' them into the structure of oppression but to transform the structure so they can become 'beings for themselves'. . . . They may discover through existential experience that their present way of life is irreconcilable with their vocation to become fully human. . . . If men are searchers and their ontological vocation is humanization, sooner or later they may perceive the contradiction in which banking education seeks to maintain them and then engage themselves in the struggle for their liberation.
>
> (Freire 1990: 61–2)

Echoes of Hegelianism here. Freire invokes the familiar humanistic Marxian project: the revolution's aim is to transform what Frantz Fanon terms 'the wretched of the earth' from 'beings for others' to 'beings for themselves,' a transformation that entails changing the conditions of material existence such as relations of ownership and control of labor and the lordship–bondage relation which is the psychosocial expression of the same thing.

Freire invokes the notion of the 'ontological vocation' to become human. In a brief dialogue with Lukács who, in his tribute to Lenin (Lukács 1970), endorses the role of the political vanguard to 'explain' the nature of the oppression to the masses, since their consciousness has been victimized by commodity fetishism Freire emphasizes the idea of self-liberation, proposing a pedagogy whose task is to unlock the intrinsic humanity of the oppressed. Here the notion of ontological vocation is identical with the universal, humanizing praxis of and by the most oppressed rather than 'for' them. For a genuine liberatory praxis does not cease even with the revolutionary act of self-liberation. The true vocation of humanization is to liberate humanity, including the oppressors and those, like teachers, who are frequently recruited from among the élite classes to work with the oppressed, but who unwittingly perpetuate domination through teaching.

Note here that Freire theorizes the class struggle, not as a zero sum game in which the victory of the oppressed constitutes a defeat for the oppressor, but as a praxis with universal significance and, more to the point, universal gain. For, as Freire argues, as oppressors of their fellow humans, the 'dominant elites' lose their humanity, are no longer capable of representing the general will to complete the project of humanization. *This* is the significance of working with the most oppressed, who in Brazil and the

13

rest of Latin America, are poor agricultural laborers and the unemployed huddled in the city's *flavellas*, shantytowns, which in São Paulo, for instance, harbor a million and a half people. Many of these are migrants from forest and agricultural regions that are in the process of being leveled for wood processing, mining and 'modern' corporate farming.

As we can see in the citation above, Freire plays ambiguously with Marx's notion that the working class is in 'radical chains.' Where Marx sees the working class 'in' but not 'of' society Freire insists they are 'inside the structure' that oppresses them. As we shall see, this phrase signifies Freire's move toward psychoanalytic theory as a sufficient explanation of which material circumstances are the necessary conditions for accounting for the reproduction of class domination.

In the light of this admittedly humanistic discourse, what can be said about Freire's philosophy that rescues it from the dread charge of essentialism, and thereby relegates the entire underpinning of Freire's pedagogy to its own historicity? A closer examination of the crucial category of the 'unfinished' shows the tension between his secular theology of liberation and the open futurity of the pedagogy. Taken at face value 'liberation', 'emancipation,' and 'self-transcendence' are teleologically wrought categories that presuppose an outcome already present in the 'project.' In this aspect of the question the goal, liberation, has the status of a *deus ex machina* of revolutionary action. For some critics, intellectuals, not the oppressed themselves, have designated the telos. It is intellectuals who have nominated themselves to deliver the subaltern from the yoke of material deprivation and spiritual domination. The oppressed must be the agent of universal humanization which, for Freire, is the real object of praxis. Taken at the surface of discourse, Freire can be indicted for reproducing the Leninist dictum according to which the task of the avant-garde intellectuals – in this case teachers – is to lead the masses into liberation.

But, as we shall see this judgement, however plausible, turns out to be misleading. I want to show that Freire's specific deployment of both pyschoanalytic theory and phenomenological Marxism leads to exactly opposite directions. Moreover, Freire is aware that his rhetorical moves may easily be interpreted as another kind of élitism and takes up this issue. Freire's overt debt to Erich Fromm's psychological equivalent of material oppression *the fear of freedom* comes into play (Fromm 1940). Freire takes from Freud, Reich, and especially Fromm the insistence that oppression is not only externally imposed but that the oppressed introject, at the psychological level, domination. This introjection takes the form of the fear by members of the oppressed classes that learning and the praxis to which it is ineluctably linked will alter their life's situation. The implication is that the oppressed have an investment in their oppression because it represents the already-known, however grim are the conditions of

14

everyday existence. In fact, Freire's pedagogy seems crucially directed to breaking the cycle of psychological oppression by engaging students in confronting their own lives, that is, to engage in a dialogue with their own fear as the representation within themselves, of the power of the oppressor. Freire's pedagogy is directed, then, not only to the project of assisting the oppressed to overcome material oppression but also attain freedom from the sado-masochism that these relationships embody. For Freire, profits and accumulation may account for exploitation of labor, but are insufficient explanations in the face of brutal domination. The dominating élites have a collective sadistic character corresponding to the masochism of the dominated. Freire quotes Fromm:

> The pleasure in complete domination over another person (or other animate creature) is the very essence of the sadistic drive. Another way of formulating the same thought is to say that the aim of sadism is to transform man into a thing, something animate into something inanimate since by complete and absolute control the living loses one essential quality of life – freedom.
>
> (Freire 1990: 45)

Freire goes on to say that 'sadism is a perverted love – a love of death, not of life.' The specific form of masochism is the 'colonized man', a category developed by Frantz Fanon and Albert Memmi. Memmi (1973) argues that the colonized both hate and are fatally attracted to the colonizer. In the educational situation this takes the form of deference to the 'professor'; the student may begin to generate themes but suddenly stop and say, 'We ought to keep quiet and let you talk. You are the one who knows. We don't know anything' (Freire 1990: 50). Although Freire does not mention the term 'masochism' that in this context manifests itself as the will to be dominated through introjecting the master's image of the oppressed, psychoanalysis insists that it is the dialectical inverse of sadism and that the two are inextricably linked. This introjection is, of course, the condition of consent without which sadism could not exist without resorting to utter force to impose its will. Or, to be more precise, would be met by resistance and a violence directed not horizontally among the oppressed, but vertically against the master.

It is not at all excessive to claim that the presuppositions of psychoanalytic theory are as fundamental to Freire's pedagogy as the existential Marxism that appears, on the surface, as the political and theological motivation of his discourse. For by positing the absolute necessity that the oppressed be self-emancipated rather than 'led' on the basis of struggles around their immediate interests by an avant-garde of revolutionary intellectuals, Freire has turned back upon his own teleological starting-point. For, the achievement of freedom, defined here as material, i.e. economic and political as well as spiritual liberation is a kind of *permanent* revolution in which the achievement of political power is merely a preliminary step.

Freire posits the absolute necessity of the oppressed to take charge of their own liberation, including the revolutionary process which, in the first place, is educational. In fact, despite occasional and approving references to Lenin, Freire enters a closely reasoned argument against vanguardism which typically takes the form of populism. In contrast to the ordinary meaning of this term in American political science and historiography, Freire shows that populism arises as a 'style of political action' marked by mediation (he calls this 'shuttling back and forth between the people and the dominant oligarchies' (Freire 1990: 147)). Moreover, he makes a similar criticism of some elements of the 'left' which, tempted by a 'quick return to power', enter into a 'dialogue with the dominant elites.' Freire makes a sharp distinction between political strategies that 'use' the movement to achieve political power (a charge often leveled against the Bolsheviks as well as the Communist parties) and 'fighting for an authentic popular organization' in which the people themselves are the autonomous sources of political decisions.

Freire's political philosophy, in the context of the historical debates within the revolutionary left, is neither populist, Leninist, nor, indeed, social-democratic in the contemporary sense, but libertarian in the tradition of Rosa Luxemburg, and the anarchists. Recall Luxemburg's sharp critique of Lenin's conception of the party as a vanguard organization, particularly his uncritical appropriation of Kautsky's claim that the working class, by its own efforts, could achieve merely trade union but not revolutionary consciousness. Inspired, in part, by Mao's conception of the *cultural* revolution in which the masses are, ideologically and practically, the crucial force or the movement is nothing, Freire's pedagogy can be seen as a set of practices that attempts to specify in greater concreteness than Mao did, the conditions for the fulfilment of this orientation.

Having proclaimed the aim of pedagogy to be the development of *revolutionary initiative from below*, Freire, none the less, rejects what he views as the two erroneous alternatives that have plagued the left since the founding of the modern socialist movements: on the one hand, leaders 'limit their action to stimulating . . . one demand' such as salary increases or they 'overrule this popular aspiration and substitute something more far reaching – but something which has not yet come to the forefront of the people's attention.' Freire's solution to this antinomy of populism and vanguardism is to find a 'synthesis' in which the demand for salaries is supported but posed as a 'problem' that on one level becomes an obstacle to the achievement of full 'humanization' through workers' ownership of their own labor. Again, workers pose wage increases as a solution to their felt oppression because they have internalized the oppressor's image of themselves and have not (yet) posed self-determination over the conditions

16

of their lives as an object of their political practice. They have not yet seen themselves *subjectively* (Marx 1975).

Freire's philosophy constitutes a tacit critique of poststructuralism's displacement of questions concerning class, gender and race to 'subject-positions' determined by discursive formations. The oppressed are situated within an economic and social structure and tied to it not only by their labor but also by the conditions of their psychological being. The task of his pedagogy is to encourage the emergence of a specific kind of discourse which presupposes a project for the formation of subjectivities that is increasingly separate from that of the structure. Freire's construction does not, *necessarily*, repudiate the theoretical principle that the world and its divisions is constituted as a series of discursive formations within which subjects pour themselves. But, he is addressing himself not to the bourgeois subject to which the old humanism refers – an individual 'consciousness' seeking the truth through reason, including science – but to the possibility of working with a new problematic of the subject. Unlike twentieth-century Marxism, especially in Third World contexts, which accepts the ineluctability of domination based upon its position that underdevelopment breeds more or less permanent dependency (just as Lukács and the Frankfurt School essentially hold to reification as a permanent barrier to self-emancipation) in all of its aspects, Freire's is a philosophy of *hope*.

Recall Freire's statement, 'problem posing education is revolutionary futurity.' Its prophetic character crucially depends on specific interventions rather than declarations of faith. The teacher/intellectual becomes a vehicle for liberation only by advancing a pedagogy that decisively transfers control of the educational enterprise from *her/himself* as subject to the subaltern student. The mediation between the dependent present and the independent future is *dialogic* education:

> Dialogue is the encounter between men *[sic]*, mediated by the world, in order to name the world. Hence dialogue cannot occur between those who want to name the world and those who do not wish this naming – between those who deny other men *[sic]* the right to speak their word and those whose right to speak has been denied to them. Those who have been denied their primordial right to speak their word must first reclaim and prevent the continuation of this dehumanizing aggression.

> (Freire 1990: 76)

Thus, Freire's deployment of psychoanalysis is not directed toward *personal* liberation but instead to new forms of social praxis. The basis of this praxis is, clearly, the overriding notion that humans are an unfinished project. This project, for Freire is grounded in his conception that to be fully human, in contrast to other species of animals, is to shed the image

17

according to which only the 'dominant elites,' including leftist intellectuals, can be self-directed. His pedagogy, which posits the central category of *dialogue*, entails that recovering the voice of the oppressed is the fundamental condition for human emancipation.

FROM REVOLUTION TO RADICAL DEMOCRACY

I have deliberately abstracted Freire's social, psychological, and political philosophy from the social context in which it emerged in order to reveal its intellectual content. However, one cannot leave matters here. Without completely historicizing the significance of this intervention, we are compelled to interrogate this revolutionary pedagogy in the light of the sweeping transformations in world economic, political, and cultural relations, to re-place Freire's philosophy and pedagogy in the emerging contemporary world political situation.

Of course, I need not rehearse here, in detail, the extent of the changes that have overtaken revolutionary Marxism since, say, the fall of the Berlin Wall in December 1989. It is enough for our purposes to invoke the world-transforming events in Eastern Europe. They were simultaneously liberating – the Soviet Union and the nations of that region may be entering a new epoch of democratic renewal – and disturbing. We are witnessing the collapse of bureaucratic and authoritarian state rule in favor of liberal democracy, the emergence of capitalism, or at least radically mixed economies, but also nationalism, accompanied by a burgeoning anti-Semitism and racism, even signs of resurgent monarchism.

In Latin America, the site of Freire's crucial educational practice not only in his native Brazil but also in pre-Pinochet Chile, revolutionary perspectives have, to say the least, suffered a palpable decline, not only after the defeat of the Sandinistas in the Nicaraguan election, but also in the choice by much of the erstwhile revolutionary Marxist left to place the struggle for democracy ahead of the class struggle and the struggle for socialism. Some have even theorized that, despite deepening poverty and despair for much of the population, socialism is no longer on the immediate agenda of Latin American societies in the wake of the world shifts that have decimated their economies, shifts that also encourage the formation of totalitarian military dictatorships. In this environment, recent political liberalizations have shown themselves to be fragile. For example, presidential democratic regimes in Argentina and Chile had hardly taken root before the military threatened to resume power to restore 'law and order.'

Some political theorists of the left, notably Norberto Bobbio, have forcefully and influentially argued that parliamentary democracy within the framework of a mixed economy dedicated to social justice is the farthest horizon of socialist objectives (Bobbio 1987a and 1987b). Following him, many leaders of the Brazilian left have acknowledged the limits of political transformation under conditions of underdevelopment. Others, while agreeing with the judgement according to which the revolutionary insurgencies of the 1960s and 1970s were profoundly misdirected, dispute Bobbio's thesis that *radical* democratic perspectives suffer from romantic nostalgia and would inevitably fail. What is important here is, in either case, a decisive scepticism concerning the prospects for revolutionary socialism, at least for the present.

Which raises the question of whether there can be a revolutionary pedagogy in non-revolutionary societies. Is it not the case that Freire's philosophy has been historically surpassed even if, in the context of its formation, it possessed the virtues of perspicacity? Under present circumstances, is it not enough to preserve Freire's work in a more modest form, as a teaching method? To be sure, Freire himself is excruciatingly aware of the changed circumstances of the late 1980s and the 1990s. On the occasion of his appointment to the post of secretary of education for the newly elected Workers' Party (PT) municipal administration in São Paulo, Freire told an interviewer that he saw in this unexpected victory 'a fantastic possibility for at least changing a little bit of our reality' (Williams 1990). The prospect for this radical left democratic administration was to achieve some reforms in health, transportation, and education. His perspective in accepting the post was to 'start the process of change' during the PT's four years of elective office.

Even before assuming office, Freire was aware of the severe limits to change posed by the economic and political situation. But he was also facing schools in which 60–70 percent of students dropped out and had barely four years of schooling, the majority of whom will be day laborers working for minimum wages. He was responsible for 30,000 teachers in the city's school system, many of whom lacked training for the awesome task of helping students break from the fatalism of Brazilian society.

In 1990, after a year of reform, Freire and his associates were speaking about democracy – social democracy – rather than 'revolution' in the strict political sense. The term 'popular democratic school' is counterposed to the 'capitalist' school. The capitalist school 'measures quality by the quantity of information it transmits to people,' says Freire's associate, Gadotti (Williams 1990). The popular school, on the other hand, measures quality by 'the class solidarity it succeeds in establishing in the school.' In order to achieve this objective the school must be 'deformalized,' debureaucratized, a measure that entails democratizing schools so that 'the community' elects the school director and there is direct accountability. This means the director can be removed at any time by the base but also that curriculum and other decisions are broadly shared. Freire uses the term 'accountability' to describe this desired relationship.

In the post-dictatorship period, one might say in the postcolonial situation, the popular-democratic philosophy has not changed, but the discourse is now eminently practical: as a schools administrator Freire speaks the language of praxis, rather than merely invoking it. The PT and its education secretary must address issues of teacher training, school-based decision-making, administration and curriculum, but from the base of a *working-class-oriented political formation that holds radical democratic reform toward popular power as its core ideology*. Freire is still trying to transfer power to the oppressed through education, now framed in the context of state-financed and controlled schooling.

SHARING POWER

In his 'spoken' book with Antonio Faundez, *Learning to Question* (1989) prepared before the PT victory, Freire had already altered his discursive practice. Throughout the text, Freire returns to the vexing relation between theory, ideological commitment, and political practice. Here, I want to give just one example of the degree to which his fundamental framework remains constant, even in the wake of the shift from revolutionary to democratic discourse. In one section Faundez and Freire engage in fascinating dialogue on intellectuals.

Faundez begins by reiterating a fairly well-known Marxist idea: that there is a social 'science,' a body of knowledge which is not merely descriptive of the present state of affairs, but 'guides all action for social change, how can we ensure that this scientific knowledge . . . actually coincides with the knowledge of the people' (Freire and Faundez 1989: 55–6). At this point Faundez contrasts the science possessed by intellectuals with the 'ideology' of the dominant classes that suffuses the people's knowledge as well as the diverse elements of practical knowledge, inconsistency between theory and practice, and so forth. The intellectuals as bearers of science find themselves caught in an excruciating paradox. On the one hand, they are bearers of scientific knowledge owing not so much to their talent as to their social position which gives them access to it. On the other hand, only by merging their science with the internalized knowledge of the people and, more particularly, fusing their vision of the future with popular imagined futures can the élitism of the various political vanguards be avoided.

As in most leftist discussions of intellectuals, Faundez draws from Gramsci's undeniably pioneering writings especially themes which Mao and Foucault are later to elaborate and develop: that all knowledge is specific, and that they are situated in a national context. Freire responds by objecting to the view that the future is *only* particular. He wants to preserve the universal in the particular and argues that we already have, in outline, a vision. But the nub of the problem remains: are the radical intellectuals prepared to share in the 'origination' of new visions with the masses or are these fixed so that the problem of coincidence is confined to strategy and tactics? Freire presses Faundez here to clarify the role of intellectuals in relation to the popular movements. Freire is plainly uneasy with the formulation that intellectuals are the chief bearers of scientific knowledge and wants to assert that to achieve radical democratic futures a fundamental shift in the relationship between intellectuals, especially their monopoly over scientific knowledge, and the movements must take place. Moreover, he is concerned to remove the curse 'bourgeois' from the concepts of democracy. A radical democracy would recognize that there are no fixed visions. And, if visions are fashioned from knowledge of the concrete situations gained through practice, there can be no science that provides certitude, either in its categories, its descriptions, much less its previsions.

Reporting on a conversation with workers' leaders in São Paulo, Freire *defines* class consciousness as the power and the will by workers and other oppressed and exploited strata to *share* in the formulation of the conditions of knowledge and futurity. This demand inevitably alters the situation of power: intellectuals must be consistent in the translation of their democratic visions to practice. In other words, they must share the power over knowledge, share the power to shape the future.

This exchange is a meditation on Latin American revolutionary history and current political reality, most especially the failure of Leninist versions of revolutionary Marxism and socialism. Explicitly, Freire warns against defining the goal of radical movements exclusively in terms of social justice and a more equitable society since these objectives can conceivably be partially achieved without shared decision-making, especially over knowledge and political futures. *The key move away from the old élitist conception in which the intellectuals play a dominant role is to challenge the identity of power with the state.* Faundez sets the stage for this shift:

> I think that the power and the struggle for power have to be rediscovered on the basis of resistance which makes up the power of the people, the semiological, linguistic, emotional, political and cultural expressions which the people use to resist the power of domination. And it is beginning from the power which I would call primary power, that power and the struggle for power have to be rediscovered.
>
> (Freire and Faundez 1989: 64)

Freire's reply sets a new ground for that rediscovery. Having focused traditionally on workers' and peasant movements, he now enters significantly into the debates about the relationship between class and social movements. He names movements of the urban and rural poor who, with the assistance of priests from the liberationist wing of the Catholic Church, began in the 1970s to redefine power as the power of resistance. But he goes on to speak of movements of 'environmentalists, organized women and homosexuals,' as 'new' social movements whose effectivity must inexorably influence the strategies of the revolutionary parties:

> It is my opinion today that either the revolutionary parties will work more closely with these movements and so prove their authenticity within them – and to do that they must rethink their own understanding of their party, which is tied up with their traditional practice – or they will be lost. Being lost would mean becoming more and more rigid and increasingly behaving in an elitist and authoritarian way vis a vis the masses, of whom they claim to be the salvation.
>
> (Freire and Faundez 1989: 66)

With these remarks, Freire distances himself from elements of his own revolutionary Marxist past, but not from a kind of open Marxism represented by Gramsci's work. For there can be no doubt that this comment is directed towards those in the revolutionary left for whom class defines the boundaries of political discourse. Without in any way renouncing class as a fundamental category of political struggle, Freire places himself in the company of those theorists, some of whom are situated in the social movements and not within the parties, who have challenged the priority of class over other social categories of oppression, resistance, and liberation. His intervention is also postmodern when he puts into question the claim of political parties to 'speak in behalf of a particular section of society.' In his latest work, Freire takes a global view, integrating the democratic ideology of the Guinea-Bissauan leader Amilcar Cabral with whom he had forged a close relationship.

Freire is sympathetic to Faundez's reminder that knowledge and its bearers are always specific, that historical agency is always situated in a national context. Yet, with Cabral, he reiterates the need to 'overcome' some features of culture. This overcoming means that tendencies towards the valorization of 'localism' which frequently are merely masks for anti-intellectualism among populist-minded leaders, should be rejected. So, Freire's postcolonial, postmodern discourse does not sink into the rigidities that have frequently afflicted these perspectives. Finally, at the end of the day we can see that to appreciate difference does not resolve the knotty issues of judgement. Freire is an implacable opponent of bureaucracy that throttles popular initiative but suggests that workers for social change must retain their 'overall vision' (Freire and Faundez 1989: 123).

Redefining power democratically entails, at its core, interrogating the concept of 'representation.' The claim of revolutionary parties to represent workers, the masses, the popular majority rests in the final analysis on the status, not of the demand for social justice, for liberal parties may, under specific conditions, also make such claims. Instead, it rests on the rock of scientific certainty, at least as to the descriptive and prescriptive propositions of a body of knowledge whose bearers, the intellectuals, thereby legitimate their own right to leadership. Freire's call for *sharing* recognizes the unique position of intellectuals in the social and technical division of labor and thereby disclaims the stance of populism that, almost always, renounces the role of intellectuals in social movements and, with that renunciation, is left with a vision of the future in the images of the present. But, by breaking with the 'state', i.e. coercion and representation as its key features, it also rejects the notion that liberation means the hegemony of intellectuals – political, scientific, cultural – over the movements.

In this way, any attempt to interpret Freire's recent positions as a *retreat* from the revolutionary pedagogy of his earlier work is entirely unjustified. On the contrary, Freire reveals his undogmatic, open thought in his most recent work. In fact, it may be argued that the Christian liberation theology of the past two decades is a kind of vindication of his own secular theology with its categories of authenticity, humanization, and self-emancipation. The paradoxes in his political thought are not apparent, they are real. For like the rest of us, Freire is obliged to work within his own historicity, an 'overall vision' that is, at once, in global crisis and remains the only emancipatory vision of a democratic, libertarian vision we have.

NOTES

1 'Pedagogy – The work or occupation of teaching. . . . the science or art of teaching.' *Oxford English Dictionary* (complete edition), (New York, Oxford University Press, 1971), p. 604.
2 See, especially, Stephen W. Melville, *Philosophy Beside Itself: On Deconstruction and Modernism* (Minneapolis, University of Minnesota Press, 1986).
3 John Dewey, himself, is a model for the idea of *collective* self-transformation; see his *Democracy in Education* (Glencoe, Illinois, Free Press, 1959).

REFERENCES

Althusser, L. (1970) *For Marx*, New York. Vintage.
Bobbio, N. (1987a) *Future of Democracy*, Minneapolis, University of Minnesota Press.
—— (1987b) *Which Socialism?*, Minneapolis, University of Minnesota Press.
Feuerbach, L. (1964) *The Essence of Christianity*, New York.
Freire, P. (1990) *Pedagogy of the Oppressed*, New York, Continuum.
Freire, P. and Faundez, A. (1989) *Learning to Question: A Pedagogy of Liberation*, New York, Continuum.
Fromm, E. (1940) *Escape from Freedom*, New York, Holt, Rinehart and Winston.
Habermas, J. (1979) 'The reconstruction of historical materialism,' in *Communication and the Evolution of Society*, Boston, Beacon Press.
Lukács, G. (1970) *Lenin*, London, New Left Books.

Marx, K. (1975) 'Thesis on Feuerbach,' in *Early Writings*, ed. D. Fernbach, New York, Vintage.
Memmi, A. (1973) *The Colonizer and the Colonized*, New York, Holt, Rinehart and Winston.
Williams, E. (1990) Interview with Paulo Freire, São Paulo.

2

EDUCATION IS POLITICS
Paulo Freire's critical pedagogy
Ira Shor

LIBERATING VERSUS DOMESTICATING EDUCATION

'To be a good liberating educator,' Paulo Freire wrote to literacy teachers in Chile in 1971, 'you need above all to have faith in human beings. You need to love. You must be convinced that the fundamental effort of education is to help with the liberation of people, never their domestication. You must be convinced that when people reflect on their domination they begin a first step in changing their relationship to the world' (Freire 1971: 62).

Freire's passion for justice, for critical knowledge, and for social change stand out when you meet him or read his work. For Freire, teaching and learning are human experiences with profound social consequences. Education is not reducible to a mechanical method of instruction. Learning is not a quantity of information to be memorized or a package of skills to be transferred to students. Classrooms die as intellectual centers when they become delivery systems for lifeless bodies of knowledge. Instead of transferring facts and skills from teacher to students, a Freirean class invites students to think critically about subject matter, doctrines, the learning process itself, and their society.

Freire's social pedagogy defines education as one place where the individual and society are constructed, a social action which can either empower or domesticate students. In the liberating classroom suggested by Freire's ideas, teachers pose problems derived from student life, social issues, and academic subjects, in a mutually created dialogue.

This pedagogy challenges teachers and students to empower themselves for social change, to advance democracy and equality as they advance their literacy and knowledge. His critical methods ask teachers and students to question existing knowledge as part of the questioning habits appropriate for citizens in a democracy. In Freirean critical classrooms, teachers reject the methods which make students passive and anti-intellectual. They do not lecture students into sleepy silence. They do not prepare students for a life of political alienation in society. Rather, Freirean educators pose

25

critical problems to students, treat them as complicated, substantial human beings, and encourage curiosity and activism about knowledge and the world.

PROBLEM-POSING: THE KEY TO CRITICAL DIALOGUE

A Freirean critical teacher is a problem-poser who asks thought-provoking questions and who encourages students to ask their own questions. Through problem-posing, students learn to question answers rather than merely to answer questions. In this pedagogy, students experience education as something they do, not as something done to them. They are not empty vessels to be filled with facts, or sponges to be saturated with official information, or vacant bank accounts to be filled with deposits from the required syllabus.

Freire's famous metaphor for traditional education, the 'banking' method, focused on the stifling of creative and critical thought in mass education. In 'banking'-style classrooms, Freire wrote that:

> Education thus becomes an act of depositing, in which the students are the depositories and the teacher is the depositor. Instead of communicating, the teacher issues communiques and makes deposits which the students patiently receive, memorize, and repeat. . . . In the banking concept of education, knowledge is a gift bestowed by those who consider themselves knowledgeable upon those whom they consider to know nothing. . . . The more students work at storing the deposits entrusted to them, the less they develop the critical consciousness which would result from their intervention in the world as transformers of that world.
>
> (Freire 1970: 58, 60)

Instead of banking education which domesticates students, problem-posing offers a search for knowledge. In this mutual search, the teacher and students develop 'co-intentionality,' that is, mutual intentions, which make the study collectively owned, not the teacher's sole property. This mutuality helps students and teacher overcome the alienation from each other developed year by year in traditional banking classrooms, where a one-way monologue of teacher–talk silences students. Co-intentionality begins when the teacher presents a problem for inquiry related to a key aspect of student experience, so that students see their thought and language (subjectivity) in the study.

Knowing, to Freire, means being an active subject who questions and transforms. To learn is to recreate the way we see ourselves, our education, and our society. 'We wanted a literacy program,' Freire wrote in *Education for Critical Consciousness* (1973), 'which would be an introduction to the democratization of culture . . . a program which itself would be an act of creation, capable of releasing other creative acts, one in which students would develop the impatience and vivacity which characterize search and invention' (p. 43).

Searching and inventing, the liberating classroom is a politics for cultural democracy. In *A Pedagogy for Liberation* (1987), Freire said:

> This is a great discovery, education is politics! When a teacher discovers that he or she is a politician, too, the teacher has to ask, What kind of politics am I doing in the classroom? That is, in favor of whom am I being a teacher? . . . The teacher works in favor of something and against something. Because of that she or he will have another great question, How to be consistent in my teaching practice with my political choice? I cannot proclaim my liberating dream and in the next day be authoritarian in my relationships with the students.
>
> (Shor and Freire 1987: 46)

Freire insists on consistency between the democratic values of this critical pedagogy and its classroom practices. The critical teacher must also be a democratic one. If the critical teacher criticizes inequality and the lack of democracy in society, and then teaches in an authoritarian way, she or he compromises her or his credibility. The empowering education Freire suggests is not a new data bank or doctrine delivered to students; it is, instead, a democratic and transformative relationship between students and teacher, students and learning, and students and society.

In this theory of learning, Freire argues that *the whole activity of education is political in nature*. Politics is not *one* aspect of teaching or learning. All forms of education are political, whether or not teachers and students acknowledge the politics in their work. Politics is in the teacher–student relationship, whether authoritarian or democratic. Politics is in the subjects chosen for the syllabus and in those left out. It is also in the method of choosing course content, whether it is a shared decision or only the teacher's prerogative, whether there is a negotiated curriculum in the classroom or one imposed unilaterally.

Politics also resides in the discourse of the classroom, in the way teachers and students talk to each other, in the questions and statements from teachers about the themes being studied, in the freedom students feel when questioning the curriculum, in the silences typically surrounding unorthodox questions and issues in traditional classrooms. Further, there is politics in the imposition of standardized tests, in grading and tracking policies, in the physical conditions of classrooms and buildings which send messages to students about their worth and place in society. Moreover, politics also resides in the punitive attitude of the curriculum towards everyday speech and non-standard English spoken by students, in the diminished role of art, dance, and music in lower-income schools, in the 'partnership' between local schools and businesses without partnerships

27

between schools and labor organizations, in the way schools are unequally funded depending on the economic class of students served, and in the unelected bureaucracy running most institutions.

'Education is politics' suggests that the entire school experience has political qualities and consequences. In schools and colleges governed from the top down by administrators, new generations of people develop. Schools construct people year by year, developing the way they think about the world and act in it. Traditional education orients students to conform, to accept inequality and their places in the status quo, to follow authority. Freirean critical education invites students to question the system they live in and the knowledge being offered them, to discuss what kind of future they want, including their right to elect authority and to remake the school and society they find. Education is politics because it is one place where individuals and society are constructed. Because human beings and their society are developed in one direction or another through education, the learning process cannot avoid being political.

Underlying Freire's definition of education as politics is a critique of domination and a commitment to challenge inequality and injustice. From a democratic point of view, Freire sees society controlled by an élite which imposes its culture and values as the standard. In schooling, this imposed standard is transferred by required syllabuses, mandated textbooks, tracking, and standardized exams. Freire wrote that, 'Any educational practice based on standardization, on what is laid down in advance, on routines in which everything is predetermined, is bureaucratizing and anti-democratic' (Freire and Faundez 1989: 41). For Freire, curriculum is controlled from above as a means to impose the dominant culture on each new generation of students. Knowledge is not neutral. Rather, it is the expression of historical moments where some groups exercise dominant power over others. That domination in school includes a traditional curriculum which interferes with the democratic and critical development of students. After years in passive classrooms, students do not see themselves as people who can transform knowledge and society.

INTERFERENCES TO TRANSFORMATIVE EDUCATION

Democratic dialogue in a critical classroom often faces resistance from school authorities, from students, from teachers, and from parents, who may defend traditional methods for complex reasons which cannot be examined fully here. The problem of student resistance to critical pedagogy is the most fascinating interference and the one faced most often by teachers experimenting with critical–democratic methods. Henry Giroux and Peter McLaren have written brilliantly on this problem in a number of works. Marilyn Frankenstein has placed student resistance into the context of maths education in her pathbreaking book *Relearning Mathematics* (1989).

I discussed it in some detail in *Critical Teaching and Everyday Life* (1987). Paul Willis explored the phenomenon of student resistance to schooling in a remarkable book on British working-class boys, *Learning to Labour* (1981). Briefly, in a school system devoted to banking pedagogy, students internalize values and habits which sabotage their critical thought. They develop as alienated and anti-intellectual adults after years in mass education and mass culture, where they are treated as objects filled with official ideas and supervised by authorities. Uncritical citizens who deny their own intellects and blame themselves for their own failures are the easiest to control, so it is understandable for the mass education system (invented decade by decade by authorities) to under-develop most students.

In traditional classrooms, students develop authority-dependence; they rehearse their futures as passive citizens and workers by learning that education means listening to teachers tell them what to do and what things mean. Freire points out that if a liberating teacher asks students to co-develop the class with her or him, the students often doubt that this is 'real' education. ('Real education' is something done to students, not something they do; 'real education' means the teacher telling students what to think and what to do instead of dialoguing and negotiating with them.) Or, in a liberating classroom emphasizing self-discipline and collaboration, students often think that *no* discipline is functioning because the teacher is not an authoritarian, giving them license to ignore the work or misbehave. Or, they sense that the democratic process and critical problems challenge the authoritarian, dominant values they have learned before, and they reject the invitation to question their internalized ideas, official knowledge, and the mainstream politics of their society.

This authority-dependence of students is matched by the authority-dependence of many teachers, who follow the traditional syllabus and resist democratic transformation, a problem Freire and I discussed in *A Pedagogy for Liberation* and which Giroux investigated in *Theory and Resistance in Education* (1983) and *Teachers as Intellectuals* (1988b). The transformation of teachers and students from authoritarian to democratic habits is a long-term project. After long years in traditional schools, teachers become conditioned to lecture, to assert their authority, to transfer official information and skills, as the proper way for professionals to do their work. It is not easy for them to share decision-making in the classroom, to negotiate the curriculum, to pose problems based in student thought and language, to lead a dialogue where student expression has an impact on the course of study, and to learn with and from students. 'A major problem in setting up the program,' Freire wrote about his literacy projects in Brazil, 'is instructing the teams of coordinators. Teaching the purely technical aspects of the procedure is not difficult. The difficulty lies rather in the creation of a new attitude – that of dialogue, so absent in our upbringing and education' (Freire 1973: 52). Freire referred impatiently to the 'instilled certainty' teachers learn, that to teach means to lecture, to maintain a one-way monologue in the classroom.

The banking method is the model from which teachers and students draw their instilled certainties about education. Not only does this method reduce the students' ability to question authority, but it is also posed as the high standards of a serious teacher. 'What I am concerned above all to do,' Freire said in *Learning to Question*, 'is to resist, theoretically and practically, two connections which are generally made. . . . The first is the connection between a democratic style and low academic standards; the second is that made between high academic standards and an authoritarian style. . . . Democracy and freedom are not a denial of high academic standards' (pp. 33, 34). His insistence on rigor and structure in liberating education preoccupied an entire chapter in *A Pedagogy for Liberation*.

Inside a rigorous dialogue, the teacher poses problems and asks questions, while encouraging students to do the same. But, the critical teacher who teaches for democracy and against inequality also has the right and the responsibility to put forward her or his ideas. The problem-posing teacher is not mute, value-free, or permissive. The democratic teacher in this pedagogy extends the critique of domination beyond teacher–student relations and the education system into a critique of the system at the root of social conditions. This critique of economics is not a teacherly lecture on good and evil. Dialogic teachers do not separate themselves from the dialogue. The teacher who relates economic power in society to the knowledge under inquiry in the classroom cannot impose her or his views on students but must present them inside a thematic discussion in language accessible to students, who have the freedom to question and disagree with the teacher's analysis. This delicate balance between teacher and students is a 'near mystery' of democratic practice, according to Freire, who suggests that teachers have to lead the class with a democratic learning process as well as with critical ideas. 'They must affirm themselves without thereby disaffirming their students,' he concludes in *Learning to Question* (p. 34).

MUTUAL AFFIRMATION: TEACHERS AND STUDENTS IN LIBERATING EDUCATION

In addition to a critique of domination underlying his pedagogy, Freire also poses an 'anthropological' notion of culture. According to this idea, culture is the actions and results of humans in society, the way people interact in their communities, and the addition people make to the world they find. Culture is what ordinary people do every day, how they behave, speak, relate, and make things. Everyone has and makes culture, not only aesthetic specialists or members of the élite. Culture is the speech and behavior in everyday life, which liberating educators study anthropologically before they can offer effective critical learning.

The anthropological definition of culture – situated in the experiences of everyday life, discovered by observing the community life of students – democratizes pedagogy because the curriculum is built around the themes and conditions of people's lives. Freirean educators study their students in their classrooms and in their community, to discover the words, ideas, conditions, and habits central to their experience. From this material, they identify 'generative words and themes' which represent the highest-profile issues in the speech and life of the community, as the foundational subject matter for a critical curriculum. These generative subjects are familiar words, experiences, situations, and relationships. They are 'problematized' by the teacher in class through a critical dialogue, that is, re-presented back to students as problems to reflect and act on. Inside problem-posing dialogue, students reflect on the lives they lead, asking questions to discover their meaning and value. They no longer live unreflectively in relation to these themes. Their experience now includes a self-reflective dimension because of problem-posing around generative themes from daily life. With dialogic reflection among their peers, they gain some critical distance on their conditions and can consider how to transform them.

Applied to academic courses, problem-posing situates special knowledge inside the language, experience, and conditions of the students. The subject matter is not presented as academic jargon or as theoretical lectures or as facts to memorize, but rather as problems posed in student experience and speech, for them to work on. In problem-posing, in teaching subject matter dialogically, academic material is integrated into student life and thought. Students do not simply memorize academic information about biology or economics or nursing, but rather face problems from their lives and society through the special lens offered by an academic discipline. This reflective posture is what Freire calls an 'epistemological relationship to reality,' that is, being a critical examiner of your experience, questioning and interpreting your life and education rather than merely walking through them.

In contrast, traditional education invents its themes, language, and materials from the top down rather than from the bottom up. In the official curriculum, culture is defined scholastically as the Great Books, or as a Great Tradition of literature, music, painting, etc., or as the correct usage of the upper classes, or as the information and experience familiar to the élite. This culture and language are alien to the lives of most students. Faced with unfamiliar scholastic culture, denied an anthropological appreciation of their own culture, students become cultural deficits dependent on the teacher as a delivery system for words, skills, and ideas, to teach them how to speak, think, and act like the dominant élite, whose ways of doing these things are the only ones acceptable.

31

QUESTIONING SOCIETY, POWER, AND KNOWLEDGE: CRITICAL CONSCIOUSNESS

Besides the critique of domination in society, the rejection of 'banking' methods, and the anthropological notion of culture, Freire's pedagogy includes the goal of 'critical consciousness.' Freire outlines several stages in consciousness growth which culminate in critical thought. The lowest stage is the most dominated, 'intransitive thought,' where people live fatalistically, thinking that their fate is out of their hands. Only luck or God can influence their lives. They do not think their action can change their conditions. Disempowered, they are stuck in time, under the thumb of the dominant élite now and forever, as far as they can tell. The next level of thought is 'semi-transitive,' where people exercise some thought and action for change. Partly empowered, they act to change things and make a difference, but they relate to problems one at a time in isolation, rather than seeing the whole system underlying any single issue. Semi-transitive people may also naïvely follow strong leaders with populist rhetoric, in the hope that one strong man can set the world right rather than they themselves having to make the changes needed.

Those people who do think holistically and critically about their conditions reflect the highest development of thought and action, 'critical consciousness.' Freire refers to this group's thought as 'critical transitivity,' to suggest the dynamism between critical thought and critical action. Here, the individual sees herself or himself making the changes needed. A critically transitive thinker feels empowered to think and to act on the conditions around her or him, and relates those conditions to the larger contexts of power in society.

Critical consciousness, the goal of Freirean education, could also be described as having four qualities:

1 *Power Awareness*. Knowing that society and history can be made and remade by human action and by organized groups; knowing who exercises dominant power in society for what ends and how power is currently organized and used in society.

2 *Critical Literacy*. Analytic habits of thinking, reading, writing, speaking, or discussing which go beneath surface impressions, traditional myths, mere opinions, and routine clichés; understanding the social contexts and consequences of any subject matter; discovering the deep meaning of any event, text, technique, process, object, statement, image, or situation; applying that meaning to your own context.

3 *Desocialization*. Recognizing and challenging the myths, values, behaviors, and language learned in mass culture; critically examining the regressive values operating in society, which are internalized into consciousness – such as racism, sexism, class bias, homophobia, a fascination with the rich and powerful, hero-worship,

32

excess consumerism, runaway individualism, militarism, and national chauvinism.

4 *Self-Organization/Self-Education*. Taking the initiative to transform school and society away from authoritarian relations and the undemocratic, unequal distribution of power; taking part in and initiating social change projects; overcoming the induced anti-intellectualism of mass education.

The Freirean pedagogy which tries to develop this critical consciousness is a student-centered dialogue which problematizes generative themes from everyday life as well as topical issues from society and academic subject matter from specific disciplines. An agenda of values for that pedagogy could describe it as:

1 *Participatory*. From the first hour of class, students are asked to participate in making their education by decoding thematic problems. The learning process is interactive and co-operative so that students do a lot of discussing and writing instead of listening to teacher-talk.

2 *Situated*. The course material is situated in student thought and language, beginning from their words and understandings of the material, relating the material to their conditions.

3 *Critical*. The class discussion encourages self-reflection and social reflection in terms of how we talk about issues, how we know what we know, how we can learn what we need to know, and how the learning process itself is working or not working. The students reflect critically on their own knowledge and language as well as on the subject matter, the quality of their learning process, and the relation of knowlege to society.

4 *Democratic*. The classroom discourse is democratic in so far as it is constructed mutually by students and teacher. Students have equal speaking rights in the dialogue as well as the right to negotiate the curriculum. They are asked to co-develop and evaluate the curriculum.

5 *Dialogic*. The basic format of the class is dialogue around problems posed by teacher and students. The teacher initiates this process and guides it into deeper phases. By frontloading questions and backloading lectures, the teacher invites students to assert their ownership of their education, building the dialogue with their words. They are doing education and making it, not having education done to them or made for them.

6 *Desocialization*. Freirean dialogue desocializes students from passivity in the classroom. It challenges their learned anti-intellectualism and authority-dependence (waiting to be told what to do and what things mean). It interferes with the students' silence, submission, and sabotage which they learn in traditional classrooms. Freirean education also desocializes teachers from the dull and domineering teacher-talk they are socialized into, transforming them into problem-posers and dialogue-leaders instead.

33

7 *Multicultural*. The class recognizes the various racial, ethnic, regional, age-based, and sexual cultures in society. It takes a critical attitude towards discrimination and inequality. It examines the cultures of dominant and non-dominant groups. The curriculum is balanced for gender, class, and race.

8 *Research-Oriented*. This critical pedagogy is based in classroom and community research by the teacher into the speech, behaviors, and conditions of the students, as well as into their levels of cognitive and affective development. It also expects students to be researchers inquiring into problems posed about daily experience, society, and academic material.

9 *Activist*. The classroom itself is active and interactive thanks to problem-posing, co-operative learning, and participatory formats. The critical dialogue also seeks action outcomes from the inquiry wherever feasible. Is knowledge power? How do people act on knowledge and from knowledge to gain power, to change things?

10 *Affective*. The critical, democratic classroom is interested in the broadest development of human feeling as well as the development of social inquiry and conceptual habits of mind. The problem-posing, dialogic method includes a range of emotions from humor to compassion to indignation.

This is one way to define some of the educational and political ideas which Freirean critical pedagogy offers to teachers and students. This educational terrain is still a frontier. There are many open spaces yet to be discovered. To be a critical, empowering educator is a choice to be what Henry Giroux has called a 'transformative intellectual.' Giroux's notions of 'civic courage' and a 'pedagogy of possibility' invite teachers to become change-agents in school and society, for critical thought and action, for democracy, equality, ecology, and peace, against domination, manipulation, and the waste of human and natural resources.

Inside the frontier of critical education, Freire has provided guidance and inspiration. But in making his contribution, he denies that his ideas or methods should be followed as rigid models. We have to reinvent liberating education for our own situations, according to Freire. One superb example of this local reinvention of Freirean ideas is the Adult Learning Project (ALP) in the Gorgie-Dalry district of Edinburgh, analyzed and chronicled by Gerri Kirkwood and Colin Kirkwood (1989) after a decade of development. Cool, northern Scotland is some distance from tropical Brazil, and the Kirkwoods report how their local conditions shaped the limits and possibilities for liberatory learning:

> It is important not to give the impression that ALP simply represents the uprooting of Freire's ideas from their Latin American setting and their transplantation into the foreign soil of Gorgie-Dalry.

Translation and adaptation are more appropriate metaphors, suggesting the need for sensitivity to the meaning of words in different cultures, and to changes of environment in the widest sense.

(Kirkwood and Kirkwood 1989: 26)

Our specific settings and conditions teach us the limits and openings for making change. These specific situations are the first and final arbiters of the methods we choose, the language we speak, and the ways we organize for change. About this challenge to adapt and reinvent his ideas, Freire observed:

That is exactly why I always say that the only way anyone has of applying in their situation any of the propositions I have made is precisely by redoing what I have done, that is, by not following me. In order to follow me it is essential not to follow me!

(Freire and Faundez 1989: 30)

Freire has opened a frontier of liberating education which we will have to develop in our own places, on our own terms, in our own words.

REFERENCES

Frankenstein, M. (1989) *Relearning Mathematics: A Different Third R – Radical Maths*, London, Free Association.

Freire, P. (1970) *Pedagogy of the Oppressed*, New York, Continuum.

—— (1971) 'To the Coordinator of a Culture Circle', *Convergence* 4(1), 61–2.

—— (1973) *Education for Critical Consciousness*, New York, Continuum.

Freire, P. and Faundez, A. (1989) *Learning to Question*, New York, Continuum.

Giroux, H. (1983) *Theory and Resistance in Education: A Pedagogy for the Opposition*, South Hadley, Bergin & Garvey.

—— (1988a) *Schooling and the Struggle for Public Life: Critical Pedagogy in the Modern Age*, Minneapolis, University of Minnesota Press.

—— (1988b) *Teachers as Intellectuals*, Minneapolis, University of Minnesota Press.

Kirkwood, G. and Kirkwood, C. (1989) *Living Adult Education: Freire in Scotland*, Milton Keynes, Open University Press.

McLaren, P. (1986) *Schooling as a Ritual Performance: Towards a Political Economy of Educational Symbols and Gestures*, London, Routledge.

—— (1989) *Life in Schools: An Introduction to Critical Pedagogy in the Foundations of Education*, New York, Longmans.

Shor, I. (1987) *Critical Teaching and Everyday Life*, Chicago, University of Chicago Press.

Shor, I. and Freire, P. (1987) *A Pedagogy for Liberation*, Westport, Connecticut, Bergin & Garvey.

Willis, P. (1981) *Learning to Labor: How Working Class Kids Get Working Class Jobs*, New York, Columbia University Press.

3

KNOWLEDGE UNDER SIEGE
The Brazilian debate

Tomaz Tadeu da Silva and Peter McLaren

The recent history of education and, particularly, of pedagogical ideas in Brazil, cannot be understood without reference to political events that have occurred since the early 1960s. In April, 1964, a military dictatorship ousted a democratically elected civil government following a brief period of intense popular agitation and participation demanding reforms. That military ruling lasted until 1985, when a civil president was elected, though still under the rules established by the military. The educational debate that we are going to analyze here must be viewed against this political background.

Freire's ideas and activities had their origins in those intensely political years of the early 1960s. The economic and social structure was one of great inequality and disparity (as it remains today). Most of the people were denied participation in the economic and social benefits deriving from development and capitalist expansion. In this context, adult illiteracy was only one of many outcomes of a system that was actively engaged in preventing a more egalitarian distribution of material and social resources.

Freire's ideas and activities were initially directed towards the creation of an educational alternative that could increase the political involvement of disenfranchised peoples in order that they might participate more directly in transforming those archaic and unjust political and economic structures that held the country in social limbo for so many years. Freire believed that this educational alternative should be developed within the existing order – the objective was to modernize it, not to revolutionize it (Beisiegel 1982). The climate of intense political radicalization that characterized the last moments of the João Goulart government, just before the military coup of March 1964, gave to the so-called Freirean System of Literacy a radical aspect not intended by Freire himself. Of course, Freire's thinking has changed since then, and has over the years acquired an intense and radical political character.

It was this re-elaboration of his initial ideas, whose most textured and definitive form is contained in his *Pedagogy of the Oppressed* (written in the years which followed the military coup of 1964 and his exile) which

36

came to be associated with Freire's name. Many of his conceptions have been adopted in educational programs around the world since then and have been very influential. Of course, this is the case also in his native Brazil. Following the coup (backed by US economic support and aid at the military and trade union level), the military government began a project of economic and social modernization, along with an intense political repression that included a suppression of civil liberties. In a wave of barbarism unprecedented in the country's history, thousands were arrested, tortured, or killed by both military and paramilitary assassination squads. Among the first to be targeted were priests, religious and lay persons active in movements for social change, and educators and university professors. In fact, education was one of the prime targets of the military government's crackdown.

The educational policy of the military government included the following:

1 A rationalization and modernization of the universities. The main lines of this project were drawn up through an agreement with USAID which came to be known as the MEC–USAID Accord (MEC means Ministry of Education).
2 A campaign of mass literacy which could presumably contribute to the integration of the great mass of illiterates into the global project of social modernization, which became known as MOBRAL (Movimento Brasileiro de Alfabetização).
3 A project of reform of elementary and secondary education in order to fit the outcome of education to the manpower needs of a modernizing economy.

These were the objectives of the educational project of the military dictatorship. Whether this was achieved as it was intended is another matter. It can even be debated whether the project was successful by its own criteria. What is certain, however, is that the educational debate in Brazil during the fifteen years or so that followed the coup was polarized between those government officials who planned and conducted the educational policy and those who opposed it.

The opposition came from many directions and also took many forms. Protests against the MEC–USAID Accord came primarily from social movements within the university – students and some professors. But it also came from rank-and-file teachers and researchers from disciplines such as sociology whose analysis of the educational policy of the military dictatorship revealed it to be a political instrument of its disastrous general social and economic policy. Research by Cunha (1975) and Freitag (1977) constituted exemplary and pioneering analyses which inaugurated a long and productive tradition of political and sociological critiques of governmental educational policy. Of course, Freire's thinking was very much present during these years. It served both as a theoretical framework to analyze some of the educational initiatives of the military dictatorship as well as an alternative basis for conducting pedagogical projects outside of the official sphere.

However, the vast majority of this opposition occurred within the limits of a very restricted political climate. Book publishing was permitted, but collective political activities were prohibited. It was only with the so-called *abertura* (political liberalization), initiated during the Geisel government (1974–9), and completed during the Figueiredo government (1979–85), that opposition to the educational policy of the military government achieved full expression. Its most visible and important symbol was the First Brazilian Conference on Education (Primeira CBE), held in São Paulo in 1980. It should also be noted that, with the process of political liberalization, many political exiles were permitted to return to the country, among them Paulo Freire.

Political liberalization allowed, among other things, state governors to be elected directly instead of being merely nominated by the central government. The first election of this type after the 1964 coup occurred in 1982. As a result, some of the opposition parties – mainly the PMDB, an ample alliance of opposition which ranged from the left to liberals, and the PDT, the party led by Leonel Brizola, an historical political leader – were able to come to power in some important states (PMDB in São Paulo, Minas Gerais, and Paraná; PDT in Rio de Janeiro). This new development meant that some of the ideas developed by educators who were critical of the educational policy of the dictatorship could be put in practice. In fact, some of those educators were to obtain prominent positions in the educational apparatus of those states.

All of these events – the political liberalization, the Conference of Education, the 1982 elections – meant that the politics of opposition in education was to be fractured, that radical educators were to be divided among different political positions that assumed distinctive objectives and strategies. The return of Paulo Freire to Brazil also meant that he was not a distant thinker anymore, someone only to be honored and praised as the symbolic figurehead of liberatory education. He was now an active participant in the political struggle, and he made this clear from the start by becoming affiliated with the Partido dos Trabalhadores (Workers' Party) which, together with the two Communist parties, represented Brazil's political left.

It is in this context that some educators on the left began to pose some questions to Freire's conceptions. There had already been an early critical study of Freire's thinking by Vanilda Paiva (1980), who connected the genesis of Freire's ideas and activities to the reformist ideology of the ISEB, a think-tank established during the Juscelino Kubitschek government (1956–61) to design and legitimate his model of economic and social development. But that was an analytical work which posed no practical alternatives.

Soon afterwards, the questioning came from an educational philosopher who intended to build a real alternative to Freire's pedagogy. Certainly this thinker, Dermeval Saviani, a researcher and professor at the Universidade de Campinas (a university financed by the State of São Paulo), and at PUC (Catholic University of São Paulo) knew that this was not a small and light task, given the prestige and respect that Paulo Freire had achieved not only in Brazil but throughout the entire world. It is the very prestige surrounding Freire's work that makes it hard to fathom how Saviani's ideas gained a momentum and an importance that perhaps he, himself, had not even dreamed.

What are the main elements of Saviani's refutation of Freire's pedagogy? It is well known that the main contribution of Paulo Freire was to politicize education. Freire saw educational practices to be infused with political objectives and to be reproductive of the existing, social, cultural, and economic relations of oppression and exploitation. Any alternative educational practice, including one oriented by emancipatory objectives, cannot be other than politically oriented because no educational practice can be neutral. And in a society organized around principles of hierarchization, inequality, and exploitation, education should be committed to exposing these relations, to making people aware of these asymmetries of power and to help them overcome these exploitative relations.

However, what makes Freire's pedagogy distinctive is that he links political content with pedagogical form. In a manner similar to educators connected to the 'new sociology of education,' Freire views knowledge to be closely connected to the contestability of social relations. Submissive and passive relationships with knowledge and among knowers (as between teacher and students) tend to be associated with corresponding relations among groups in the larger society. When students become the passive receptacles into which teachers deposit uncontested the meanings and interpretations of the dominant culture, students assume a subordinate position not only with respect to that knowledge but also with respect to corresponding class relations within the larger society where such knowledge is affirmed and legitimated. Thus Freire proposes a dialogical pedagogy in which learners and teacher engage in active interaction with knowledge in conditions of mutuality and respect. In other words, what makes education political for Freire is both its content and form and its relationship to the larger economic and social structure.

Saviani gives a drastic twist to Freire's argument.[1] For him, educational practice is distinctive from political practice. The two kinds of practice should not be conflated:

Any analysis, as superficial as it may be, of educational practice makes us see that, differently from political practice, education

39

is a relationship between non-antagonists. It is a presupposition of any educational relationship that the educator is acting in favor of the interests of the learner. . . . As for politics, the inverse is true. The most superficial analysis shows that the relationship here occurs fundamentally between antagonists. In the political arena there is a struggle between interests and perspectives which are mutually contradictory. As a consequence, in politics, the objective is to win, not to convince. . . . Conversely, in education the objective is to convince, not to win.

(Saviani 1983: 86)

Thus the fundamental concern of Saviani is not to make education and politics identical. If they were made so, then education would dissolve into politics and would lose its specificity. None the less, this does not mean that they are independent and autonomous. For Saviani, every educational practice has a political aspect to it just as every political practice has an educational aspect:

The political component of education means that as education is addressed to the non-antagonists it empowers them (or disempowers) in relation to the antagonists and thus empowers (or disempowers) their political practice. . . . The political dimension of education implies, thus, the appropriation (by the non-antagonists) of the cultural instruments which will be used in the struggle against the antagonists.

(Saviani 1983: 88)

Saviani makes a clear separation between politics and education. Education has a role in the transformation of society, but that role is not directly political. It is political in so far as it performs in an appropriate way its function of transmitting knowledge to the oppressed classes:

The political practice is supported by the truth of power; the educational practice by the power of truth. Now, we know that truth (knowledge) is not disinterested. However, we also know that, in a society divided by class, the dominant class is not interested in truth because this would make visible the domination it maintains over other classes. In contrast, the dominated class has the utmost reason to want truth to manifest itself, because this alone would show the exploitation to which it is submitted, stimulating it then to engage itself in the struggle for liberation.

(Saviani 1983: 91)

Saviani concludes that the political importance of education is situated in its function of knowledge socialization, that is, in its transmission of vledge. It is only in its specific role in knowledge socialization that education becomes political. Thus Saviani rejects the idea (obviously connected to Freire's work) that 'education is always a political act' (Saviani 1983: 94).

Of course, Saviani is not so naïve as to believe that knowledge should be uncritically transmitted. Throughout history, knowledge has been used as a vehicle by the dominant class for its own purposes and interests and so it should be submitted to criticism, challenged, and perhaps selectively appropriated by the dominated classes. This is why Saviani calls his perspective 'Pedagogia Histórico–Crítica' (historical–critical pedagogy) although it became known in Brazil simply as 'Pedagogia dos Conteúdos' (Pedagogy of Contents) which is a shorthand for 'Pedagogia Crítico–Social dos Conteúdos (Social–Critical Pedagogy Based on Contents) a label created by one of Saviani's prominent followers, José Carlos Libâneo.

Before we discuss Saviani's ideas we should say something about their most immediate sources. Perhaps the thinker that has exerted the greatest influence on Saviani's pedagogical ideas is Antonio Gramsci, if we are to judge by the many quotations he makes of Gramsci's works.[2] Another important influence has been George Snyders, a professor affiliated with the French Communist Party who has also been active in attacking the pedagogies based on active methods (Snyders 1974 and 1976).

While the syllogistic thinking of Saviani is frequently brilliant (and we have not done justice to it here), it is also conceptually limited. At the same time as it was acquiring a wide acceptance in leftist educational circles, it was being submitted to intense and serious criticism. We are not going to summarize this criticism here (see, for example, Nosella 1986 and Freitas 1987); rather we are going to limit ourselves to sketching our own critique of Saviani's ideas.

First of all, by failing to make a sociological analysis of the connections between knowledge, education, and power, Saviani is unable to build a pedagogical alternative which is distinct from existing liberal statements about education. He makes prescriptive assertions about what the connections between education and politics *should be* without analyzing what the present connections *are* like. He also ignores what critics like Bourdieu, Althusser, and others have taught us about those links. The most that Saviani can do is to make idealist statements about the role of education in relation to politics. Saviani is depoliticizing education at the same moment he proclaims that education is all the more political when it performs its specific function of transmitting existing knowledge, albeit in a critical way. How is it possible to challenge existing knowledge without challenging the connection between knowledge and politics?

Another problem with Saviani's perspective is the separation he makes between politics and education. In his view one becomes political in and through education by learning the truth about reality and society in order to (albeit instrumentally) act politically afterwards and outside of

41

education, presumably in the larger society. In school, one can *talk about politics, but not make politics*. Education becomes then *a preparation* for politics. Let us assume that Saviani is talking about children's education because it is immediately apparent that no adult education program can, in any strict sense, be separated from politics. Even so, to admit that one first learns to be political in school and then act politically in society, is equivalent to asserting a separation between theory and practice, between mind and action that would make of the individual a political schizoid. Here Saviani absolutely fails to take account of the discursive underpinnings of knowledge and the power/knowledge couplet so assiduously addressed by writers such as Foucault. Saviani adopts a position that, while retaining the language of the left, is fundamentally one which ignores both the vision and the intellectual power that social theory has bequeathed the left. This also raises the question of what is the appropriate arena for political struggle. For Saviani, this place is located somewhere in the larger society, presumably in the political parties. He is, however, not very clear about this, but it is clear that he is not referring to the school. School is presumably safeguarded against political conflicts because of the disinterested engagement of the participants in the educational encounter (teachers and learners) who seek out 'truth,' as seen above. Schools are then politically aseptic places, located outside the messy web of social conflict. But to say that politics is limited to a specific site is to accept weak liberal assumptions about the place and workings of power and thus to lose ground in the struggle over power. This obviously runs against the thrust of the most important ideas of Saviani's mentor, Antonio Gramsci, for whom the fight for cultural hegemony in all institutions of society is an important element in the strategy for its radical transformation.

The separation between politics and education advocated by Saviani is also made possible by the absence in his analysis of a theory of the state. By not placing education in the context of state apparatuses, a lesson Saviani should have learned, he is able to see it floating freely in a field of non-conflict. As an analysis of the state would show, the schooling system is part of the apparatus of the state, as both an *object of* political struggle and a *place for* political struggle. Perhaps educators should ideally be people concerned only with truth, as Saviani advocates, but any superficial analysis of the school system that reveals its interests in conflict within the state apparatus will also reveal that neither educators nor other aspects of the educational encounter (programs, curricula, textbooks, methods, etc.) are as neutral as Saviani wants them to be. Again, to ignore these connections is equivalent to making one powerless to break them. Disempowerment, not empowerment, is the result, just the opposite of what Saviani seeks in his pedagogy. Not unlike other educational critics of schooling, Saviani tends to take existing knowledge for granted even when he admits that it should be criticized. He approaches the problem of knowledge exclusively from the standpoint of its distribution and transmission, neglecting the examination of its circuits of production. It is this oversight that contributes to an idealized view of knowledge. For instance, absent in Saviani's analysis are the ways in which knowledge and science are produced and their connection to economic production and relations of power. As a consequence, it is easy to slip into the view that knowledge is 'out there,' waiting to be selected and transmitted. Again, there is no way of being critical about existing knowledge without analyzing how knowledge and power are connected and this means to act politically in relation to knowledge and knowledge acquisition, that is, to act politically *in education*, which is what Saviani initially rejects. Moreover, an approach which ignores the connections between existing knowledge and its discursive contexts of production tends to equate knowledge in general with school knowledge, which is what Saviani does. As a consequence, the complex ways in which knowledge is turned into school knowledge and the power relations involved in this transformation never get discussed. Again, politics is left outside only because Saviani wants to see it outside, for it is obvious that politics is there.

Many other objections could be raised against Saviani's approach. Most of them are related to the adoption itself of the notions of 'contents' and 'its transmission' as central concepts of his theory (da Silva 1987). It is very problematic to conceptualize pure 'content' as a stock of information as the crucial element in the process of cultural and social reproduction or in its inverse, the act of resistance. As Bourdieu and others have taught us, there is more to social reproduction and cultural domination than just the mastering of some set of factual knowledge. There is *habitus*, there is a *relationship* with knowledge, there is a socially situated relationship with language, all notions that take us far beyond the reductive notion of 'content'. In addition, the notions of 'content,' 'systematized knowledge,' 'socialization of knowledge,' all frequently used by Saviani, have a very positivist flavor. It implies that there is some stock of knowledge out there, not problematic at all, about which there is a general accord. This view ignores even the minor discrepancies among producers of knowledge in the so-called natural sciences, not to mention the obvious discrepancies in the social sciences. It ignores the always conflictual, socially constructed nature of knowledge by reducing it to a mausoleum of dead facts.

Moreover, these notions carry the connotation that any 'systematized knowledge' is benign, that knowledge only helps to 'organize' experience. As the so-called 'aid for development' given to underdeveloped countries by the United States in recent years has shown, 'modern information' has only helped to disorganize and to make more dependent many communities in the Third World. Again, the adoption of a model of knowledge transmission that does not take into account the implicit relations of power and does not challenge those relations in the very

43

act of knowing, as Paulo Freire so aptly taught us, cannot be emancipatory in any sense.

An emphasis on 'content' ignores the importance of form and the relationship between form and content. Here, too, Paulo Freire's view is more lucid. Freire emphasizes (but does not monumentalize) the question of method because he rightly finds that the way we come to know is inextricably connected to knowledge and its object. The form in which we know, the form in which knowledge and information are transmitted to us, helps to 'make' our consciousness. As any television producer or advertising executive has known since the age of McLuhan, the format may be more important than the content itself in transforming minds and hearts. Take, for example, any news show. The intended effect and affective investment are obtained as much by the format (dramatization, segmentation, fragmentation, events presented as spectacle, etc.) as by the content.

These are some of the problems involved in Saviani's approach. In sum, the reified notion of curriculum and knowledge implied in the emphasis given to 'content' as something to be transmitted, makes Saviani's theory very problematic as an educational project of emancipation. Contrary to his claims, an adoption of his approach entails social reproduction instead of social liberation. His neglect of the relationship between knowlege and power, and between culture and politics, is inimical to a project of emancipation because we cannot break those connections by simply ignoring them.

An alternative approach should, in our view, adopt the opposite view and would take advantage of the many insights Paulo Freire has given us about the relationship between power and knowledge. This approach would seek to locate knowledge, and particularly school knowledge, in a circuit of production, circulation, and acquisition in which social relations among different groups with differential access to power are considered. It would give priority to an analysis of the conditions in which different types of knowledge are produced, fought for, and established as valid. A theory about the relations among cultures, and the tensions and struggles for hegemony within and among them, constitutes a much more powerful basis for an emancipatory theory of curriculum than the belief in the existence of an abstract, universalized, and transcendental 'systematized knowledge' to be transmitted to the subaltern classes as an instrument of emancipation. A truly emancipatory theory of curriculum must see the field of production and distribution of knowledge itself, and consequently of education, as a field of struggle and search for hegemony.

In this chapter we have used Saviani's opposition to Freire's ideas to illustrate the current status of the pedagogical debate in Brazil. Although we have emphasized the differences between them, we should emphasize that the educational left in Brazil is more united around common objectives and strategies than separated by the differences we have described above. The alliance among the many and varied left constituencies during the writing of the New Constitution (1986–8) (which was drafted to guarantee some progressive educational principles) is only one example of this struggle for common goals. Perhaps the current debate around Freire's ideas could be viewed more as an affirmation of the vitality and fertility of leftist educational thinking of that same Latin American tradition to which Paulo Friere has contributed.

Nevertheless, the problems facing Brazilian educators are as great as ever. Like the distribution of wealth and other goods, education is still distributed in disproportionate amounts according to one's economic status. The most important struggle is still the one to guarantee access to and permanence in the public educational system for all. This is an objective around which there is full agreement. There is also agreement on the objective of the internal democratization of the educational structure. Instead of schools being directed by a distant and centralized bureaucracy, progressive educators are pressing for more voice and action for the people directly involved in the educational encounter – teachers, students, parents.

In conclusion, we can say that Paulo Freire's continued activism since his return to Brazil protects him against being reified and sanctified while still alive. If for nothing more, Saviani's objections to some of his ideas remain a useful and laudable contribution to radical pedagogical thinking and practice in Brazil.

NOTES

1 In one instance he builds an argument against the Escola Nova (as progressivism is known in Brazil) and Dewey's ideas. He argues that progressivist methods tend to be reactionary in that they are based on the assumption that learners should be engaged themselves in 'research' – that is, in the elaboration of knowledge. Children of the oppressed classes have been unable to get access to knowledge through such means, thus depriving them of possessing an important instrument of emancipation. This objection extends to Freire's pedagogy, which Saviani calls *Escola Nova Popular* (Saviani 1983). In contrast, he sees a pedagogy centered on the transmission of relevant content as essentially democratic.
2 Saviani's interpretation of Gramsci's educational ideas is similar to that of Entwistle in *Antonio Gramsci – Conservative Schooling for Radical Politics* (Entwistle 1979).

REFERENCES

Beisiegel, C. (1982) *Política e Educação Popular, A Teoria e a Prática de Paulo Freire no Brasil*, São Paulo, Atica.
Cunha, L. A. (1975) *Educação e Desenvolvimento Social no Brasil*, Rio de Janeiro, Francisco Alves.

Entwistle, H. (1979) *Antonio Gramsci – Conservative Schooling for Radical Politics*, London, Routledge & Kegan Paul.

Freitag, B. (1977) *Escola: Estado e Sociedade*, São Paulo, EDART.

Freitas, L. C. de (1987) 'Projeto histórico, ciência pedagógica e "didática"', *Educação e Sociedade* 27 September, 122–40.

Nosella, P. (1986) 'Educação tradicional e educação moderna. Debatendo com Saviani', *Educação e Sociedade* VIII (23), 106–35.

Paiva, V. (1980) *Paulo Freire e o Nacionalismo-Desenvolvimentista*, Rio de Janeiro, Civilização Brasileira.

Saviani, D. (1983) *Escola e Democracia*, São Paulo: Cortez/Autores Associados.

Silva, T. T. da (1987) 'Conteúdo: um conceito com falta de conteúdo?', *Revista de Educação*, AEC 16 (63), 20–4.

—— (1988) 'Production, knowledge, and education: the missing connection', paper given at the International Sociological Association, Salamanca, Spain (August).

Snyders, G. (1974) *Pedagogia Progressista*, Coimbra, Almedina.

—— (1976) *Para Onde Vão as Pedagogias Não-Diretivas*, Lisboa, Moraes.

4

DECENTERING PEDAGOGY

Critical literacy, resistance and the politics of memory[1]

Peter McLaren and Tomaz Tadeu da Silva

It is a commonplace assumption in both the United States and Brazil that educators are growing increasingly hesitant about the educational system; yet it is becoming singularly more difficult, if not impossible, for educators to ignore the relationships – in their most opprobrious sense – that obtain among educational policy and practice, the discourses and attendant symbolic economies that help constitute them, and the occlusion of issues of race, class, gender, and subjectivity from the purview of what has been touted as the current 'crisis of education'. In fact, it is no exaggeration to describe the present historical juncture as both perilous and challenging: as a time of political guile and improbity; a time of moral instability and social injustice; and yet a time when new possibilities and enablements present themselves as a means of reversing and perhaps even transforming the direction of governments that over the last decade have witnessed a steady attenuation of democracy. In short, we are facing with a mixture of optimism and deep unease a disenchanted modernity and the dawning of a portentous new postmodern epoch of shifting paradigms, degenerating borders, and an increasing contestability of familiar dichotomies of thought.

The current historical juncture has become a site where grotesque and sublime hybridizations of our social worlds and identities compete for the political space opened up by the erosion of certainty and the bankruptcy (and impossibility) of liberal humanism. It is further a site where identity has become annexed by advertising and marketing industries and where the nihilistic extrapolation of the mass-produced image provides the fundamental referents for structuring and 'promoting' human agency.

Global capitalism's theatre of terror continues to shape the social imagination of both the First and the Third Worlds with its insipid colonizing logic and its delusion-producing politics of desire. Its shift from organized to disorganized capitalism (post-Fordism in the West) has been accompanied by a shallow optimism, a grandiose banality and vulgarity, an increasing need for the production of autonomous pleasure and a growing indifference to the issue of class and cultural oppression. The geopolitical world arena, with its industrial and corporate co-efficients and the steady encroachment of multinationals, is producing just not just a monopoly on information but what could also be called empires of consciousness – regimes which structure our desires transculturally.

It is within such empires of consciousness (produced in part by the global race for ownership of the media industry by a half-dozen 'lords of the global village') that the meaning of literacy is taking on a new immediacy and importance; (see Bagdikian 1989). In this historical juncture – one in which illiteracy rates in the United States and Brazil are increasing in alarming proportions and everyday cultural life in more and more countries is witnessing a postmodern flight from historical meaning – the production of literacies takes on increasing importance.

This chapter examines the relationship among language, experience, memory, and the development of historical agency. It does so in the context of exploring recent work in the areas of critical literacy and critical pedagogy and rethinking the project of literacy in Western educational contexts. Our discussion takes its bearings from the work of Brazilian educator Paulo Freire, described in a recent interview with Carlos Alberto Torres (1990: 12) as 'the prime "animateur" for pedagogical innovation and change in the second half of this century.' In part, this chapter stands as a poststructuralist and postcolonialist rereading of Freire that, while to a certain extent 'reinventing' Freire's work in light of perspectives selectively culled from contemporary strands of critical social theory, attempts to remain faithful to the main contours of the Freirean problematic. More specifically, we shall draw upon some recent feminist and poststructuralist discussions of the relationship among language, experience, and memory to highlight the respects in which the Freirean perspective on literacy can be deepened. In Chapter 3 we examined Freire's work in the context of recent criticisms it has provoked in Brazil. In doing so, we hoped to bring to light some new perspectives for engaging Freire's work as a resource with which educators might enhance their general theoretical store in a way that enables them to situate their pedagogy as a fit converse between critical thought and emancipatory practice.

Our central argument is that pedagogies always produce specific forms of practical competencies – i.e. literacies – which, for the most part, have been pressed into the service of the dominant culture. This occurs through the particular ways in which knowledge is differentially inscribed into the social such that certain linguistic competencies, forms of ethical address (Giroux 1988), and ideological and political configurations are privileged over others and carry greater currency within the larger social order. We argue that, if appropriated with prescience and care, Freire's work can enable teachers to acquire a greater purchase on forms of critical practice that might serve to interrogate, destabilize, and disorganize dominant strategies of power and power/knowledge relations and in doing so envisage a means of enlisting pedagogy into the construction of a contestatory space where a radical and plural democracy might begin to take root.

We shall begin by addressing a concern that follows from a poststructuralist assumption: namely, that theory is a form of practice that involves the imbrication of experience, language, and power. In attempting to understand how knowledge is produced, one cannot simply give primacy to experience without taking into account how experience is structured and power is produced through language, whether this language refers to a tabloid editorial, local argot, or treatises on popular culture by critical theorists. In a similar fashion, one cannot simply privilege language because ideology is lived not only through language, but also through experience, that is, through discursive, non-discursive, and extratextual forms of knowing of the body (de Certeau 1984; McLaren 1988).

Experience takes into account the events we encounter, social practices we engage, choices we make, and accidents of history that befall us. For instance, reading about racism and oppression is not the same thing as living as its victim. A major consideration for the development of contextual, critical knowledge is affirming the experiences of students to the extent that their voices are acknowledged as an important part of the dialogue; but affirming students' voices does not necessarily mean that educators should take the meaning that students give to their experiences at face value, as if experience speaks romantically or even tragically for itself. The task of the critical educator is to provide the conditions for individuals to acquire a language that will enable them to reflect upon and shape their own experiences and in certain instances transform such experiences in the interest of a larger project of social responsibility (Giroux and McLaren 1989). This language is not the language of the metropolitan intellectual or the high-priests of the post-avant-garde, although it may borrow from their insights. It is a language that operates critically by promoting a deep affinity for the suffering of the oppressed and their struggle for liberation, by brushing commonsense experience against the grain, by interfering with the codes that bind cultural life shut and prevent its rehistoricization and politicization, by puncturing the authority of monumental culture and causing dominant representations to spill outside their prescribed and conventional limits. In the pages that follow, we will examine these issues in relation to Freire's perspective and his development of critical literacy.

Specifically with reference to the current literacy debate and the struggle with the academy over the canon, Freire's position eschews a tendency to see the world in Manichean terms, as gripped by a titanic struggle between forms of civilized high culture and the contaminating forces of the culture

49

of the masses. Freire's approach to literacy opposes the position of critics such as Allan Bloom, whose *Closing of the American Mind* (1987) has served as a reactionary bludgeon in debates over the liberal arts curriculum. In the mawkish elegance of Bloom's highbrow paradise (which consists of Victorian salons and Tudor libraries populated by white, bourgeois males and *belles-lettristes* from ivy league schools, and other descendants from the white European) the Freirean educator confronts colonialism's vertiginous intoxication with the selective tradition of knowledge production in our schools. In Bloom's universe, the non-Western thinker who traffics in magic and ritualism or the toxic eschatology of Nietzschean perspectivism becomes the debased and inverted image of the hyper-civilized metropolitan intellectual who deals in ideological artifacts. In other words, both non-Western knowledge and the uncultivated knowledge of the masses become a primitive non-knowledge that serves as a conduit to savagery and barbarism – a descent into Hell, reason's Negative Other.

Empires of consciousness collide in Bloom's theatre of the mind (the radiantly civilized high culture of Hellenism of which Bloom himself is a prime representative and the dark, primitive culture of the mob) where a fantasy narrative is played out that is common to many bourgeois male academics and one that the hegemony of the universalized and eternalized language and tropes of the colonizer makes easier to script: Euro-American civilization is keeping the grandeur of the savage at bay in the name of Truth. Freire's work offers a direct challenge to this perspective.

After nearly twenty years since his exile from his native Brazil and subsequent work in literacy campaigns throughout the world (Brazil prior to 1964, Chile, Nicaragua, Guinea-Bissau, São Tomé, Cape Verde, Principe, and Tanzania), Paulo Freire has returned to the city of São Paulo and recently served as secretary of education for the newly elected Workers' Party (PT). Currently he is acting as a consultant in a campaign called Mova São Paulo, which involves literacy and post-literacy training in a city where it is estimated that 1.5 milion people cannot read or write (Torres 1990). Freire's high level involvement in education is a very gratifying if not peculiar turn of events for a man who was once imprisoned by the Brazilian military regime as a dangerous revolutionary, and whose classic book, *Pedagogy of the Oppressed* (a break from the incipient liberalism which informed his earlier work, *Education as Practice of Freedom*), is still revered by many educators as a revolutionary and landmark text, in both Third and First Worlds. Freire's vision and special calling to the project of emancipatory political praxis through critical literacy has made him an extraordinary scholar/teacher.

In an epoch permeated by global mechanisms of oppression, ever more sweeping machineries of surveillance, and increasingly brutal structures of violence which tunnel through the flesh and marrow of everyday life and into the very core of what Raymond Williams calls our 'practical consciousness,' only to burrow further to the domain of the unconscious, Freire continues to exhibit courage and a persistent commitment to freedom and social justice. Despite the pressing and insurgent power contained in Freire's revolutionary project of social transformation, his work runs the risk of being reconfigured doxologically by a generation of liberal educators who would hold him captive as a benevolent Father and benign eminence to be venerated because of his experiential 'method.' Western canonizers of Freire too often identify him with a 'learning by doing' methodology of perfumed liberalism. As a consequence, language arts educators in the public schools and liberal arts mavens in the academy ignore the immanently sociopolitical character of dialogical praxis. This reduces conscientization to a 'cognitive consciousness' that floats and swirls like metaphysical ether in a cloud of Eurocentric paternalism. Such an overly precipitate appropriation of Freire has been damaging. We wish to emphasize that Freire's work cannot be appropriated or appreciated if it is absorbed into hagiolatry or a celebratory apologetics or abstracted by liberals from its sociopolitical and geopolitical roots in their lapidary quest for a foundational method and universal epistemology.

Freire's distinct contribution to contemporary social thought goes well beyond his appropriation by liberal educators into an innocuous liberal pluralism. The politics of difference that underwrites Freirean pedagogy does not locate identity in a centrist politics of consensus that leaves individuals to function and flounder as unwitting and obeisant servants of the state but rather in a politics of location that invites them to be active shapers of their own histories (Freire 1985). Freire's position is not accretive in the sense that it simply promotes other voices to be added to the menu of mainstream cultural perspectives in the form of a depotentiated multiculturalism. In the sense that Freire 'thinks from the margins,' his viewing the oppressed not as ethnocentric special interest groups to be fulsomely added on to the already harmonious pre-existing pluralism but rather as offering in themselves valid and legitimate articulations of everyday experience ('dialogical angles') invites comparison to Bakhtin's conception of social and ethnic diversity (Stam 1991). The lived experiences of oppression of peripheralized and marginalized groups provide them and their oppressors with an epistemological vantage point in deconstructing the mystifications of the dominant social order.

So that critical pedagogy does not fall prey to forms of evangelizing or enunciating its call for liberation as if it were the sole theoretical representative of the oppressed, teachers should give the oppressed a preferential option for developing their own language of analysis as a means of interrogating the conditions of their own oppression (we shall argue that such an analysis is largely based on but not limited to experience). Like

51

Bakhtin's dialogism, Freirean pedagogy is not unilateral but a reciprocal and dialogical negotiation of power in the sense that both interlocutors (teacher and student) are changed in any dialogical exchange (Stam 1991).

Freire's move away from the pseudo-equality of liberal pluralism is evident in his challenge to deepen our understanding of how individuals can gain a greater purchase on social agency through a critical narrativization of their desire, through the naming of their own histories, and through claiming the necessary power to resist their imposed subalternity and the deforming effects of social power. For nearly two decades, Freire's work has been employed by teachers, social workers, literacy workers, theologians, and others to construct an educational vision in which self-development and social transformation go hand in hand in the struggle for social justice.

Freire has devoted a lifetime to understanding how subordinate groups in both totalitarian regimes and liberal democracies become depoliticized, deracinated, and recontained by the dominant culture. In the First World especially, political subversion by oppressed peoples has been continually displaced by a countersubversiveness made all the more subtle and menacing by the ideological machinery of sophisticated media technology. Despite such obstacles, Freire's project can offer much to educators in the United States whose legacy of educational modernism has unified coercively the heterogeneous culture of the Other through the values of patriarchy, self-perception, and individual autonomy. These values have been forced upon the culture in part by the conflation of the logic of the marketplace with Eurocentric views of rationality. While to a certain extent Freire's work shares some of the metatheoretical concerns of post-Enlightenment Western thinking, we wish to stress how Freire's work in the main constitutes an agenda of dissent by breaking away from modernism's foundational unities (subject/object, fact/value, self/other) to the extent that he perceives a need to ground all knowledge of social life in human history, culture, and relations of power.

Perhaps more than any other educator in this century, Freire has revealed to us that literacy practices are practices of power. As a practice or act of power, literacy may serve to link hope to possibility through developing various means of resisting the politics of oppression so that a qualitatively better world can be summoned, struggled for, and eventually grasped (Freire 1970; Giroux and McLaren 1989). Or, on the other hand, literacy may serve as a political restraint which uncouples hope from possibility, inhibiting the development of a world less terrorized by the conflict between subordinate and superordinate groups, between those who have and those who hunger, those who need very little and those who are in grave need of life's barest essentials (Lankshear 1987).

The former type of literacy refers to a critical assessment of the prevailing cultural hegemony in which the word is not read at the expense of the world and the cultural spaces of everyday life are understood as being formed within asymmetrical relations of power and privilege, relations which need to be struggled against in order to construct a more equitable and just society (cf. Freire and Macedo). The latter type of literacy refers to that which is merely functional, which harnesses ideology to 'necrophilic' social relations of domination, encouraging individuals to form their values, politics, and reading of the world in static, reified images produced in the 'machine ecstasy' of the dominant culture. It is a literacy that fails to see beyond the necropolis of Baudrillard's *hyperbaton*, where resistance becomes a mere doubling of the same, where to contest conformity becomes an act of hyper-conformity (see Hebdige 1988: 209). It is to the former, liberatory type of literacy that Freire's work is directed.

All language, according to Freire, works to reproduce dominant forms of power relationships, but it also carries with it the resources for immanent critique, for dismantling the oppressive power structures of the social order, and also for articulating a more transformative and liberating vision of the future. Freire has made it clear that an important correlation exists between advancing and deepening the democratic socialist project and our access to discourses that encourage self-reflexivity about the literalness and otherwise unrecognized and passively accepted meanings of our own reality and those of our fellow human beings. He argues that we need to understand the historical contexts, social practices, cultural forms, and ideologies that give these discourses shape and meaning. Freire teaches us that contradictions in the larger social order have parallels in individual experience and that educators for liberation must restore the political relation between pedagogy and the language of everyday life. Since all pedagogical practices are constituted within regimes of truth, privileging norms, and ruling social arrangements, the important questions for educators become: What pedagogical forms permit emancipation of human potentialities and what social and what institutional structures should be in place for such human capacities to develop politically unimpeded in both the classroom and the larger society (see Simon 1987)?

Freirean-based literacy programs involve an examination of society's hidden economies of power and privilege and how these help to inform students' subjectivities. Too often words that are intimately connected to social relations and cultural power recapitulate the asymmetrical relations of power and privilege of the larger society. As social agents, we are geopolitically arranged by dominant literacies. For example, Enrique Dussel (1980) has tellingly pointed out in his discussion of analectics that the Cartesian *ego cogito*, which informs the subjective voice of First World subjects, enjoys an imperial legacy from 'I conquer' and 'I vanquish' to 'I enslave.' He maintains that the ontology that justifies the empires of the center (i.e. England, Germany, France and the United States), and the ideologies which give them a 'good conscience' are carried in the subjectivities of the colonizer, the oppressor who is unaware of his or her status with respect to the 'other.'

Refusing to fall prey to the modernist illusion of the self as self-cohering, self-situating, self-explaining, non-differential, self-identical, and mono-centric, Freire assumes the position that the self is constituted dialectically within language and social action and is capable of exercising a critical consciousness. Even though human subjectivity is not an irreducible nexus of action, desire, belief, and intention, individuals can still assume the position of 'contrary antagonists' to the educational system and its role as a cultural medium for acceptance, passivity, reconciliation, resigna-tion, and accommodation. Under the impress of Freirean pedagogy, individuals are seen as capable of forming a praxis of liberation. Liberating praxis acknowledges that even though knowledge may be embedded, situated, constructed, and temporal, it can still establish the necessary conditions for emancipation, even though these conditions may be contingent, partial, and provisional.

Liberating praxis is not the creature of reason alone, but is a certain type of reasoning process that is undertaken as part of action both in and on the world. Freirean pedagogy makes it clear that theory and practice work in concert, are mutually informing, and together constitute a dialectical praxis. What makes this insight especially important for educators is precisely the disclosure that it is futile and counterproductive for teachers to view critical pedagogy as essentially a theoretical exercise that is primarily descriptive. Rendering theory as a form of practice that is intrinsic to human social activity and the implied opposition between theory and practice as eminently contextual, Freire's work has consis-tently illustrated how theory and practice always work together and unite in the dialectical and political act of knowing. As Freire (forthcoming) notes, 'there is a "politicity" of education in the same way, that there is an "educability" of the political; that is to say there is a political nature to education just as there is a pedagogical nature to the political act.' Freire's radicalism, as Robert Mackie (1981: 97) points out, is not sectarian, but rather is built upon *conscientizaçao*. In this regard, Freire (1972a: 53) writes that 'consciousness of and action upon reality are therefore inseparable constituents of the transforming act by which people become beings of relation.'

Following in the tradition of Hegel, Marx, and Dewey, Freire empha-sizes individual and collective intentionality or agency as a precondition for knowing. According to Henry Giroux (1987: 11), this 'includes a view of human agency in which the production of meaning takes place in the dialogue and interaction that mutually constitute the dialectical relationship between human subjectivities and the objective world.' From this perspective, the bourgeois mode of subjectivity which privileges private, inner experience and valorizes high culture is rejected in favor of understanding the various types of segmentarity that divide up social life and the concatenated levels and the arborescent interrelationships of power that make up the antagonisms and contradictions of ordinary and mundane social experience.

Freire could be charged with positing reality as relational, but this is hardly the same thing as labelling him a relativist. The distinction is worth emphasizing. Freire does not consider all ideas to be of equal merit, but rather argues that they must be understood contextually as historically and culturally informed discourses that are subject to the mediation of the forces of material and symbolic production – part of what Giroux (1987: 11) calls 'the relational nature of how meaning is produced, i.e., the intersection of subjectivities, objects, and social practices within specific relations of power.' In this sense, Freire considers knowledge not through the atomized logic and postivist/empirical explanations bequeathed by Enlightenment thinking, but as always occupying a tension between the specific and the universal. Freire's position on knowledge is quite clearly post-Cartesian: We cannot hide the word's inherence in, its constitutiveness of, and its ingress to the world. This is a position which, rather than vitalizing the sovereign objectivity of knowledge, underscores its insinuation into human interest, social power, and the brute facticity of everyday pain and pleasure. The subject and object of knowledge are coeval.

According to Freire, the act of knowing is action-reflexive; it takes the form of an active transformation on and through the world, not an accommodation to the world. Dialogical knowing always renders problematic an individual or group's existential predicament in relation to a larger sociopolitical context. While it is true that Freire's work is concerned with self-transformation, grounded as it is in the concept of conscious intentionality and volition, it is equally true, if not more so, that it concerns itself with social transformation, assuming as a central referent the reconstruction and reconstitution of the structural arrangements of the existing social order. Given these dual foci in Freire's work, it is easy to see why, for Freire, critical reflection cannot occur in antiseptic isolation from the world of others, removed from the public sphere.

Critical reflection is a social act of knowing undertaken in a public arena as a form of social and collective empowerment. To reflect critically is not something which can be achieved in isolation from others, for this merely valorizes personal transformation or empowerment at the expense of collectively making and remaking history with and for others. Personal history is always embedded in social forms which are part of our collective cultural present, and they always owe an ideological debt – whether good or bad – to the past.

Critical or dialogical reflection is a part of a long political and historical process, a battle waged on behalf of the peripheralized and immiserated subordinate classes who seek freedom from the cultural and moral hegemony of the dominant culture. Freedom, in the Freirean sense of the term, means unmasking the social and cultural mechanisms of power as a basis for engagement in emancipatory action. Freire recognizes, as does Foucault, that the distinction between truth and power needs to be blurred, and that sociocultural power is a double-edged sword that can sever the bonds of domination yet can also be wielded by oppressors. Even when sheathed, such power can be dangerous since it can conceal or camouflage its own means of operation.

Freire's conception of literacy involves acknowledging and understanding both the frequency and the means by which large numbers of marginalized groups refuse to be absorbed into the hegemonic articulations of the dominant culture and to become docile bodies split off from empowering processes. In this case, dominant forms of literacy serve as a process of colonization whereas illiteracy often signals a resistant act of refusing, as Giroux (1987: 13) puts it, 'to learn the specific cultural codes and competencies authorized by the dominant culture's view of literacy.'

Critical dialogue is a process which Shor and Freire (1987: 104) refer to as 'situated pedagogy' – a collaborative discourse and reciprocity in which thought, action, and reflection combine in informed, enlightened, and committed action to dismantle and counter the hegemonic structures that support oppression. In this way, students can take their places as historical actors in the social drama of critical transformation of both the self as social and the social as self. This suggests self transformation cannot occur without social or structural transformation and that the latter cannot occur unless individuals are able to both understand and work against their personal implication in the process of social repression.

It must be emphasized, however, that Freire does not equate revolutionary consciousness with achieving human potential through dialogue, that is, by constructing a new social semiotic or an epochal shift in what Volosinov (1973) calls 'behavioral ideology' (which would make Freire vulnerable to attacks of mere reformism or pedagogism); revolutionary consciousness not only involves changes in forms of subjectivity but also structural change in the larger social order. This can be achieved both within the field of signifying practices (i.e. undermining the discourses of patriarchy, the unicity of the Cartesian order and liberal humanism's conjunction with positivistic science) and through direct political challenges to oppressive public policies and institutions.

The generic distinction we have drawn between Freire's critical literacy and conventional strands of cultural and functional literacy approaches highlights the former's potential for institutional and/or representational critique, analysis or address and the latter's deep-seated inability to recognize the rhetoricity of knowledge, literacy's own status as discourse, and the role of literacy as a servant of power.

Freire's project illuminates the essential praxis necessary for establishing a critical literacy in classrooms and for actively contesting the power arrangements that structure the politics of the everyday. Language is understood as something that does not give us transparent access to reality or a means of discovering Plato's universe of Hellenistic truths but rather serves as a medium for constructing rather than discovering meaning. Consequently, knowledge is not a hidden reality that can be revealed through the linguistic aperture of language.

Language plays a constituent role in the social construction of that reality. If knowledge is inseparable from the language that gives it birth then it stands to reason that language does not simply incarnate reality without implicating itself in relations of power – usually as a totalizing system situated in the dominant strain of modern Western thought in which interpretive strategies are employed to categorize and classify the way 'we' understand the social and cultural practices of 'them.' In other words, language is more than an arbitrary system of differences in which meaning is guaranteed by the linguistic system itself and the values given to signifying practices within particular linguistic communities. There is no Rosetta Stone – no privileged access to meaning in the sense of discovering the master code that explains how the elements of a social text function together – the unalterable linchpin that holds together the chain of signifiers that is said to constitute culture (which is not to claim that there exists no access to extratextual reality or that reality is an endless deferral or deformation of meaning or an abyssal plummet into infinite semiotic regression). Rather than granting codes a transcendental status that serve as privileged referents around which other meanings are positioned, Freire puts much more emphasis on meaning as a contested event, a terrain of struggle in which individuals take up often conflicting subject positions in relation to signifying practices.

Poststructuralist readings both complement and extend Freire's position on language. As subjects, we are always constituted by language and cannot step outside of it in order to reflect upon how we are positioned in it. We are always already inscribed in the system of differences that constitute a language. While the structures of language are ontologically dependent on specific communities of speakers, there are no *a priori* rules of language and the relations between signifiers and signified are arbitrary *vis-à-vis* other languages. We effectively follow the rules of language *as if* they were necessary (Pheby 1988). As Keith Pheby notes, discourse is always finite, transitory, and historically situated. Signs are always inhabited or populated by other signs and meanings:

No discourse, not even that concerning the constitution of subjectivity is innocent of 'ulterior motives'. All discourse is inextricably tied to the political conditions of a culture at any point in its history.
(Pheby 1988: 63)

While taking some liberties in positioning Freire's work within a poststructuralist perspective, it could be argued that meaning for Freire is not the function of the speaker because signs are only known in the context of other signs; meanings are always designated and cannot exist outside of the world of language. Meaning is lived within and through the materiality of discourse as linguistic 'gestures' that are constructed within and through bodies. Inscription through the flesh – 'enfleshment' (in the sense that metaphor is a correlate of patterns of bodily action and interaction; see Jackson 1983 and McLaren 1989) – is the seat of discursive power and the founding act of culture. Freire foregrounds the fact that we can only know the real through regimes of signs, through systems of representation that are historically lived in suffering and celebrating bodies and are the result of class, race, and gender struggles. Meaning consists not only of signs operating in a context but also as concrete struggles over naming reality. This makes signification an eminently political enterprise and involves a relationship among discourse, power, and difference. Signs actively 'perform' in the material world, but their movements and shifts are neither indeterminate nor predetermined. Their meanings are contingently activated by contextually specific material struggles and historical circumstances involving human labor, suffering, and celebration. The reality of the signifying subject has not radically displaced human agency. As such, historical agency (how we act in and through history) is not something that just happens to us or that we automatically acquire; it does not arrive adventitiously or even serendipitously or as a full-blown developmental stage. Historical agency is decidedly not inevitable. Neither is it capricious.

We are using the term 'historical agency' here because Freire's ideas are forged within an interactive nexus of philosophical *topoi* such as exile, oppression, struggle, history, and identity (or large-scale *topoi* such as 'the people speak their word,' 'the popular library,' 'the illiteracy of literacy in the US'), in which the struggle to release the oppressed from their historical bondage is the primary *leitmotif* (and a very elegiactic one). Freire's project here differs from many poststructuralist currents in which critical advocacy often lapses into the form of the jeremiad, or else is reduced to a synecdochal subtext within a larger deconstructive narrative. As historical agents, we are surely not self-identical. Even with semiotic tools such as poststructuralism, individuals are not able to prise open the Pandora's box of self-identity in order to possess transparent access to their own best interests – especially if they happen to be female and find themselves defined phallocentrically as lack, absence, other – according to what male is not. Or if they happen to be black and female and are also defined by the invisible norm of colonial whiteness.

According to Freire, historical agency acquires its grounding in emancipatory acts as individuals challenge the everyday language and social practices that social agents use to give shape and meaning to their world;

it is an ongoing process involving the development of a plurality of critical literacies. Such 'postmodern' literacies can assist in the formation of alternative subject positions so that the multifarious, multi-layered and many-sided agent of history can exercise some determinate, ethical action that is self-reflexive and critically contemplative. In other words, the critical historical agent needs to self-consciously shape the direction of his or her desiring and the will to struggle against the decline and deformation of the possible. Regrettably, Freire does not place enough emphasis on the race and gender barriers to and possibilities for liberation and what kinds of 'wars of position' are needed in a leftist politics of resistance that takes race and gender seriously.

Dialogue emerges from Freire's pedagogy as a real, practical option for teachers and students for replacing the traditional authoritarian mentor approach based on forms of Cartesian rationalism. In contrast to functional or cultural literacy's claims to a self-containment and palpable presence of knowledge, Freire's approach emphasizes the dependency of knowledge on already existing and highly conventionalized meanings – on a socio-linguistic system or 'language games.' As one reads through Freire's vast corpus of writings, the act of knowing is invariably made critical, reflexive, and necessarily incomplete precisely as it is put into the service of uncovering the interests that inform conventionalized meanings.

Paradoxically, it is in its incompleteness and provisionality that Freire's concept of knowledge derives its dialectical strength. Emancipatory knowledge is never realized fully, but is continually dreamed, continually revived, and continually transformed in the hearth of our memories, the flames of our longing and the passion of our struggle. Similarly, the words and concepts that make up our everyday frames of intelligibility are a result of the ongoing material and discursive struggles within the domain of the sign (see Volosinov 1973).

Because Freire implicitly recognizes that discourses are always prag-matically negotiated and adjusted through difference, to establish a priori universal principles with which to objectively and unambiguously shape pedagogical practice with onto-theological authority is antithetical to Freire's own theory of pedagogy and to most contemporary models of Freirean-based liberatory praxis. Freire's position has much in common with the counter-positivist dissent found in the sociology of knowledge, existential phenomenology, and certain strands of poststructuralism. From these vantage points, knowledge that aspires to the condition of empirical science and that falls into the classical encyclopedism, atomized logic, and generic conceptualizing of logical positivist understanding betrays a meta-theoretical commitment to dualized categories of meaning and logocentric strategies of identity and hierarchization: in short, to a tendency towards grand theory. And it is precisely against such grand theorizing that Freire's work has gradually taken shape and development.

Freire's treatment of language is multiplex and is geared to locating the sources of interest and unfreedom in the reproduction of race, class, and gender relations. While Freire's theoretical formulations are not formally situated within the disciplinary trajectories of structuralism and poststructuralism, it remains the case that they often support certain advances made within these perspectives. This is especially true in so far as Freire's work continually acknowledges the relation among language, social structure, and consciousness and maintains that knowledge and meaning are always *produced* rather than expressed or discovered. This perspective gives Freire's recent work an affinity with certain strands of poststructuralism (although, as Stanley Aronowitz points out in his chapter in this volume, Freire speaks to certain limitations within poststructuralism when he recognizes that the oppressed are more than subject positions constituted discursively, but rather are subjectively produced by the material effects of economic, social and psychological conditions).

LANGUAGE AND THE POLITICS OF EXPERIENCE

We shall now turn to the topic of language and experience in order to discuss a particularly troublesome situation in the work of some Freirean-influenced educators. Our concern here is with certain pedagogical approaches which, like Freire's, are grounded in student experience. The problem arises when (as it so often happens) direct experience is thought to speak for itself. It is not uncommon to confront a self-styled Freirean (or Deweyan, for that matter) educator who insists upon privileging 'raw' experience over the practice of theory. However, as Giroux (1985: xxi) points out, Freire neither romanticizes experience nor fails to render it problematic.

Roger Simon and Donald Dippo (1986) highlight an ongoing concern in critical pedagogy when they argue that educators must avoid the conservatism inherent in confirming what people already know. By this they mean that experience should never be celebrated uncritically; student voices must be affirmed while simultaneously encouraging the interrogation of such voices. Experience does not speak for itself, but is a way in which individuals confront the contingency of the present and the politics of daily living. Though one should not deny the importance of non-discursive experience, experience is an understanding constructed largely linguistically as an interpretation over time of a specific concrete engagement with the world of symbols, social practices, and cultural forms.

No experience is pristine and unmediated. How we think and talk about our world through the particular languages and theories made available to us largely shapes our understanding of why things are the way they are, which images of 'that which is not yet' are possible and desirable, and what needs to be done for things to be otherwise. For instance, E. L. Doctorow believes that 'a book can affect consciousness – affect the way people think and therefore the way they act. Books create constituencies that have their own effect on history' (cited in Trenner 1983: 43). This is not to suggest that a physical encounter such as being cracked on the head by police during a political demonstration does not teach you something directly (and we have deliberately chosen an example provided by Myles Horton of the Highlander Center in Tennessee who claims that, as a young man, being struck on the head by a police baton during a May Day Parade in New York City profoundly and permanently radicalized his politics) – or does not leave an experience directly inscribed in memory's flesh.

We are suggesting that the way we understand and respond to such encounters is largely linguistically determined through whatever competing discourses are available and on the basis of how these discourses resonate ideologically with and are affectively invested in by the individual interpreting the event. The striking police baton is transformed into a signifier of state brutality; society writes its law into the flesh of the body – a process which McLaren (1988) terms 'enfleshment'[2] and de Certeau (1984) calls 'intextuation.'

At the same time as individual body/subjects are inscribed within the body politic, they are offered a number of dominant and subordinate subject positions to assume: innocent victim, casualty of state-inflicted barbarism, wounded protestor, martyr, freedom fighter. Or perhaps some new subject position is forged in the process. But these 'choices' are made largely on the basis of the affective and symbolic economy in which such an event is situated, the discourses available to subjects, their reading formations, and the selection process undertaken.

The point that we are accenting here is that the language of teaching too often serves as a coercive text by restricting or shaping the way in which both teachers and students make sensuous and linguistic sense of their experience. In order to escape an idealized liberalism that too often inflicts the incarnation of patriarchy upon feminine subjectivity, teachers especially need to recognize how much their own personal histories, ideological assumptions, and Eurocentric and patriarchal narrative forms (not to mention those of their students) are grounded in a discursive economics of liberal capitalism. We want to suggest that cultural workers need to recognize that the knowledge and understanding that students are *prevented* from bringing to their experiences is as important as the knowledge and understanding which students are *permitted* to narrate with respect to their lived experiences. It is important, too, to recognize that students may reject certain forms of 'professional' adult knowledge as catachrestically invasive of their own identity and meaning.

Krystyna Pomorska (1980) writes that the nature of the language we use determines, at least in part, *how we make sense of our experiences and the type of social action we choose to engage in as a result of interpreting our experiences*. It also determines the range of possibilities we have to organize our social world, to develop new forms of sociality and, as teachers, new forms of pedagogy. If experience is largely understood through language, and language shapes how we see and act *with and on the world*, then it follows that experience itself does not guarantee truth since it is always open to conflicting and contradictory interpretations. That is, our experience is not some fixed or fluid essence, or some concrete reality that exists prior to language, waiting to be reflected by language (Brown 1987). Rather, experience is largely constituted by language.

Experience – 'events and behaviors occurring in social formations' (de Lauretis 1987: 42) – is highly constitutive of subjectivity. Since language enables us to interpret our experience, it follows that language is also constitutive of subjectivity, that is, of an individual's conscious and unconscious understandings. Subjectivity is constituted in language to the extent that while we construct language we are simultaneously constructed by it. Language and subjectivity are interanimating. As William Gass writes,

> language is . . . more powerful as *an* experience of things than *the* experience of things. Signs are more potent experiences than anything else, so when one is dealing with the things that really count, then you deal with words. They have a reality far exceeding the things they name.
>
> (cited in Hutcheon 1988: 149; italics added)

We have noted that experience does not speak for itself, outside the frames of reference (discourses) associated with the language we select *or are given* in order to make sense of that experience. And we have also noted that language cannot give us an untroubled access to the real from, say, a God's-eye perspective that can see beyond the world of social discourse. The serious issue here deals with *the ways in which we have been inserted into language both as teachers and students* and to connect these with our occupancy in certain class and material locations as well as those of gender and race. To reflectively situate ourselves in discourse – in language – is to historicize our role as social agents. *If we conjure only those ideas that we already have the words to express, then our presence in history remains more or less comfortably static.* Part of the state of this crisis is reflected in the unavailability of subject positions in which students are permitted to practice forms of radical critique and engage in social practices informed by a commitment to establishing a more democratic social order.

While experience is important in the act of knowing, it is frequently 'blind.' Consequently, it is in 'the political *interpretation* of experience that existence becomes fruitful' (Eagleton 1985/6: 104; italics added). In a similar fashion, Donald Morton and Mas'ud Zavarzadeh (1988: 163) attack the concept of direct or intuitive experience when it is presumed that such experience is 'transdiscursive . . . free of all political, social, economic, and linguistic constraints . . . [and outside] . . . the opacities of culture.' Experience is not an 'unmediated, and direct, intuitive knowing of the body of the world.' Rather, they cite Catherine Belsey (1983: 17) who argues that 'experience itself is the location of ideology, not the guarantee of truth.' Experience is a constitutive and regulatory site of selective knowledge.

John Shotter (1989: 141) follows Wittgenstein, C. Wright Mills, and Bakhtin (especially the latter's notion of 'addressivity') in assertng that 'the main function of language is not the representation of things in the world, or the giving of "outer" expression to already well formed "inner" thoughts, but its use in creating and sustaining social orders.' Experience does not speak for itself, because, as Shotter notes, all our experiences are held accountable 'in terms that are intelligible and legitimate within this order' (p. 142). If we are able to act routinely and in an accountable manner in the social order, the requirements of our everyday media of communication necessitate the reproduction of a dominant social ordering. If the ways in which we speak to each other are constrained, then it follows that 'our experience of ourselves, will be constrained also' (p. 141). And we would add here that the choice of our actions in and on the world would be qualitatively affected. Shotter claims that there exists a great deal of pressure on us as individuals to sustain our status and that this means that we must express ourselves in ways approved by others – 'that we feel our reality must be of a certain kind' (p. 141).

We are emphasizing the point that only certain languages (terms, vocabularies, narratives, concepts) are deemed legitimate within the communities of discourses used by educators. And often those languages are those of management and technical efficiency that fail to adequately capture the complexity of social life.

We are not trying to suggest that educators and students should only converse with one another in arcane, elaborated codes, but rather that a variety of critical languages should be made available to the discerning student. And, of course, students should learn the limitations of the critical languages that are made available for helping them to understand their everyday experiences, forms of social engagement, and feelings of intuition. And we should begin to explore with more exigence how meanings and hegemonic articulations are manufactured outside of purely discursive modes and the actions of social agents (McLaren 1989).

GENDERED EXPERIENCE: ESSENTIALISM AND BEYOND

A point we wish to emphasize is that experience should be recognized as a form of cultural politics that is *always historical and gendered*. Rejecting the failure of Marcuse and Adorno to provide an analysis of woman as historical actor (in so far as they consider woman to be dominated both by recognizing her difference and by denying it), Patricia Jagentowicz Mills stresses the importance of articulating woman's experience. She writes that:

> Woman's experience is to be found in the traces of memory reformed through the process of 'naming.' Although naming can never capture the immediacy of the experience – what is articulated is never *the same as* the experience – we must name experience in order to understand it; without naming, experience is simply passed through or endured. When concepts are linked to experience so that experience is understood, not just undergone, we are led to a rediscovery of philosophy as critical theory. . . . The naming of woman's experience . . . remains silent on the relations between women and on woman's self-experience of desire. In this way, woman's experience is distorted and denied. Woman's voicelessness reveals reification as silencing. By giving voice to her experience, by naming the unnamed for herself, woman challenges the reification of the name through silence and she initiates the political project.
>
> (Mills 1987: 207–8; italics original)

In Mills's view, not all dominant ways of thinking and understanding are linked to the Leviathan-like reservoir of raging hormones located in the male genitalia which, according to some radical feminists, biologically shape the logic of male domination; nor does she feel that 'the content of knowledge must come solely out of "woman's experience" as some sanctified and truth-producing zone' (Cocks 1988: 19). While it is true that a pedagogy of liberation that does not attend to the specificity of experience – but instead attempts to universalize experience in terms of race, class, and gender – is doomed to further entrap women, minorities, and the poor, what needs to be stressed in order to escape a naïve essentialism is *the nature of the theoretical discourse brought to bear on the sensuous specificity of experience*. This means engaging theoretical discourses that are not based on the subordination of the female by the male, reason's subordination of nature, or the marginalization and oppression of the 'other' by patriarchal and Eurocentric narratives of the self that within our current culture so tenaciously shape desire and agency.

Experience is never transparent to itself and always occurs *within* particular social and cultural forms that have been produced within specific relations of power and regimes of discourse serving particular interests. With specific reference to feminist pedagogy, Diana Fuss writes:

> the problem with positing the category of experience as the basis of a feminist pedagogy is that the very object of our inquiry, 'female experience,' is never as unified, as knowable, as universal, and as stable as we presume it to be. . . . The appeal to experience, as the ultimate test of all knowledge, merely subtends the subject in its

64

fantasy of autonomy and control. Belief in the truth of Experience is as much an ideological production as belief in the experience of Truth.

(Fuss 1989: 114)

Fuss notes that the 'politics of experience' can lead individuals and groups to itemize and rank identities, in which case certain considerations of difference can then occlude other considerations and delegitimate them. It can also cause them to see only one part of a subject's identity – as 'male,' as 'Asian,' as 'lesbian,' etc. Hierarchies of identities are sometimes set up *within* speaking subjects as well as between them (p. 116). Ranking of identities is used as a means of authorizing individuals to speak or de-authorizing them on the premise that 'some essences are more *essential* than others' (p. 116). Fuss also makes the point that, 'The anti-essentialist displacement of experience must not be used as a convenient means of silencing students, no matter how shaky experience has proven to be as a basis of epistemology' (p. 117).

However, Fuss needs to acknowledge to a greater extent how students in classroom settings are *always already* inscribed in institutional, cultural, and social systems of domination, oppression, and power/knowledge relations that reify and demonize the Other in essentialist ways. As bell hooks (1989) has noted, essentialism or identity politics is not something that is misused only or primarily by marginalized groups. Essentialism is abused most often by dominant groups whose subjectivities are constituted in cultural forms and practices that both silence difference and delegitimate and devalue the personalized experiences and voices of the marginalized Other.

Today feminists are often faced with the dilemma of either adhering to essentialist doctrines or fostering the dissolution of feminist struggles into localized, regional, specific struggles representing the interests of particular women (Grosz, 1989). The way out of this dilemma, argues Elizabeth Grosz (1989), comes in recognizing that feminists need not take on universalist and essentialist assumptions in the same way as patriarchs. We would add to this insight bell hooks's (1991) observation that marginalized groups should not be the only groups singled out for exclusionary practices attributed to essentialism; after all, dominant groups employ essentialist strategies that produce exclusionary behavior firmly buttressed by institutionalized structures of domination that do not criticize or check it. And while it is important to oppose essentialist practices that construct identities in exclusionary, monolithic ways, it is important not to relinquish the power of naming one's experience in ways that can help to formulate theories of experience. The complexity of experience – for instance, knowledge of suffering that is often inscribed in the bodies of marginalized peoples – needs to be engaged through what hooks calls 'multiple locations' – and what she terms 'the passion of remembrance.'

65

Gloria Anzaldúa speaks to the task ahead as one of trying to formulate marginal theories

> that are partially outside and partially inside the Western frame of reference (if that is possible), theories that overlap many 'worlds.' We are articulating new positions in these 'in-between,' Borderland worlds of ethnic communities and academies, feminist and job worlds. In our literature, social issues such as race, class and sexual difference are intertwined with the narrative and poetic elements of a text, elements in which theory is embedded. In our *mestizaje* theories we create new categories for those of us left out or pushed out of the existing ones. We recover and examine non-Western aesthetics while critiquing Western aesthetics; recover and examine non-rational modes and 'blanked-out' realities while critiquing rational, consensual reality; recover and examine indigenous languages while critiquing the 'languages' of the dominant culture. . . . If we have been gagged and disempowered by theories, we can also be loosened and empowered by theories.
>
> (Anzaldúa 1990: xxvi)

The critical theory to which Freire's work speaks must be extended in order to allow women as well as minorities to emerge as critical, social actors on the stage of human transformation and struggle. Furthermore, the conceptual frameworks that purport to uncover and transform the constructions of subjectivity need to be purged of their phallocentrism, Eurocentrism, and masculinist ideologies.

Within educational approaches in the United States, the privileging of experience over theory has led to an unashamed celebration of empirical realism, impartial and disinterested knowledge, and a refusal to recognize that all forms of analysis are simultaneously forms of advocacy. It has fostered the development of an epistemology in which there exists a stress on validity and measurement, an analytic cleavage of description and exhortation, a temporal separation of knowledge and desire, the sundering of analysis and social criticism, and the refusal of teachers to narrate their own ideological contingency within networks of power relations (Agger 1989). Iris Marion Young (1990) observes that since particularities always operate in the context of social action, the ideal of impartiality not only creates a dichotomy between the universal and the particular, public and private, reason and passion, but also serves debilitating ideological functions by masking the ways in which dominant perspectives claim universality and justify forms of domination.

It is important that methodology-based Freirean educators reject what Ben Agger has termed 'methodological pluralism.' According to Agger, methodological pluralism assumes that the world is really all of one piece – a terrain expunged of ideology and sublimely absolved of all human interest; a place where there exists no contradiction with the self – but can be read differently through different critical approaches. In other words, the same world can be explained differently, it is simply a question of the educator's personal ontological co-ordinates. This view prevails in many social and literary theory courses that teach different interpretive approaches (i.e. new criticism, historiographic metafiction, Marxist literary theory, postmodern poetics). The problem with explaining knowledge through a variety of supposedly equal but different interpretive approaches is that it often 'assumes a single, simple world named differently,' and therefore 'misses the constitutiveness of writing entwining a theory of being and explanation' (Agger 1989: 315). What Agger underscores with such sharpened insight is that when the educator neglects how knowledge has been historically produced within a nexus of power relations, the world's own self-understanding and self-referentiality then becomes the basis of the educator's criticism of the social world and thus critical interpretations of social life can become dismissed and domesticated and ultimately discarded as weakened versions of other forms of analysis. A critical social theory such as Freire's can become, in this view, just another 'gloss' on reality. And presumably the classroom instructor, who is standing in a site putatively unspoiled by ideology, can invoke critical literacy as one item in an entire menu of theoretical approaches in a shopping-mall version of social and cultural life. Epistemological pluralism is decidedly anti-Freirean in that it operates as a form of neopositivism; it is a discursive fiction in which social life is *always already* 'preontologically available' for the educator to use as a backdrop for different textual 'readings' of the world.

Yet the centrist position of slicing up the world into a 'balanced curriculum' comprising conservative, liberal, and critical positions really works to usurp critical research under a liberalism that locates it as an example of the 'openness' of the social system. Within such a logic, even critical approaches can become 'ironically a genuflection to an *uncritical* discipline' (p. 316). This amounts to nothing less than the subordination of advocacy to analysis and desire to knowledge.

It is important to stress here that educators teach not just in a classroom but within a field of competing discourses that help structure a variegated system of socially constituted human relationships. The classroom as social site is not simply the physical location where learning takes place, or the geopolitical vectors of power crosscutting the cultural terrain where pedagogy occurs, it is also the site of the teacher's embodiment in theory/discourse and his or her own disposition as a theorist within a specific politics of location. Critical pedagogy necessitates recognizing the complexity of social relations and the educator's own socially determined position within the reality he or she is attempting to describe.

The status of teachers as truth-bearers from the culture of whiteness and maleness putatively imbues them with an impartial and rational intelligence, reinforces the idea that the student's anecdotal logics and local knowledge are of lesser status, and binds power and truth together in such a way as to both privilege and normalize existing relations of power. This only habituates students to the established direction of pedagogy and the cultural–political regime of truth ascribed to by the dominant culture. It is also why teachers and students need to enter the pedagogical encounter *collaboratively* rather than purge difference through the universal calculus of putatively disinterested objective analysis. Teachers need to share with students the discourses at work that are shaping classroom relations, and how the teacher's own personal and intellectual biography is contributing to them.

The analytic mode of Freire's pedagogy recognizes that subjectivities are forged in asymmetrical relations of power, and historical subjects are created *non-synchronously* within various hierarchies of discourses, cultural forms, and social practices according to one's race, class, and gender location in the larger social order. For instance, a working-class black female's subjectivity is shaped out of discourses, social practices, and cultural memories which are qualitatively different from those of a white, middle-class male. At times gender relations will assume a greater place in our critical project of resisting and transforming oppression. At other times, race and social class will figure more prominently. The formation of race, gender, and class all work to produce modes of subjectivity, but not always synchronously (McCarthy 1988).

Critical pedagogy based on Freirean principles creates what we call an arch of social dreaming (McLaren 1992), that is, a forum for sharing and engaging stories of pain and suffering but also for constructing a new narrative of hope through the development of a pedagogy capable of uniting those whose racial gender, and class subordination appears to have foreclosed the possibility of an active struggle for emancipated subjecthood. To engage in critical pedagogy is to recall how, as subjects, we have become disproportionately constituted within dominative regimes of discourses and social practices through race, class, and gender identities. The purpose of such remembering is to actively free us from the mystification that results from living unreflectively in such discourses and material constraints. But critical pedagogy is also *always already* a form of Utopian dreaming. Here we want to reject the standard critique of Utopian thinking that rests on the ontological claim that the nature of things is given, on the regional claim that Utopia is not grounded in the real world, and on the psychological claim that we depart from reality when we feast on dreams of perfection beyond the limitations of everyday reality (Hudson 1982). Freire's Utopia is not the Utopia of 'unbridled subjectivism' or 'totalistic, adolescent psychological states' that provides 'an illusory basis for human action' (see Hudson 1982: 50–1).

Freire's Utopian thinking is provisional rather than categorical. To embrace Utopia categorically is to lock one's vision of the future in blueprint. A provisional Utopian thinking invites a constant promotion of alternatives to present asymmetrical distributions of power on the basis of race, class, gender, and other interests (Dauenhauer 1989). It not only demystifies the present by allowing us to recognize ourselves from a critical/historical perspective as, disproportionately, oppressors and oppressed, but it also carries traces of future possibility in its reconstruction of the present moment. It is in this sense that Paulo Freire's notion of *critical reflection can be compared to a form of redemptive remembrance and social dreaming*.

Critical pedagogy must serve as a form of critique and also a referent for hope. And it must provide a way for the non-poor to recognize their privilege in order to make alliances with the oppressed. Histories of oppression and suffering must be recounted, including unaddressed instances of domination that take the form of institutional and social practices, universal claims to truth, as well as racism, sexism, and classism. Memories of hope must also be offered that can reclaim the historical agency of the revolutionary subject.

Liberation is an unfinished process that entails changing not only the material conditions of oppression but also the psychological conditions (see Aronowitz, this volume). Not surprisingly, liberal educators often launder the political import of psychological liberation in Freire's work to refer to ameliorating individual forms of distress (in which case, everybody is oppressed) and lose sight of his concern with the pathogenic social reality that produces structural forms of collective victimage.

Following Freire's lead, it becomes the task of critical pedagogy to invite students to engage the discursive and conceptual means through which they produce the ideological dimensions of their experiences, deep memories, psychological blockages, and passionate investments in everyday life and relate these to the material and symbolic structures of power that operate in the larger context of social life. It becomes the challenge of critical educators to confront the authority of the signifier and the 'social void' this has produced. In some of the work done in present-day Freirean analysis, we are left with the impression that student experience should be accorded a privileged status, often with little consideration for developing a critical vernacular outside of the language of analysis which students and teachers frequently use to mediate among their own reality, the lived situatedness within their own community, and their ideological and material location or positionality within the larger social order. This privileging of experience over critical understanding works against the very premises of Freirean pedagogies and other critical approaches to schooling.

This does not mean that the choice of language and theoretical constructs used to analyze experience should not be open to debate, because it is important that the particular language of theory that educators endorse is, for instance, able to move outside the constraints of Name-of-the-Father vocabularies and, further, is able to serve as a stronger medium for voices of people of color. It also remains undeniable that critical reflection requires a language that highlights the contingency and situated character of everyday discourse, and that calls subjectivity into question. Theoretical language must resymbolize ordinary social life in order to bring into relief its supposedly inevitable imprisonment in existing relations of power and to locate transformative 'openings.' This has never been more urgent than within the 'cultural dominant' of late post-Fordist capitalism – what has been termed 'the postmodern condition.'

Freire recognizes that it is not enough to recognize language as a carrier of specific interests; more important is the recognition of the political ends such interests serve in the context of the dominant social order. At the same time Freire insists that critical language not serve as a language of imposition, as a vocabulary of indoctrination and violence that positions individuals in such a way that they are made to see the world and where they stand in it from the perspective of the Eurocentric white, male theorist. The development of a critical literacy for global decolonization must always be sensitive to the fact that the wholesale adoption and translation of new theoretical paradigms may need to be modified due to the semantic context surrounding the geopolitical specificity of their origins (Lash 1990). While we must situate problematically the sexism of Freire's early writings and his phallocentric paradigm of liberation in which freedom and the experience of patriarchal manhood are conflated, this criticism of Freire's 'blind spot' – as bell hooks puts it – should not overshadow his valuable insights (see hooks, this volume).

It is important that discourses of liberation do not unproblematically reflect a European, masculinist, or teleological view of history. That is, it is important that they not unqualifiedly endorse an Anglo-European scholarly axis. Critical theory, in the United States in particular, must lose its specific character by incorporating critical discourses of non-Western liberation struggles (for instance, Latin American and African counter-narratives that fracture the philosophical time of concepts and surmount the categorical oppositions of philosophical logic (see Coste 1989). Care must be taken in appropriating such discourses so that they do not recover the colonialism they contest. At the same time, it must be recognized that African and Latin American knowledges are *transcultural* and not antiseptically free of western ideological and technological influences.

Freire's pedagogy is one that reveals social consensus to be social difference dressed up in discourses of equality that hide the real face of domination behind it. But his interrogation of the limits of these discourses does not transcend the culture in which they are embedded in the form of a dogmatic system of thought or totalizing critique. Freire does not need to take shelter in a transcendental citadel that stands above the messy terrain of concrete struggle, lived history, and the contradiction, complexity, and paradox of enunciation in contemporary social life. Yet we would like to emphasize that while Freire's work is centered around the task of affirming the local knowledges of individuals within the contextual specificity of particular struggles, Freire's pedagogy in no way abandons the concept of totality outright. As Fred Jameson remarks:

> Local struggles . . . are effective only so long as they remain figures of allegories from some larger systematic transformation. Politics has to operate on the micro- and the macro-levels simultaneously; a modest restriction to local reforms within the system seems reasonable, but often proves politically demoralizing.
>
> (Jameson 1989: 386)

George Lipsitz underscores this idea, arguing that while totality can potentially do violence to the specificity of events, a rejection of all totality would likely

> obscure real connections, causes, and relationships – atomizing common experience into accidents and endlessly repeated play . . . [and that] . . . only by recognizing the collected legacy of accumulated human actions and ideas can we judge the claims to truth and justice of any one story.
>
> (Lipsitz 1990: 214)

Without a shared vision of democratic community we risk endorsing struggles in which the politics of difference collapses into new forms of separatism. As Steve Best (1989: 361) points out, poststructuralists rightly deconstruct essentialist and repressive wholes, yet in so doing they often fail to see how repressive and crippling the valorizing of difference, plurality, fragmentation, and agonistics can be. He writes:

> The flip side of the tyranny of the whole is the dictatorship of the fragment . . . [and] . . . without some positive and normative concept of totality to counter-balance the poststructuralist/postmodern emphasis on difference and discontinuity, we are abandoned to the seriality of pluralist individualism and the supremacy of competitive values over communal life.
>
> (Best 1989: 361)

Best is correct in suggesting that what needs to be abandoned are the reductive uses of totality, and not the concept of totality itself. Otherwise we risk undermining the very concept of the democratic public sphere.[3]

Freire's understanding of knowledge as always a creature of cultural

71

limits and theoretical borders can assist educators in recognizing how certain literacies are necessarily implicated in particular 'selective' economics of truth, value, and power. Knowledge is always indexical to the context of the knower and the known. In other words, knowledge is always implicated in relations of power and power is distributed laterally and historically, which is to say unequally among groups differentiated by race/ ethnicity, gender, and class. If we believe the human mind to be quintessentially creative and that schools should be in the business of enhancing, deepening, and developing creativity for its own sake, we are vulnerable to privileging the 'creative experience' as the centerpiece of a transformative practice. This, of course, reflects the bourgeois standards and petrified harmony of many liberal arts programs. Even if schools were to provide opportunities for students to acquire knowledge in the five main modes of artistic understanding – the aural, visual, verbal, kinesthetic, and enactive – these forms of knowledge production would never be innocent in themselves. The production of knowledge in schools always occupies specifiable locations in relations of power. All forms of knowledge – including those we profess to be creative – are inescapably linked to evaluative choices. Such choices need to be seen as social practices that are themselves historically and socially constructed; educators need to examine cultural choices and consider the degree to which they are liberating or oppressive.

THE FLESH OF MEMORY AND REDEMPTIVE REMEMBRANCE

Freire stresses the importance of affirming the stories that students tell — stories that are based on their own experiences. The importance of students' stories should not be overlooked by educators, for these form the 'warrants' that can eventually serve as guideposts to liberating praxis.

Students' voices are codified and emplotted in stories and in the often vivid descriptive accounts of their lives that students piece together from their daily experiences. Each society has its treasured stock of stories. However, Freire has stressed that not all stories share a similar status and there are those which exist devalued within society's rifts and margins. The stories students bring into the classroom often reflect the ethos and spirit of the community and, if not its collective memory, then the structured silences which make up its repressed unconscious. Such stories need to be voiced, heard, affirmed but also criticized when they embody, often unconsciously, racism, sexism, or antagonisms which oppress others. As Giroux points out:

Freire does more than argue for the legitimation of the culture of the oppressed. He also recognizes that such [cultural] experiences are contradictory in nature and harbor not only radical potentialities but also the sedimentations of domination. Cultural power takes a twist in this instance and refers to the need to work on the experiences that make up the lives of the oppressed. This means that such experiences in their varied cultural forms have to be recovered critically in order to reveal both their strengths and weaknesses. Moreover, this means that self-critique is complemented in the name of a radical pedagogy designed to unearth and critically appropriate those unclaimed emancipatory moments in bourgeois knowledge and experience that further provide the skills the oppressed will need to exercise leadership in the dominant society.

(Giroux 1985: xxiii)

Stories help us to remember and also to forget. They help shape our social reality as much by what they exclude as what they include. Narratives provide the discursive vehicles for transforming the burden of knowing into the revolutionary act of telling. These include the magisterial tropes and master narratives of the empire, as well as narratives of refusal searching for co-ordinates outside of the binary oppositions that consolidate the Manichean universe of Eurocentric time and space and the phallomilitary dynamics of postmodern citizenry. In fact, making an experience into a story is perhaps the most fundamental act of human understanding. Terry Eagleton (1981: 72) notes that, 'We cannot think, act, or desire except in narratives; it is by narrative that the subject forges the "sutured" chain of signifiers that grants its real condition of division sufficient imaginary cohesion to act.' Our histories have referents but our access to them takes textualized forms, meanings, and feelings – all of which become narrativized. Dana Polan (1986: 18–19) remarks that 'dominant ideology . . . seems to find in narrative structure a promising form for the mediation of social conflicts and their resolution through the enveloping power of narrative.' The structures that underlie narrative flow privilege certain resolutions over others, serving what Jameson calls 'strategies of containment' (Polan 1986: 19).

Whereas memories can potentially liberate the subject of history from the ideological sedimentations of experience by hastening the flight of repressed thought from the threshold of the unconscious to the progressively enlarged horizons of insight, it is the narrative or story which gives memory shape and meaning; of course, one has to acknowledge that there may be some meanings repressed by the narrative structure. Not every narrative will fit snugly into a Eurocentric master narrative or modernism's 'imagined communities' – some will indeed brush against the grain of the logocentric tradition.

To remember *in a critical mode*, however, means, in Freirean terms, to confront the social amnesia of generations in flight from their own collective histories – the subjugated knowledges of the marginalized, the excluded, the disenfranchised, and immiserated groups. This process has, of course, been described by Foucault as a form of 'counter-memory' or 'the interaction of subjugated knowledges.' In Freirean terms, critical remembrance of this kind can establish the ethical referents needed for an ongoing struggle for social change. John O'Neill (1976: 4) notes appositely that, 'Remembrance is the womb of freedom . . . [and] . . . the body infrastructure of political knowledge and action.' It holds 'justice to account and sustain the utopian hope that underlies the will to freedom and equality.' In a similar fashion, Sharon Welch (1985) adopts the term 'dangerous memory' to describe a category of remembering which serves both to describe and critique specific histories of oppression and human suffering often 'unaddressed and tacitly tolerated.' It is not only a memory of exclusion and conflict but also of freedom and resistance, even if such resistance is often contingent and in danger of being obliterated (p. 39). Dangerous memory has to do with acknowledging the history of subjectivity and history's often hidden promise of liberation. It often takes forms of pretheoretical commitments, which are more immediate than reflective. This, however, does not diminish the importance of 'critical reflection by intellectuals on the symbolic expression and political action of those who are oppressed' (p. 43).

We can give voice to the subjugated knowledges of oppressed peoples by providing structures that allow the oppressed to speak for themselves. In this way insurrections of subjugated knowledges provide not only new forms of critique, solidarity, and struggle but also a deeper identification with the victimized. This is what Giroux (1987) means when he refers to Freirean literacy as 'liberating remembrance.'

Critical remembering is something more than simply creating a mindful space for residues of the past to be activated. Critical remembering is an historically attuned 'motive power' blasting through the forgetfulness of all reification. As Marcuse reminds us:

> the authentic utopia is grounded in recollection. . . . Forgetting past suffering and joy alleviates life under a repressive reality principle. In contrast, remembrance spurs the drive for the conquest of suffering and the permanence of joy. . . . The horizon of history is still open. And if the remembrance of things past would become a motive power in the struggle for changing the world, the struggle would be waged for a revolution hitherto suppressed in the previous historical revolutions.
>
> (Marcuse 1978: 73)

The concept of memory invites further consideration. For instance, following Walter Adamson's (1985) employment of the term, it can be used as a heuristic device to bring us into a deeper conversation

74

with Freire's problematic. Adamson has developed a very illuminating distinction among what he calls modes of 'memorizing,' 'memory,' and 'remembering.'

Adamson associates the mode of *memorizing* with the Enlightenment idea of a mental 'faculty' or memory through which individuals seek to recall or capture a factual record of historical events 'as they really were.' Memorizing as a mode of realism and historical understanding considers the historical past to be something that already exists as a sociocultural artefact, waiting to be discovered. The mode of *memory* is quite different, and is associated by Adamson with nineteenth-century idealism, which asserted that while memory may not be able to provide an accurate (in the sense of 'factual') account of history, it can, nevertheless, provide individuals with an interpretive account of the past which is 'better than the past understood itself.'

Remembering is, according to Adamson, the most significant mode around which one can establish an emancipatory political project. Emerging as a break with historical tradition after World War I, remembering is to modernism and French 'textualism' what memory is to idealism and historicism, and memorizing is to the Enlightenment and Cartesianism. Whereas memorizing tries to recall what was, and memory dreams of discovering the master code – the Rosetta Stone – with which to uncover the correct interpretation of the past, remembering is a critical and redemptive mode which attempts not to understand the past better but to understand it *differently*.

This emancipatory mode seeks not to establish our radical difference with the past but rather 'seeks to restore our relation to it' (Adamson 1985: 233). It is a critical mode in the sense that 'it recognizes that we are always operating within a changing horizon – of expectations, problems, needs – that leads us to ask different historical questions and to be offered different answers' (p. 233). In this view, history is not conceived of as a linear succession of events in which oppressed victims are forced 'to absorb an alien, desiccated, sterile memory fabricated by the oppressor, so that they will resign themselves to a life that isn't theirs as if it were the only one possible' (Galeano 1973: 288). Rather, history is engaged as a *lived discourse* within the fullness of time in the sense that it provides us with an ethical and political vantage point not for recovering or discovering the past but for *entering a dialogue with the past*. Remembering in this instance conceives of history not as a constraint on the present but rather as a 'source or precondition of power' that can illuminate our political project of emancipation. History, therefore, becomes a source of imaginative power as remembering invites us to remember in different ways so as to comprehend our social and policital situatedness, and in this sense remembering bears an affinity to Benjamin's concept of 'redemptive history.' This notion is far removed from the simplistic notion of 'those

75

who fail to remember the past or ignore history are condemned to repeat it' and is closer to Freire's notion of *conscientizaçao*.

Consciousness is constantly seeking to escape remembering, preserving itself from being overstimulated by remembering, rather than preserving its integral relation with past experience. This is why Adamson, following Benjamin, insists that in the present era remembering must take the form of a radical disruption – a blasting – that is strong enough to break through unconscious repression. According to Arendt (1956), remembering must always mediate between the sense impressions and thought. Rather than freeze-frame events for a disinterested inspection, it must dislodge and summon forth hope. Especially in the present 'idealist culture of memory,' it is important to develop a critical/historical perspective that is able to 'arouse dormant emancipatory energies'.

We would like to take Adamson's typology a step further and thereby extend Freire's pedagogy in such a way as to underscore the importance of speaking from multiple subjectivities in a present that is relentlessly careening forward, imploding into itself. We also share a concern with the speaking subject as a multilayered social agent who is able to assume a number of conflicting subject positions. In doing so, we wish to stress the importance of developing a *mode of redemptive remembering*. Redemptive remembrance contests social amnesia and challenges relations of domination. It recognizes that social life is radically decentered and individuals inhabit a cultural terrain that is unevenly and unequally occupied by conflicting discourses. It is a mode of social dreaming that has a redemptive capacity in that it not only recognizes the partial, contingent, and uncertain character of all knowledge and the heterogeneity of social, cultural, and institutional life but seeks to transform knowledge in the interests of the power and powerless. But it is more than the dreaming of the postmodern *flâneur* or *bricoleur*, who capriciously seeks out the 'shock of the new'! It is, rather, the daydreaming of Ernst Bloch that sets out to rescue emancipatory moments from the 'depravation of history'. It is a dreaming that acknowledges that oppression is not seamless and all of one piece. Redemptive remembering speaks to a critical engagement of and resistance to the dominative society – a society that possesses a crippling potential to disable the oppressed to a supplicatory attitude that is placatory toward regimes of domination.

Redemptive remembering is more than a nostalgic recalling of our past. It follows Linda Hutcheon (1988) in recognizing the danger of a view of history that tends to see the past only as the site of positive values in contrast to a view which acknowledges the capitalist present in its complicity with domination. Against nostalgia, Hutcheon defends the perspective offered by historiographic metafiction which argues that the historical past can never be represented except by transparent conventions. Postmodernism, according to Hutcheon, implies an anti-idealist distinction between the real past and the past as object of knowledge. Following Hutcheon, not only is history full of contradictions, but our means of constructing history is always implicated in ideological interests and relations of power. To engage in redemptive remembering is to recall how, as subjects, we have become disproportionately constituted within dominative regimes of discourses and social practices, through our race, class, and gender identities. The purpose of such remembering is to actively free us from the mystification that results from living unreflectively in such discourses and material constraints. But redemptive remembering is also *always already* a form of Utopian dreaming. It not only demystifies the present by allowing us to recognize ourselves from a critical/historical perspective as, disproportionately, oppressors and oppressed, but it also carries traces of future possibility in its reconstruction of the present moment. It is in this sense that Paulo Freire's notion of *critical reflection can be compared to a form of redemptive remembrance and social dreaming* – an approach to the *Aufhebung*, a passing into the *not yet*.

A redemptive remembering must serve as a form of critique and also a referent for hope. And it must also provide a way for the non-poor to recognize their privilege in order to make alliances with the oppressed. Histories of oppression and suffering must be recounted, including unaddressed instances of domination that take the form of institutional and social practices, universal claims to truth, as well as racism, sexism, and classism. Memories of hope, too, must be offered – that reclaim the revolutionary subject and the historical conditions of resistance. These should include the voices of the oppressed and respect for their integrity and subjugated knowledges (Welch 1985).

The conception of memory that we are advancing follows the Utopian lilt of Walter Benjamin's dialectical images in their attempt to 'blast open the continuum of history' in order to overthrow bourgeois history, not by replacing it with a Marxist narrative, but rather by bringing 'to consciousness those repressed elements of the past (its realized barbarisms and its unrealized dreams) which "place the present in a critical position"' (Buck-Morss 1989: 338).

Benjamin's dialectical images operate unlike present-day deconstructive methods. Such methods do not contain an image of the present as a moment of revolutionary possibility – only as novel interpretations or the tropological displacement of discursive familiarity. Rather than serve as a form of radical politics, they function only as 'fashion masquerading as politics.' In contrast, Benjamin's dialectical image focuses 'on the past that made the present, as revolutionary "now-time," its vanishing point' (Buck-Morss 1989: 339). This puts modern efforts at deconstruction in Benjamin's 'image realm' of the proletariat 'without thereby being in the least allied to the working class' (Buck-Morss 1989: 290). Historical memory is recalled in dialectical images, not as a surrogate for experience

77

but as a means of providing with a voice, undistorted by the echoes of industry or the motors of progress, those memories which have been policed into silence. History, in this instance, is recognized as more than an artefact of the past, or as simply the replacement of the temporal narratives of our political unconscious by the tyranny of the sign (Lash and Urry 1987: 292). Rather, the dialectical images of history become the birth pangs of the liberating moment, of Freirean critical praxis, of awakening from the 'nightmare' weighing on the brain of the living from which Marx proclaimed our legacy of the past. Memory needs to be linked both to historical narratives that have become repressed and an identity forged out of such a linkage that is firmly grounded in a commitment to the *metanarrative* and not the *master narrative* of human freedom. Metanarratives are *metacritical* and do not succumb to the transcendental unity of subject and object or their transfiguring coalescence (Saldivar 1990: 173).

Richard Kearney (1987) speaks of a form of 'anticipatory memory' that 'rediscovers in history many narrative prefigurations of possible truth, now repressed or forgotten' (p. 54). He reminds us that the development of an ethical imagination in the age of postmodernism presupposes the existence of a certain narrative identity which 'remembers its commitments to the other (both in its personal and collective history) and recalls, that these commitments have *not yet* been fulfilled' (p. 55). Metanarratives discredit magisterial narrative's 'phallic projectory' into the telos of historical destiny while at the same time recuperating a provisional or formative totality that is unifying without dominating, that is always in need of supplementation, that seeks to understand social relations in their implications of totality and not in terms of a false universalism (Murphy 1991).

Within narrative identity, historical agency is understood as assuming authorship of one's life, as a narrator who constantly revises and reinterprets one's own story in relation to its historical and discursive connections to the cultural archives of the wider community such that personal identity is always located in the interests of the broader public. Personal history in this view is always the history of a collective past and future, the relation of self to other.

Redemptive rememberance is a form of counter-memory. Counter-memory employs stories and narratives as a mode of contestation. It provides a backdrop – a provisional totality – from which to interpret and judge the claims to truth and justice of any one story. Lipsitz describes counter-memory as follows:

> Counter-memory is a way of remembering and forgetting that starts with the local, the immediate, and the personal. Unlike historical narratives that begin with the totality of human existence and then locate specific actions and events within that totality,

78

counter-memory starts with the particular and the specific and then builds outward toward a total story. Counter-memory looks to the past for the hidden histories excluded from dominant narratives. But unlike myths that seek to detach events and actions from the fabric of any larger history, counter-memory forces revision of existing histories by supplying new perspectives about the past. Counter-memory embodies aspects of myth and aspects of history, but it retains an enduring suspicion of both categories. Counter-memory focuses on localized experiences with oppression, using them to reframe and refocus dominant narratives purporting to represent universal experience.

(Lipsitz 1990: 213)

Counter-memory moves beyond history and myth, especially the historical narratives of Western capitalist countries. In fact, counter-memory plays myths *against* history, pointing 'the way toward a new synthesis, one that offers dignity interchangeably to all peoples without first forcing them into an imaginary identity constructed from a top-down perspective on human experiences' (Lipsitz 1990: 227). Counter-memory combines linear history with orally transmitted popular history; this involves mixing 'subjective understanding of . . . oppression with objective evidence about the pain suffered by others' (p. 225). Counter-memory does not focus exclusively on the cursive time of linear history nor the monumental time of private life cycles and rituals, but rather 'women's time' which is the time of oppressed and marginalized groups. Counter-memory as 'women's time' 'celebrates the subversive visions and stubborn *jouissance* of monumental time while still insisting on relating local oppositional practices to macro-social causes and consequences [cursive time]' (p. 229).

Counter-memory is forged in the margins of popular collective consciousness which contain Utopian dimensions that serve both as a form of critique and as a form of popular vision of what could and should be. The concept of counter-memory (as brilliantly articulated by Giroux 1990) constitutes part of the language of public life, a vision of optimism, and a witness to history; it provides the ethical and epistemological grounds for a politics of difference within solidarity. The postmodern mode of redemptive remembrance recognizes the fallibility of metaphysical inquiry, the radical undecidability of knowledge, the speculative nature of theory, and that the totality in which all differences are recognized cannot exist. These recognitions are not a cause for despair but rather the beginning of a radical hope which rejects the quest for certainty and the craving for absolutes. It is a hope that affirms the partiality of all knowledge, that is open to difference and otherness and demands that one be responsive to the other's claims. It is a hope grounded in the necessity of freedom, in a politically responsible totalization that always recognizes the gaps

79

produced by the metaphoricity of imagined communities and the disjunctive temporality of the sign-gaps where culture can be transformed through minority subaltern voices (Bhabha 1990). It is a hope that is formed outside the classical epic forms, literary devices, and metropolitan tropes hewed in the drawing rooms and rooming houses of our *modernista* mega-fathers. Rather, it is reflected in the passion of prophetic voices and the rhetoricizing moves of preachers; it asserts the priority of dialogue over totalizing discourses; it places our ethical relation to the other prior to our ontological, cosmological, and epistemological relation to ourselves (Levinas 1969). It is a hope of passionate remembrances, of finding a common ground of struggle rather than a common culture, of new spaces of possibility rather than arenas of despair and manufactured doubt. It is a hope that is fundamentally Freirean.

CONCLUSION

Art is not a mirror held up to reality but a hammer with which to shape it.

Bertolt Brecht

The strength of Freire's pedagogy is that it presents a way of transcending the unacknowledged violence inherent in the binary thinking that positions the 'colonizer' against the 'colonized.' The problem of binary thinking has been discussed at length by thinkers as diverse as Nietzsche, Benita Parry, and Michel Pêcheux and is worth summarizing.

In his *Genealogy of Morals*, Nietzsche discusses the revolt of the slave against the master. His perspectivist account locates the discourse of the master in terms of the evaluative polarity of the existing anonymical pairs, 'good' and 'bad' (Nietzsche 1968; cited in Redding 1990). According to Nietzsche, the noble is the measure of all that is 'good' while his 'other,' the slave, is the measure of all that is 'bad.' But as Paul Redding (1990) notes, when the slave conceives of the master as 'the evil enemy,' he reactively inverts the evaluative polarity of the good/bad couplet, leaving the original pattern of indexicality intact. That is, the indexical 'center' is still the way of life of the noble speaker. The slave's actions are determined from the perspective of the noble and since the slave had no means of encoding any other way of life except from the perspective of the master, there was no way of making 'action-guiding' judgements of his own. All that the slaves were capable of doing was to reverse the evaluative polarity of the existing antonymic pairs, 'good and bad.' In this regard, Steven Connor (1989: 236) notes that in its defense of the colonized and marginalized, critical theory must be 'prepared to surrender its sense of its own territorial right to codify and manage the margins, determining the conditions under which speech from margins is possible.' This must be done in order to avoid the 'romance of the marginal' which leads to 'a Manichean Universe of absolute opposites which is barely responsive to the actual complexities and overdeterminations of the situation under determination.'

Michel Pêcheux has constructed a useful typology for understanding how discourses are engaged by various groups in contemporary social life: to *identify* with a discourse means that a group lives within the terms generated by the discourse; to *counteridentify* with a discourse means living within its governing structure of ideas but to reverse its terms; to *disidentify* with a discourse means going beyond the structure of oppositions and sanctioned negations which it supplies. As part of a pedagogy of liberation, to *disidentify* means to refuse the very frames of reference which splits off the marginalized from the dominators and to create, in pedagogical terms, new vocabularies of resistance which do not separate curriculum from gender politics, values from aesthetics, pedagogy from power (cited in Connor 1989: 236–7).

In Benita Parry's (1987: 28) terms, a critical practice must do more than repossess 'the signifying function appropriated by colonialist repre-sentation' or demystify or deform the rhetorical devices that 'organize colonialism's discursive field.' Rather, the founding concepts of colonial-ism's 'received narratives' and 'monolithic figures and stereotypes of colonialist representations' must be refused. For Parry, resistance must include a critique of imperialism that does not conflate race, class, ethnic, gender, and sexual discrimination and that enables counter-discourses to develop that are able to displace imperialism's dominative system of knowledge from a position outside of its cultural hegemony. That is, it must confront dominant structures of knowledge from a disidentificatory vantage point outside of those structures.

While disidentification seems the most urgent option for critical educa-tors, there is a danger in the possible abandonment of a universal application of the principles of freedom and justice in an attempt to get outside the metanarratives of value and morality. We need, in other words, to ground our theory of resistance (counterhegemony) as we struggle to negotiate between competing interests and among multiple centers of identity. Unless we recognize that totality and universality should not be rejected outright, but only when they are used unjustly and oppressively as global, all-encompassing, and all-embracing warrants for thought and action in order to secure an oppressive regime of truth, we court disaster (Best 1989). Unless we have a moral, ethical, and political ground – albeit a provisional one – from which to negotiate among multiple interests, we could establish pedagogies and curricula which flirt dangerously with the very error which critical educators seek to correct, which duplicate the original silencing of the Other which they so passionately rail against, which replicate the concepts and systems of power they seek to revoke, which resurrect in reverse millenarian myths of imperial conquest, and which re-legitimize those very discursive regimes they seek to reject.

That is, by repudiating domination without at the same time establishing some ethical 'bearings' for a universal struggle for freedom, critical pedagogy could recover such domination in different forms. We need to ask the question: Are our pedagogies built upon a normative backdrop which privileges Eurocentric and patriarchal representations and interests? Are our multicultural and feminist pedagogies mortgaged to theoretical formulations which, however ruthlessly deconstructed, still reaffirm the primacy of Western individualism, patriarchy, class privilege, and a partitionist politics?

Freire's work makes clear that a postcolonial pedagogy must always be tied, conceptually, politically, and ethically, to a larger pedagogy of liberation. In this context, resistance to domination and oppression must consist of more than a reactive transvaluation of dominant forms of knowledge and social practices – more than moral injunctions against dominant evaluative judgements and cultural forms. As long as resistance is 'reactive,' it positions itself as 'other-centered' discourse (Redding 1990). Within a larger pedagogy of liberation, resistance must also be an *active* transvaluation of dominant perspectives in order for it to constitute a project of possibility. It must be active if it is to generate new 'action-guiding' perspectives that can allow cultural workers to escape the larger logic of domination which continues to underwrite many anti-colonialist struggles and resistances. That is, resistance must not only consist of the struggle against oppression but *through* oppression by means of dialogical engagement *with* and a transformation *of* oppressive social relations. It not only means defamiliarizing the borders that demarcate established conventions of teleological closure and narrative meaning, but also generating a new language of critique and hope that can challenge the transparency of representation that undergirds dominant enunciative systems and regimes of discourse. The challenge of a pedagogy of liberation is to rupture the binary thinking and self-engendered world of facts ushered in by modernism's apotheosis of imagination. Yet in doing so, it must not break with all forms of narrative expectancy, for that would be to wage war with rationality itself. For Freire, liberatory pedagogy recognizes that the oppressed cannot always transparently articulate their best interests, yet he cautions against speaking for others. Rather, he encourages dialogue that is responsible and accountable and that avoids a reinscription of colonialist attitudes through a privileging of the social location of the speaker.

Freire's pedagogy underscores the reality that one can never simply speak for oneself (as some deconstructionists and liberal humanists woefully presume). Because when one claims to be only speaking for oneself, this also entails 'participating in the creation and reproduction of discourses through which my own and other selves are constituted' (Alcoff, 1991–2: 21). Claiming only to 'speak for oneself' permits individuals to retreat from a political and ethical responsibility for their actions. Yet, we should not unproblematically speak *for* others. Freire emphasizes a 'speaking to' and 'speaking with' rather than a 'speaking for.' This issue is addressed by Linda Alcoff (1991–2) who argues that in evaluating whether or not to speak for others, we need to consider the effects of our words on the material and discursive context in which such speaking will take place. She maintains that we need to ask how our own discourse as an *event* positions us as authoritative and empowered speakers in ways that unwittingly reinscribe the discourse of colonization, of patriarchy, of racism, of conquest – 'a reinscription of sexual, national, and other kinds of hierarchies' (p. 29). Alcoff, citing Spivak, notes that we should adopt a '"speaking to," in which the intellectual neither abnegates his or her discursive role nor presumes an authenticity of the oppressed but still allows for the possibility that the oppressed will produce a "counter-sentence" that can then suggest a new historical narrative' (p. 23). Such a perspective is fundamentally Freirean.

Freire's revolutionary project can be summed up in his own words: 'There is no revolution without love, the revolution is loving' (forthcoming). The work of Paulo Freire is a compassionate fire, one in which the bourgeois world of mystification melts away as our critical imagination becomes ignited; it is a fire that heats up our spirit even as it softens the solidity and certainty of existing social relations; it is a fire whose flames of transformation invite us to take Brecht's hammer and to forge on liberation's anvil new, reciprocal discourses of knowing and freer, more equitable spaces for living.

Yet the metaphor of the anvil, while capturing the force and density of Freire's political project, does not do justice to the rich complexity and interconnectedness of his ideas. To do so, one would have to examine the warp and woof of Freire's sociological imagination. The former metaphor testifies to the power Freire's pedagogy gains from its social location in the experiences of the oppressed; the latter captures the compassionate weave of his politics spun in a language that speaks to the heart of all those who suffer.

For Freire, the most important sites for resisting enslavement to machineries of servitude are the schools. While not the only sites for social transformation, they are very necessary. That they are not sufficient for social change should not be a cause for despair but should point to the radical possibilities associated with a commitment to forms of social alliances and movements that can help realize the most radical dream of democracy, the dream of freedom.

What makes Freire's work so important for social and pedagogical struggle at this historical juncture is that it constitutes an *ethics of obligation* – an ethics going beyond liberal humanist concerns with self-esteem so prevalent in the mainstream pedagogical discourses of capitalist countries. In the final analysis, Freire offers not pedagogical rules for individuals to apply to particular social acts, but rather a pedagogical attitude situated at the level of an ethical intention, based on respect for others as a moral obligation, a principle for living informed by a narrative imagination that tells us the story of exile, humility, historical responsibility, and liberation. His task has been to return to the oppressed the values and forms of social engagements that have been usurped and alienated by colonialism's enduring imposition of the cultural forms and hegemonic social relations of the oppressor.

Freire's work presents a common ground for contextualizing oppression and for transforming the effects of conditioned fear and self-defeating patterns of alienation. His protest is mounted as a direct challenge to the categorical function of pedagogy as it is frequently understood and practiced. Freire's unique challenge has been to bend reality to the requirements of a just world, and to create new zones of transformative liminality in the home, the school, the university, the community, and in larger public and administrative contexts. His task has been largely postcolonial[4] in decentering and disorienting monolithic and imperial forms of authority that domesticate the Other, that lay siege to the power of the margins. His goal has been to question the tacit assumptions and unarticulated presuppositions – the unexamined faith in continuity and desire for familiarity – that make up the history of oppression, and to put under hermeneutical stress the privileged norms these interpretations legitimate, the self-images they create, the borders of identity that they police and the despair they foster. His contribution has been to breathe new life into historical agency and to pronounce it unfinalizable in a world that has witnessed the apocalyptic disappearance of the subject of history (Jameson 1989; Giroux and McLaren 1989) and to give encouragement to those who instead of visiting history as a curator or custodian of memory choose to live in the furnace of history, where memories are molten and can be bent into the contours of a dream, perhaps even the immanent force of a vision.

In the current historical juncture of recycled McCarthyism, postmodern pastiche, and the ironic self-detachment of artists and intellectuals, where everyday life has been brought under the *nouvelle* aesthetic sign-form of Madonna's hyper-bra and Arnold Schwarzenegger's replicant super-cut biceps, Freire's pedagogy points to a way in which we can live and shape history rather than simply rehearse it through image-produced desire. Freire's pedagogy foregrounds the failure of leadership that we have experienced from echelons of aristocratic aesthetes like Baudrillard and other impresarios of postmodernism and capital city intellectuals, whose intellectual advances have not been sufficiently mounted as contestatory practices capable of fracturing the fault lines of capitalist social relations and existing proliferations of power and privilege. Baudrillard's pataphysical projections of his own fantastic universe of runaway signs encourage academics to embrace ludic forms of postmodernism for the radical posture it affords them as a cover for their role as passive supplicants of history and to avoid the concrete politics that Freire speaks about.

The political pedagogy of Paulo Freire, if protected from reductionistic practices of liberal educators to turn it into a method, can serve as a praxis where Blacks and Latinos no longer fear and obey the white gaze of power, where bonds of sentiment and webs of social obligation can be formed among all oppressed people, where resistance can enable schools to become more than instruments of social replication, where contrasting cultural styles and cultural capital among groups (*différences de moeurs*) cease to remain tokens of estrangement that separate groups but rather the very impetus that brings them together as liminal travelers under an arch of social dreaming.

Freire's words blow like strong winds through the torpor of Western liberalism and the political quietude and apathy of generations of youth – generations increasingly held captive by the power of global capitalism and the structures of intelligibility, sepulchral identities, and social relations such power is likely to produce. They whisper with the force of a gale, calling educators to establish pedagogies that establish not only the grounds for a critical language of imagination but also the formation of a teachable heart – a heart that invites compassion, empathy, and forgiveness through a new and revolutionary way of loving.

NOTES

1 Condensed sections of this chapter will appear in *Access* (New Zealand), *The Fortieth Yearbook of the National Reading Conference*, Chicago, and *College Literature*.
2 Enfleshment refers to the mutually constitutive enfolding of social structure and desire; that is, it constitutes the dialectical relationship between the material organization of interiority and the cultural forms and modes of materiality we inhabit subjectively. Enfleshment is the 'quilting point' that results when the radical externality of the body/subject as independent and resistant to volition joins the pure interiority of subjectivity. Enfleshment, then, involves both the entextualization of desire and the embodiment of textual forms (McLaren 1988).
3 This idea has been taken from Henry Giroux and Peter McLaren, 'Radical pedagogy as cultural politics: beyond the discourse of critique and anti-utopianism,' in Donald Morton and Mas'ud Zavarzadeh (eds) *Theory/Pedagogy/Politics* (Chicago; University of Chicago Press, 1991), p. 182.
4 We wish to qualify our use of the term 'postcolonialism.' We are referring here to the importance of problematizing pedagogical discourses in light of the current trajectory towards global capitalism (while admitting its disorganized and

disjunctive character) and the narratives and cultural logic associated with and resulting from the breaking up of old imperialisms based on nation states. We are aware that in some critical circles, the term 'postcolonialism' is coming under the same kind of criticism as the concept of 'multiculturalism.' Some critics perceive both terms to be totalizing discourses that mask injustice and inequality under subtle forms of neocolonialism. Postcolonial pedagogy, as we are using it, is a pedagogy of anti-imperialism that attempts to challenge the very categories through which the history and narratives of the colonized have been written (Ashcroft et al. 1989). Explicit in this form of pedagogy is a challenge both to the way situated knowledges are produced within the larger context of the social formation and to global capitalism as a master narrative of desire and inevitability, as well as to the way that Anglo-European discourses have split off the Other and either banished or romanticized difference in politically and ethically disabling ways. Of course, the term 'postcolonial' is always to be understood in context-specific ways, and I do not seek to sketch its contours without placing it in contradiction to its possible universalist assumptions. I see postcolonial pedagogy as a temporary suspension of the colonial moment, a liminal space that, while still containing traces of colonial and neocolonial discourses, effectively allows for their suspension and for the development of a community of resistance.

REFERENCES

Adamson, W. (1985) *Marx and the Disillusionment of Marxism*, Berkeley, University of California Press.

Agger, B. (1989) *Socio (onto) logy*, Urbana and Chicago, University of Illinois Press.

Alcoff, L. (1991–2) 'The problem of speaking for others', *Cultural Critique* 20, pp. 5–32.

Anzaldúa, G. (1990) 'Haciendo caras, una entrada,' in G. Anzaldúa (ed.) *Making Face, Making Soul*, San Francisco, Aunt Lute Foundation Books, pp. xv–xxviii.

Arendt, H. (1956) *Between Past and Future: Eight Exercises in Political Thought*, New York, Penguin.

Ashcroft, B., Griffiths, G., and Tiffin, H. (1989) *The Empire Writes Back: Theory and Practice in Post-Colonial Literatures*. London and New York, Routledge.

Bagdikian, B. (1989) 'The lords of the global village', *The Nation* (12 June) 248, 805–20.

Baudrillard, J. (1973) *In the Shadow of the Silent Majorities*, New York, Semiotexte.

Belsey, C. (1983) 'Reply to John Holloway,' *Times Literary Supplement* 4, 1217.

Bennett, T. (1986) 'Texts in history: the determinations of readings and their texts,' in D. Attridge and G. Bennington (eds) *Post-structuralism and the Question of History*, Cambridge, Cambridge University Press, pp. 63–81.

Best, S. (1989) 'Jameson, totality and the poststructuralist critique,' in D. Kellner (ed.) *Postmodernism/Jameson/Critique*, Washington, Maisonneuve Press, pp. 233–368.

Bhabha, H. K. (1990) 'DissemiNation: time, narrative, and the margins of the modern nation', in H. K. Bhabha (ed.), *Nation and Narration*, London and New York, Routledge, 291–322.

Bloom, A. (1987) *The Closing of the American Mind: How Higher Education has Failed Democracy and Impoverished the Souls of Today's Students*, New York, Simon & Schuster.

Brown, R. H. (1987) *Society as Text*, Chicago and London, University of Chicago Press.

Buck-Morss, S. (1989) *The Dialectics of Seeing*, Cambridge, Massachusetts, MIT Press.

Cocks, J. (1988) *The Oppositional Imagination*, London and New York, Routledge.

Connolly, R. (1981) 'Freire, praxis and education,' in R. Mackie (ed.) *Literacy and Revolution*, New York, Continuum. pp. 70–81.

Connor, S. (1989) *Postmodern Culture*, Oxford, Basil Blackwell.

Coste, D. (1989) *Narrative as Communication*, Minneapolis, University of Minnesota Press.

Dauenhauer, B. P. (1989) 'Ideology, utopia, and responsible politics,' *Man and World* 22, 25–41.

de Certeau, M. (1984) *The Practice of Everyday Life*, Berkeley, University of California Press.

de Lauretis, T. (1987) *Technologies of Gender*, Bloomington and Indianapolis, Indiana University Press.

Dussel, E. (1980) *Philosophy of Liberation*, Maryknoll, New York, Orbis Books.

Eagleton, T. (1985/6) 'The subject of literature,' *Cultural Critique* 2, 95–104.

—— (1981) *Walter Benjamin or Towards a Revolutionary Criticism*, London, Verso.

Foucault, M. (1980) *Power/Knowledge: Selected Interviews and Other Writings, 1972–1977*, ed. C. Gordon, New York, Pantheon.

Freire, P. (1970) *Pedagogy of the Oppressed*, New York, Seabury Press.

—— (1972a) *Cultural Action for Freedom*, New York, Penguin.

—— (1972b) *Pedagogy of the Oppressed*, New York, Continuum.

—— (1985) *The Politics of Education*, South Hadley, Massachusetts, Bergin & Garvey.

—— (forthcoming) *Critique of Domesticating Pedagogy: A Dialogue with Paulo Freire*, edited by M. Escobar, A. L. Fernandez and G. Guevara, Albany, SUNY Press.

Freire, P. and Macedo, D. (1987) *Literacy: Reading the Word and the World*, South Hadley, Massachusetts, Bergin & Garvey.

Fuss, D. (1989) *Essentially Speaking: Feminism, Nature, and Difference*, London and New York, Routledge.

Galeano, E. H. (1973) *Open Veins of Latin America*, New York, Monthly Review Press.

Giroux, H. A. (1985) 'Introduction,' in P. Freire, *The Politics of Education*, South Hadley, Massachusetts, Bergin & Garvey, pp. xi–xxv.

—— (1987) 'Introduction: literacy and the pedagogy of political empowerment,' in P. Freire and D. Macedo, *Literacy: Reading the Word and the World*, South Hadley, Massachusetts, Bergin & Garvey, pp. 1–27.

—— (1988) *Schooling and the Struggle for Public Life*, Minneapolis, University of Minnesota Press.

—— (1990) *Curriculum Discourse as Postmodernist Critical Practice*, Victoria, Australia, Deakin University Press.

Giroux, H. A. and McLaren, P. (1989) 'Schooling, cultural politics, and the struggle for democracy,' in H. A. Giroux and P. McLaren (eds) *Critical Pedagogy, the State, and Cultural Struggle*, Albany, SUNY Press, pp. xi–xxv.

Grosz, E. (1989) 'Sexual difference and the problem of essentialism,' *Inscriptions* 5, 86–102.

Hebdige, D. (1988) *Hiding in the Light*, London and New York, Routledge.

Hewitt, M. (1989) 'Feminist critical theory,' *The Ecumenist* 27 (67), 86–90.

hooks, bell (1989) *Talking Back: Thinking Feminist, Thinking Black*, Boston, South End Press.

—— (1991) 'Essentialism and experience,' *American Literary History* 3 (1), 172–83.

Hudson, W. (1982) *The Marxist Philosophy of Ernst Bloch*, New York, St Martin's Press.

Hutcheon, L. (1988) *A Poetics of Postmodernism*, New York and London, Routledge.

Jackson, M. (1983) 'Thinking through the body,' *Social Analysis*, 14, 127–48.

Jameson, F. (1989) 'Afterword – Marxism and postmodernism,' in D. Kellner (ed.) *Postmodernism/Jameson/Critique*, Washington, Maisonneuve Press, pp. 369–87.

Kearney, R. (1987). 'Ethics and the postmodern imagination,' *Thought* 62, (244), 39–58.

Lankshear, C. (1987) *Literacy, Schooling and Revolution*, Philadelphia, Falmer Press.

Lash, S. (1990) *Sociology of Postmodernism*, London and New York, Routledge.

Lash, S. and Urry, J. (1987) *The End of Organized Capitalism*, Madison, Wisconsin, The University of Wisconsin Press.

Levinas, E. (1969) *Totality and Infinity*, Pittsburgh, Duquesne University Press.

Lipsitz, G. (1990) *Time Passages*, Minneapolis, University of Minnesota Press.

McCarthy, C. (1988) 'Rethinking liberal and radical perspectives on racial inequality in schooling: making the case for nonsynchrony,' *Harvard Educational Review* 58 (3), 265–79.

Mackie, R. (1981) 'Contributions to the thought of Paulo Freire,' in R. Mackie (ed.) *Literacy and Revolution*, New York, Continuum, pp. 93–119.

McLaren, P. (1986) *Schooling as a Ritual Performance*, London and New York, Routledge.

—— (1988) 'Schooling the postmodern body: critical pedagogy and the politics of enfleshment,' *Journal of Education* 170 (3), 53–83.

—— (1989) 'On ideology and education: critical pedagogy and the cultural politics of resistance,' in H. A. Giroux and P. McLaren (eds) *Critical Pedagogy, the State, and Cultural Struggle*, Albany, SUNY Press, pp. 174–202.

—— (ed.) (1992) *Postmodernism, Postcolonialism and Pedagogy*, Albert Park, Australia, James Nicholas.

Marcuse, H. (1978) *The Aesthetic Dimension*, Boston, Beacon Press.

Mathews, M. (1981) 'Knowledge, action, and power,' in R. Mackie (ed.) *Literacy and Revolution*, New York, Continuum, pp. 82–92.

Mills, P. J. (1987) *Woman, Nature and Psyche*, New Haven and London, Yale University Press.

Morton, D. and Zavarzadeh, M. (1988) 'The cultural politics of the fiction workshop,' *Cultural Critique* 11, 155–73.

Murphy, P. (1991) 'Postmodern perspectives and justice,' *Thesis Eleven*, no. 30, 117–32.

Nietzsche, F. (1968) 'On the genealogy of morals,' in *Basic Writings of Nietzsche*, ed. W. Kaufman, New York, Modern Library.

O'Neill, J. (1976) 'Critique and remembrance,' in J. O'Neill (ed.) *On Critical Theory*, New York, Seabury Press, pp. 1–11.

Parry, B. (1987) 'Problems in current theories of colonial discourse,' *The Oxford Literary Review* 9, 27–58.

Pheby, K. (1988) *Interventions: Displacing the Metaphysical Subject*, Washington, Maisonneuve Press.

Polan, D. (1986) *Power and Paranoia: History, Narrative, and the American Cinema, 1940–1950*, New York, Columbia University Press.

Pomorska, K. (1980) 'The overcoded world of Solzhenitsyn,' *Poetics Today* 1 (3), 163–70.

Redding, P. (1990) 'Nietzschean perspectivism and the logic of practical reason,' *The Philosophical Forum* 22 (1), 72–88.

Ricoeur, P. (1989) 'The human being as the subject matter of philosophy,' in T. P. Kemp and D. Rasmussen (eds) *The Narrative Path*, Cambridge, Massachusetts, MIT Press, 89–101.

Saldivar, R. (1990) *Chicano Narrative: The Dialectics of Difference*, Madison, University of Wisconsin Press.

Shor, I. and Freire, P. (1987) *A Pedagogy for Liberation*, South Hadley, Massachusetts, Bergin & Garvey.

Shotter, J. (1989) 'Social accountability and the social construction of "you,"' in J. Shotter and K. J. Green (eds) *Texts of Identity*, London, Sage, pp. 133–151.

Simon, R. (1987) 'Empowerment as a pedagogy of possibility,' *Language Arts* 64 (4), 370–82.

Simon, R. and Dippo, D. (1986) 'On critical ethnographic work,' *Anthropology and Education Quarterly* 17 (4), 195–202.

Stam, R. (1991) 'Bakhtin, polyphony, and ethnic/racial representation,' in L. Friedman (ed.) *Unspeakable Images: Ethnicity in the American Cinema*, Urbana and Chicago, University of Illinois Press, pp. 251–76.

Thiong'O, N. W. (1986) *Decolonizing the Mind*, London, James Currey and Portsmouth, New Hampshire, Heinemann.

Torres, C. (1990) 'Paulo Freire's "Pedagogy of the Oppressed" twenty years after: interview with Paulo Freire,' *Aurora* 13 (3), 12–14.

Trenner, R. (1983) *E. L. Doctorow: Essays and Conversations*, Princeton, New Jersey, Ontario Review Press.

Volosinov, V. N. (1973) *Marxism and the Philosophy of Language*, trans. L. Matejka and I. R. Titunik, New York and London, Seminar Press.

Welch, S. D. (1985) *Communities of Resistance and Solidarity*, Maryknoll, New York, Orbis Books.

West, C. (1989) 'Black culture and postmodernism,' in B. Kruger and P. Mariani (eds) *Remaking History*, Seattle, Bay Press, pp. 87–96.

Wolff, R. (1989) Review of *The Last Intellectuals* by Russell Jacoby, *Rethinking Marxism* 2 (1), 135–41.

Young, I. M. (1990) *Justice and the Politics of Difference*, Princeton, New Jersey, Princeton University Press.

Žižek, S. (1990) 'Beyond discourse-analysis,' Appendix to E. Laclau, *New Reflections on the Revolution of our Time*, London, Verso, pp. 249–60.

5

FUNCTIONAL LITERACY FROM A FREIREAN POINT OF VIEW

Colin Lankshear

THE EMERGENCE OF FUNCTIONAL LITERACY

Kenneth Levine identifies functional literacy as the key concept used in recent decades to advance a utilitarian argument for making available to illiterate populations 'a broad-based, socially "relevant" literacy' (Levine 1986: 25). He shows how the idea of becoming functional emerged as a goal to be pursued in a series of UNESCO-sponsored literacy programs in the Third World, and traces the various shifts in connotation and emphasis it underwent during its 'career' with UNESCO. At times functional literacy was reduced to very narrow instrumental terms, emphasizing the value of literate adults to a nation pursuing economic development. At other times it carried more humanistic connotations as well – recognizing the role of literacy in promoting human rights and social–cultural advancement in addition to serving economic and other national development ends. Overall, however, the meanings given to functionality within Third World literacy initiatives were predominantly instrumental or utilitarian in tone. They stressed the importance of people being able to fit more fully into existing circumstances and practices, and/or to perform a productive role within a national development plan (see Levine 1986: 25–42; Giroux 1987: 2–6; McLaren 1988: 213–34).

More recently, functional literacy has also emerged as an official goal for adult literacy programs within modern industrial capitalist countries. Considerable adult illiteracy was discovered in Britain and the United States during the 1960s and 1970s. This discovery[1] was quickly replicated in Canada, Australia, New Zealand, and elsewhere. The perceived scale of the problem in these countries prompted organized activity – with official government support – on behalf of adult illiteracy. In the United States and Britain functional literacy was adopted from the outset as the official level of attainment to be pursued in adult literacy campaigns: the best known being the 'Right to Read' campaigns.

The US Office of Education defined literate persons as those who have acquired the essential knowledge and skills in reading, writing, and computation required for effective functioning in society, and whose attainment in such skills makes it possible for [them] to develop new attitudes and to participate actively in the life of [their] times.

And in Britain,

> *A Right to Read* . . . quoted with approval the US National Reading Center's (USNRC) definition: 'A person is functionally literate when he [sic] has command of reading skills that permit him to go about his daily activities successfully on the job, or to move about society normally with comprehension of the usual printed expressions and messages he encounters.'[2]

Here, as in Third World contexts, the espoused goal of functional literacy has been overtly utilitarian. The aim is to incorporate (marginal) adults into established economic and social values and practices. Functional literacy has been conceived as a means to an end. And within this view human beings themselves have been conceived foremost as means to such ends as economic efficiency and social cohesion. Levine says that from the start the kind of 'intermediate level of attainment' which gradually evolved into a notion of functional literacy was assumed 'to be associated with employability' and 'in a loose and unclarified way, with the social "integration" and "adjustment" of its possessors' (Levine 1986: 25–6).

Minimalist approaches to adult literacy, and functionality in particular, have come increasingly under attack in Britain and the United States. While some critiques have been of a technical or conceptual nature,[3] others have gone to the very heart of the ethos of functional literacy and rejected its underlying premises. It is the latter line of attack I want to elaborate here.

Jonathan Kozol rejects functional literacy outright. It is an unworthy goal to be pursued in adult literacy programs. A functionalist philosophy minimalizes human beings. In the sense of the term that has been 'frozen into public discourse,' functional literacy is mean-spirited. 'Machines function,' says Kozol. 'People either perish or prevail. We need to find more generous delineations of our goals.' Kozol sees functional literacy reducing persons to the status of mere objects and means, rather than confirming and exalting them as ends in themselves. It aims to equip illiterate adults with just those skills and knowledges – no more – which ensure 'competence to function at the lowest levels of mechanical performance,' as workers and citizens in a print-dominated society. The stress is on illiterate adults becoming capable of coping with external demands imposed on them by the world of work and civic duty, not on their personal and collective expansion as human beings. Functional literacy demeans human beings by denying its recipients the potential inherent in print as a vehicle for discovering, expressing, and enhancing their humanness. Moreover, Kozol finds it morally repugnant, if not dangerously insane, to adjust people (through making them literate) to daily routines which are integral to one nation's pursuit of global domination, when the price of that pursuit could well be global annihilation. In Kozol's view, literacy surely has more noble and humane ends to promote:

> The competence to function at the lowest levels of mechanical performance must . . . be transcended by a humanistic vision of the uses to which literate men and women will address their new-found skills. A fundamental humane literacy is one which does not demarcate a skill from its potential application, a scientific from a humanistic purpose, a selfish ambition from its frequently destructive consequences.
>
> (Kozol 1985: 185–6)

From a different but related angle, Levine raises doubts about the political and social interests underlying the functional literacy enterprise. He is suspicious of the emphasis given to reading at the expense of writing within influential views of functional literacy. How, he wonders, can competence in reading labels and instructions, or even in filling out forms, produce the advantages promised by the way definitions of functional literacy are formulated and by the advertising and propaganda of many literacy agencies? (Levine 1986: 41). Moreover, on the whole it is writing competencies 'that are capable of initiating change'; and it is change that is needed if the most serious difficulties faced by those persons deemed functionally incompetent are to be overcome. Levine questions which/ whose interests are really served by functional approaches to adult literacy. He suggests that functional competence according (for example) with the USNRC definition would clearly be in the interests of the state, employers, and authority and power élites generally. Overall, its likely effect would be 'to domesticate and further subordinate rather than to increase the autonomy and social standing of the previously illiterate person' (Levine 1986: 41).

Such critiques provide a useful background against which to set some of Paulo Freire's central ideas. This can best be done by first taking a closer look at what functional literacy actually becomes 'on the ground,' so to speak, when it is operationalized into specific objectives, tasks, content, and skills. The model of functional literacy developed by the Adult Performance Level [APL] team at the University of Texas is, perhaps, most appropriate for this purpose.

APL: A SOPHISTICATED MODEL OF FUNCTIONAL LITERACY

In *Adult Functional Competency: A Summary* (Adult Performance Level Study 1975), APL indicates the sorts of skills and competencies they regard as necessary for being a functional person within a modern Western society. They construct their model of functional literacy on two dimensions: content and skills. Content refers to the kind of information individuals need access to and the knowledge they must be able to generate in order to function competently in daily life. APL defines five general knowledge areas which comprise the content of functional literacy. These are consumer economics, knowledge related to occupations, community resources, health, and government and law. With regard to skills, APL claims that the great majority of requirements placed on adults are accounted for in four primary skills: communication skills (reading, writing, speaking, and listening); computation skills; problem-solving skills; and interpersonal relations skills.[4]

Content and skills intersect to provide an empirical account of what is required for functional literacy. A broad goal is specified for each content area. To achieve these goals is to be functionally literate. The five goals, by content area, are:

1 consumer economics – to manage a family economy and to demonstrate awareness of sound purchasing principles;
2 occupational knowledge – to develop a level of occupational knowledge which will enable adults to secure employment in accordance with their individual needs and interests;
3 health – to ensure good medical and physical health for the individual and his [*sic*] family;
4 government and law – to promote an understanding of society through government and law and to be aware of government functions, agencies, and regulations which define individual rights and obligations;
5 community resources – to understand that community resources, including transportation, are utilized by individuals in society in order to obtain a satisfactory mode of living.

(Adult Performance Level Study 1975; Appendix)

Each goal statement is then defined more specifically in terms of detailed empirical objectives. Within consumer economics twenty objectives are identified. There are ten for occupational knowledge, thirteen for health, six for government and law, and sixteen for community resources (of which nine relate to transportation). Examples of these objectives are revealing.

For instance, consumer economics objectives include: being able to count and convert coins and currency and to convert weights and measures using mathematical tables and operations; understanding the concepts of sales tax and income tax; developing an understanding of credit systems. Occupational knowledge objectives include: being able to identify sources of information – radio, newspapers – which could lead to employment; knowing how to prepare for job applications and interviews; being aware of vocational testing and guidance methods which may help one recognize job interests and relevant qualifications; knowing which attributes and skills may lead to job promotion and the standards of behavior for various types of employment. Objectives relating to government and law include: developing an understanding of the structure and functioning of the federal government; understanding the relationship between the individual citizen and the legal system; and exploring the relationship between government and the US tax system.

At the most specific level functional literacy is defined in terms of situation-specific requirements called tasks. APL did not publish examples of tasks in *Adult Functional Competency*, partly because it is 'the objective that is the most important element in the requirements for functional literacy' (Adult Performance Level Study 1975: Appendix). Explicitly stated tasks would be guidelines at most, rather than fixed and final requirements: examples of how requirements might be met, allowing for the considerable variations that may exist within the nation between the detailed circumstances and needs of different people.

To be functionally literate in this sense comprises a minimal, essentially negative, and passive state. At best, such functionally literate people are helped to cope with their world. They manage to fill in job application forms, having read an advertisement for the job. They may even get the job and, in that event, survive in it assisted by the ability to read bus and train timetables, job instructions, order forms, and the like. To be functional here is to be not unable to cope with the most minimal routines and procedures of mainstream existence in contemporary society. (Of course, being able to read and write hardly bestows the power to create jobs where none exist, or to secure a liveable income where work is very poorly paid.) It is, then, a negative state – avoiding failure to cope – rather than any optimal achievement, or a positive expression of human capacities. It is, moreover, passive. Functional literacy equips the person to respond to outside demands and standards, to understand and follow. There is no suggestion here of leading, commanding, mastering, or controlling.

At this point we can introduce some of Freire's most important ideas relating to literacy, ideology, and the politics of teaching illiterate adults to read and write.

FREIRE ON THE PHILOSOPHY AND POLITICS OF LITERACY

Freire insists that education cannot be neutral. It either serves as an instrument to domesticate human beings or is made into an instrument of human liberation (from oppression). What holds for education holds necessarily for the process of making people literate: since within a print society becoming literate is the foundation – and, in many cases, the whole – of education. Given the links within Freire's conceptual scheme between 'domestication,' 'dehumanization,' 'objecthood,' and 'oppression'; and between 'liberation,' 'humanization,' 'subjecthood,' and 'freedom'; either teaching literacy is an act of oppression which (unwittingly) treats humans as mere objects, or it is 'a cultural action for freedom' whereby persons collectively pursue and affirm their subjecthood.[5]

To understand these dichotomies we must reveal Freire's metaphysic. The basis of this is his belief that humans have an ontological vocation to become more fully human (Freire 1972: 20–1). By 'ontological vocation' Freire means a given destiny which we have by virtue of what we distinctively are as human beings.[6] Given what they are like, humans have a particular life quest to pursue; a destiny to fulfill. This quest is to become more fully human: to become more of what, in some sense, we already are. What *are* we, distinctively?

Four features stand out in Freire's account of human distinctiveness:

1 Humans possess consciousness.
2 They are 'beings of the praxis' who live authentically only when engaged in inquiry and creative transformation of the world.
3 Humans are uncompleted beings who are humanized in dialogue.
4 Humans are historical beings.

At the point in their evolution where they achieved consciousness, humans became importantly different from other animals. Like animals, humans exist in the world and necessarily interact with it in order to survive. Unlike other animals, however, humans gradually became conscious of the world as something objectively distinct from themselves: a reality they are in relationship *with*.[7] Humans see themselves as acting on a world which stimulates their action and in turn acts back on them. They survive better in so far as their action upon the world is (more) appropriate and efficacious. This depends upon their understanding the world more (rather than less) clearly and accurately. As humans came gradually to objectify and problematize the world more and more routinely, they came to objectify themselves as well. They became capable not only of knowing the world, but also of actually knowing that they are knowing it.[8] Humans alone among sentient beings transcend mere activity or behavior in their interaction with the world. They achieve intentionality toward it: engaging in action upon the world informed by their reflection upon it. This orientation toward the world and quality of interaction with it is distinctively and characteristically human. It is the essence of consciousness:

> Consciousness is intentionality towards the world. . . . Through the problematisation of the relationships between human beings and the world, it is possible for them to recreate, to remake, the natural process through which consciousness appeared in the process of . . . evolution, precisely in the moment which Teilhard de Chardin calls 'hominisation' in the evolution of humanity. When consciousness appears there is reflection; there is intentionality towards the world. Humanity becomes . . . different from animals. We can not only know, but can know that we are knowing.[9]

These ideas help clarify Freire's notion of humans as 'beings of the praxis.' For praxis is a dialectical unity of reflection and action:

> As beings of the praxis [humans] differ from animals, which are beings of pure activity. Animals do not consider the world. They are immersed in it. In contrast humans emerge from the world, objectify it, and in so doing can understand and transform it with their labour. . . . [Human] activity consists of action and reflection: it is praxis; it is transformation of the world. And as praxis it requires theory to illuminate it. [Human] activity is theory and practice.[10]
>
> (Freire 1972: 96)

Humans live humanly to the extent that they engage in praxis. They are uncompleted beings who are humanized in dialogue, and for whom, therefore, dialogue is an existential necessity.

The essence of dialogue is 'the true word.' True words are unities of reflection and action 'in such radical interaction that if one is sacrificed – even in part – the other immediately suffers' (Freire 1972: 60). To speak a true word is to engage in praxis: to transform the world in accordance with reflection; to name the world. These are interchangeable terms for Freire. Dialogue 'is the encounter between humans, mediated by the world, in order to name the world' (Freire 1972: 61). It is the act of humans engaging together in praxis. In such acts humans live humanly: expressing, developing, re-creating, and affirming their humanity.

> Human existence cannot be silent, nor can it be nourished by false words, but only by true words, with which humans transform the world. To exist, humanly, is to name the world, to change it. Once named, the world in its turn reappears to the namers as a problem and requires of them a new naming. [Humans] are not built in silence but in word, in work, in action-reflection. . . . If it is in speaking their

96

word that humans transform the world by naming it, dialogue imposes itself as the way in which [humans] achieve significance as [humans]. Dialogue is thus an existential necessity.

(Freire 1972: 60–1)

Humans, then, are 'beings in the process of becoming.' They live humanly to the extent that they affirm and express their distinctively human powers. They are necessarily uncompleted beings since their humanity consists not in a finite finished state, but in (ongoing) engagement in dialogue. Praxis can never be complete since reality itself is forever unfinished, continually demanding of humans new namings. Freire refers to the ongoing engagement in dialogue as the process of humanization.

Humanization is our ontological vocation. When Freire speaks of our ontological vocation to become more fully human, he simply means that we are called upon continually by what we *are* to humanize ourselves – to express, nurture, and expand our humanness in permanent shared praxis. We are called to dialogue: to name the world in action-reflection with other humans.

There is more to our vocation, however. For we are *historical* beings (Freire 1976: 3–4; Freire 1972: 56, 70–1). This is to make several points. At bottom, human historicity means that we are conscious of time and of our location within time. Humans have, and know they have, a past, a present, and a future. The human differs from the cat, who is submerged in a never-ending 'today' (Freire 1976: 3). Precisely because human beings are conscious of time they can conceive causes and effects, and thereby act with intention upon the world.

As beings conscious of time, humans can conceive of themselves as incomplete beings. Humans can know that they have been different in the past (individually and generically), that they may become different in the future, and that these changes reflect transforming action by humans upon their world. This too sets humans apart from other animals, for 'in contrast to other animals who are unfinished, but not historical, humans know themselves to be unfinished; they are aware of their incompleteness' (Freire 1972: 57).

Furthermore, humans are historical beings in the sense that they live within particular historical settings: that is, within some set or other of economic, social, political, cultural, etc., structures and institutions. These settings reflect past and present human action. History is a human creation. Those institutions, economies, political structures, and cultural routines that we live within – and within which we become what we are – have been created by human thought and deed. History reflects the way that those humans possessing the (greater) power to do so have imposed their intentions upon the social world, and created the structured conditions under which people at large live. This is precisely to create conditions

97

which shape the parameters of what people at large become. Humans necessarily pursue their ontological vocation under specific material historical conditions. Consequently, becoming more fully human is not simply an ontological vocation, but also an historical vocation.

Three brief points must suffice by way of elaboration here. First, the kind of history that has been made, and that humans must live within, may be hostile to many of them pursuing their ontological vocation. It may foster dehumanization rather than humanization. For 'within history, in concrete, objective contexts, both humanization and dehumanization are possibilities for humans as uncompleted beings conscious of their incompleteness' (Freire 1972: 20). But Freire insists that humanization alone is an historical vocation. Dehumanization is a distortion of the vocation to become more fully human. This distortion 'occurs within history; but it is not an historical vocation' (Freire 1972: 21).

Second, to speak of humanization as an historical vocation calls attention to the fact that in the quest to become more fully human, people may have to confront the history that has been made, and seek through transforming action upon the world to make a different history: one which will enable human beings at large to engage on an equal basis in shaping their shared world and controlling their related destinies. Given prevailing historical conditions, pursuit of our vocation is inevitably a call to revolution: to participate in humanizing struggle for liberation from oppression. Oppression signifies any situation in which A objectively exploits B, or hinders B's pursuit of self-affirmation as a human subject in the process of affirming and re-creating their humanity (Freire 1972: 31). Oppression entails violence because it negates humanity.

Third, oppressive historical structures undermine the material, emotional, and intellectual well-being of those who are oppressed, as well as thwarting the pursuit of their ontological vocation. Where oppressed groups take up the call to remake history in a humanizing praxis, they stand to advance materially, emotionally, and intellectually, as well as ontologically. In material terms the oppressed are poor: unemployed, underemployed, at risk of unemployment, poorly paid, etc.; they endure inferior housing, health care, nutrition, and so on. In emotional and psychic terms they are vulnerable, often anxious, beset with feelings of futility and fatalism, and are fearful of freedom. They are prone to a host of dehumanizing tendencies: ranging from addictions, to violent dispositions, and the inclination to tyrannize others they see as being even weaker than themselves (Freire 1972: 23, 38). Intellectually, the oppressed are dominated by ideologies steeped in the interests and world-view of their oppressors – typically blaming themselves and/or other social victims for the conditions they endure, rather than seeking out the true causes of their circumstances. In the grip of such ideologies they inevitably play into the hands of those who negate them. Of course, ideologies which reflect and serve élite interests *are themselves* historically created and perpetuated. Confronting and overcoming them in a liberating praxis is a key aspect of struggle to create a new – humanizing – history.

Freire's view of the political options for literacy is now clear. Either teaching literacy (to illiterate marginal adults) is a domesticating act, which helps accommodate oppressed people to the ongoing denial of their ontological vocation, and maintains them in material, emotional, and intellectual poverty; or it is made into an instrument of liberation by which marginal people are invited into, and sustained within, a revolutionary praxis to (re)make history in accordance with the right of all to live their humanity as fully as possible. In referring to these as *political* options, I mean simply that they are options bearing on the exercise of power within the social structure (Lankshear and Lawler 1987: Chapter 1). As a domesticating act, teaching literacy sides with the structured investment of superior power in minority élites; enabling the élites to retain their power advantage over oppressed minorities by helping to secure the consent of the oppressed to their own domination.[11] As an instrument of liberation, literacy work aligns with those who are subject to the greater power of the élites, and seeks to foment reflection and action aimed at overturning historical and cultural structures by which, and within which, power is divested unequally in favour of élites.

In *Pedagogy of the Oppressed* Freire advances ideas about the nature and role of domesticating education which can readily be applied to much adult literacy work. We are invited to consider the extent to which teaching literacy to adults

1 takes the form of banking education within a wider paternalistic social action apparatus;
2 is anti-dialogical;
3 reflects false generosity;

and thereby serves the interests and ends of élites.[12]

Banking education refers to situations in which narrating teachers deposit information into the minds of passive receiving students. It assumes that knowledge is 'a gift bestowed by those who consider themselves knowledgeable upon those whom they consider to know nothing,' and regards humans as adaptable and manageable beings (Freire 1972: 46–7). Banking education is invaluable for maintaining an oppressive social order, for the more that students put their efforts into receiving and storing information deposited in them, the less they can attain the critical consciousness that comes from intervening in reality as makers and transformers of the world.

In banking education consciousness does not come into active contact with the world. A wedge is driven between them. Learners do not address their consciousness to the world: rather, abstracted fragments of the world are addressed at their consciousness as information to be received. Learners are made into spectators, functioning not as conscious beings but as 'possessors of . . . an empty "mind" passively open to receiving deposits of reality from the world outside' (Freire 1972: 49). The more completely learners accept the passive role imposed on them, the more they tend merely 'to adapt to the world as it is and to the fragmented view of reality deposited in them' (Freire 1972: 47).

Freire maintains that the interests of oppressors 'lie in "changing the consciousness of the oppressed, not the situation that oppresses them"' (Freire 1972: 47). The more that marginal people can be brought to adapt to the existing order the more completely they can be dominated and denied their ontological vocation:

> To achieve [domination] the oppressors use the banking concept of education in conjunction with a paternalistic social action apparatus within which the oppressed receive the euphemistic title of 'welfare recipients'. They are treated as individual cases, as marginal persons who deviate from the general configuration of a 'good, organised, and just' society. The oppressed are regarded as the pathology of the healthy society, which must therefore adjust these 'incompetent and lazy' folk to its own patterns by changing their mentality. These marginals need to be 'integrated', 'incorporated' into the healthy society that they have 'forsaken'. . . . Translated into practice the concept of banking education is well suited to the purposes of the oppressors, whose tranquility rests on how well humans fit the world the oppressors have created, and how little they question it.
>
> (Freire 1972: 47–8)

Next, to call certain educational practices 'anti-dialogical' implies three ideas. Anti-dialogue is a one-way transaction: a monologue which negates partnership in the social act of communication. It precludes the speaking of true words. It involves false communication, in the sense that it foists myths upon marginal people in the cause of conquering them.

Monologue involves vertical power relations between educators and learners. The former issue communiqués: prescriptions or directives for learners to follow (Freire 1972: Chapter 3; Freire 1976: 46). There is no idea of reciprocal communication in which the interests and intentions of all parties are given a voice within a common project to know and understand reality more fully and accurately in order better to promote the humanity of all. Language and print are reduced to vehicles by which the will and world-view of the powerful are imposed upon the weak. It is assumed that everything learners need to know has already been determined (by others who know better). Education is simply a matter of passing prescriptions on down to those whose life task it is to absorb and observe them.

In anti-dialogue the world cannot be approached as an object to be opened up for understanding and re-creation in a shared way, for those who practice anti-dialogue lack or reject the values and attitudes essential to people speaking true words together. Dialogue presupposes love, humility, and faith. The very being of oppressors and those anti-dialogical educators who (often unwittingly) serve them, negates these values and attitudes:

> Dialogue cannot exist . . . in the absence of a profound love for the world and for [human beings]. The naming of the world, which is an act of creation and recreation, is not possible if it is not infused with love. . . . It is necessarily the task of responsible Subjects and cannot exist in a relation of domination. . . . The naming of the world, through which [people] constantly recreate that world, cannot be an act of arrogance. Dialogue . . . is broken if the parties (or one of them) lack humility. How can I enter into a dialogue if I always project ignorance onto others and never perceive my own . . . if I consider myself a member of the in-group of 'pure' [persons], the owners of truth and knowledge, for whom all non-members are 'those people' or 'the great unwashed'? . . . Dialogue further requires an intense faith in [humanity], faith in their power to make and remake, to create and recreate, faith in their vocation to be more fully human (which is not a privilege of an elite, but the birthright of all). . . . Founding itself upon love, humility and faith, dialogue is a horizontal relationship of which mutual trust between the participants is the logical consequence.

(Freire 1972: 62–4)

Where literacy work cannot proceed from these assumptions – because dominant interests themselves, and the educational and wider social–cultural structures and practices created in accordance with these interests, negate them – it is necessarily anti-dialogical. It can serve only as an instrument of domestication.

The élites, of course, need to 'educate' the mass of marginal people and make them literate. For humans are 'considerers' of the world (Freire 1972: 109). So there is always the possibility that oppressed groups may come to see that their present conditions and way of life are incompatible with their human vocation. Through their interaction with the world they may come to see that reality 'is really a process, undergoing constant transformation,' and not a fixed, static 'thing' to which they must simply adapt, and which they must accept. If humans

> are searchers and their ontological vocation is humanization, sooner or later they may perceive the contradiction in which they are

maintained, and then engage themselves in the struggle for their liberation.

(Freire 1972: 48–9)

To pre-empt this possibility the élites must present a false picture of reality 'for the consideration of the oppressed and subjugated.' Through education the world must be presented as something fixed and given, to which humans 'as mere spectators, must adapt,' and not as an ongoing challenge to be met in dialogue.

The élites must approach the people in order to keep them passive. This approach, however, cannot permit true communication. On the contrary, it is achieved by depositing myths which are 'indispensable to preserving the status quo.' Within this logic literacy work will become an exercise in false communication: instilling myths in popular consciousness. Typical myths include the following: the oppressive order is a 'free society'; all people are free to work where they wish. If they do not like their work situation they can find another job; the social order respects human rights and is therefore worthy of esteem; anyone who is industrious can become an entrepreneur – and the street vendor is as much an entrepreneur as the owner of a large factory; the dominant élites, 'recognizing their duties,' promote the advancement of the people, and the people for their part should accept and conform to the words of the élites; private property is fundamental to personal development; the oppressors are industrious whereas the oppressed are lazy and dishonest; marginal groups are naturally inferior and élites naturally superior (Freire 1972: 109–10).

Freire also identifies the myth that élites are charitable and generous, whereas what they really do as a class is foster selective 'good deeds' which harmonize with their own interests and undermine the interests of the supposed beneficiaries. This relates directly to the idea that adult literacy work may comprise a form of false generosity.

False generosity refers to (paternalistic) forms of treatment bestowed on the oppressed with a view to ameliorating their condition a little, or of softening the effects of oppression but which actually *maintain intact* the concrete situations and social structures which beget oppression (Freire 1972: 26–7). They do nothing to address the causes of the conditions experienced by the oppressed. Rather, they sink marginal persons even more deeply into dependence and vulnerability. A model case of false generosity is where well-to-do people make their services available to unemployed or poorly paid workers to teach the latter how to budget their (inadequate) finances. The presumption is that the problem of poverty lies within the individual – in the low or underpaid worker – and not in the economic structure. To the extent that the oppressed come also to see the situation this way they become dependent on this external source of assistance. Yet the net effect of such 'aid' is precisely to perpetuate the very structures and routines within which oppression is practiced (e.g. by paying low wages, creating unemployment, etc.). It could not be otherwise. For

> in order to have the continued opportunity to express their 'genero-sity', the oppressors must perpetuate injustice as well. An unjust social order is the fount of this 'generosity', which is nourished by death, despair, and poverty. . . . False charity constrains the fearful and subdued, the 'rejects of life', to extend their trembling hands.
>
> (Freire 1972: 21)

In so far as élites, or their unwitting accomplices endorse, demand, or provide on behalf of the 'disadvantaged' or 'underprivileged'[13] literacy programs which domesticate their clients, we have instances of false generosity. Adult literacy programs – particularly functional literacy programs – are prime risks here. It is not enough that those who provide or operate such programs are unaware of their effects, or that they make such provision available because they see it as being at least something they can do to help the situation. As far as Freire is concerned, it *does not* help the situation. By holding the oppressed 'fast in a position of dependence' (Freire 1972: 26) and in a distorted view of reality, bestowers of false generosity (unwittingly) abet dehumanization.

DOMESTICATING FUNCTIONAL LITERACY: A CRITIQUE OF THE APL MODEL

In what follows I use Freire's work in an attempt to advance a constructive illustrated critique of the prevailing 'philosophy' of functional literacy. The particular model developed by APL is by no means the only one liable to the kind of critique that follows. It has been singled out because it is a well-researched, complex, and well-regarded attempt to operationalize functional literacy.[14] I believe that critique of a general position should be directed at the strongest representatives available. In advancing this critique I have no doubt that the last thing APL would want is to contribute to (further) domesticating marginal people. On the contrary, such initia-tives are typically undertaken with the very best intentions. Since Gramsci, however, we have been well warned about the roles (conscious as well as unconscious) of traditional intellectuals within stratified – in our case, capitalist – social orders. With functional literacy as with many other cases, good intentions may not be enough on their own. To the extent that applied social research proceeds from a mystified view of (social) reality, it may have all kinds of consequences that are unintended, unwanted, and that remain unrecognized by the researchers themselves. Freire, like Gramsci before him, challenges us to scrutinize the politics of education and the political role of intellectuals (such as the academics on the APL team) within the historical process of maintaining an existing order of unequal power and privilege. The following critique is offered as a contribution to such scrutiny.

When we examine the APL model in the light of Freire's metaphysical, ethical, and political perspective we find that it fits the logic of domestication like a glove. Given the earlier account of the nature and role of domesticating education, the following claims seem warranted.

First, the APL model is plainly underwritten by the assumption that humans are adaptable, manageable beings. The very meaning of 'being functional' here is of being adapted to the way things are. APL seeks a comprehensive range of skills and informations ('knowledges') that will help illiterate people at the bottom of the social heap operate more effectively within existing economic, social, and legal structures. The other side to this is that the APL model seeks non-coercive ways of managing people who might otherwise disrupt or complicate the 'flow' and 'efficiency' of daily routines. If, for example, enabling people to use public transport effectively makes it less troublesome for them to get to work on time, it is also true that a punctual work-force is a more profitable work-force – other things being equal. From the standpoint of those who generate profit from workers' labor, managing the work-force into punctuality is a major contribution toward maximizing profits. The more that 'at risk' people can be managed into coping with the central demands of daily life, the less need there is to provide resource-hungry helping agencies: and the more that economic resources can be directed to their 'proper' ends – like capital accumulation and optimizing private profits. We are perfectly justified in asking for whom the literacy in question here is most (or most truly) functional.

Second, the content and skills conferred by APL's program reflect the assumption that knowledge is a gift bestowed by the knowledgeable on those considered not to know what they need to know. The entire APL research exercise was about a small group of specialists producing an operational account of what people deemed functionally incompetent need in order to live more effectively. In this the learners do not address their consciousness to the world. Instead, they 'act' very much as 'possessors of "empty" minds,' receiving an account of the world outside. They receive a view of the world as being a place where, for example, credit systems are an integral part of everyday domestic economies. Of course, these systems must be operated *correctly*. Accordingly, information is proffered on how to operate credit. The knowledge provided in the name of functionality is selective and fragmented. Knowledge of credit and its requirements is in. So too is knowledge about how to dress for particular types of employment; how to pursue promotion; how to present for an interview. By contrast, knowledge about collective wage bargaining, the rights of organized labor, the rights of tenants, etc., is omitted. The recipients have no formal control over the view of the world that is transmitted simultaneously with basic literacy skills.

Third, functionally illiterate adults are indeed treated as 'the pathology of the healthy society': i.e. as individual cases who, deviating from the norms inherent in a good and well-ordered society, must be incorporated into the mainstream. Within this approach those judged functionally incompetent are encouraged to see themselves as a deficit system. If they have underachieved or are struggling in daily life it is because of their personal deficiency. The expectation is that this deficiency will be overcome if they can receive the gifts of knowledge being offered them. This is a powerful initiation into a series of life-shaping assumptions. For example:

1 The problem is within me. If I cannot get a job, or the job I want, then that is because of something about me rather than something about the world (such as a shrinking labor market, an economic crisis, a diminishing number and range of skilled or challenging jobs).
2 If others do better than I do, that is because they are better than I am. If I want to do as well, then I have to improve. The 'game' or 'race' itself is proper, legitimate, beyond question. I am just not a sufficiently skilled or competitive 'player.'
3 To get better I will have to have my faults diagnosed and be taught how to improve. Others have this knowledge. It is not for me to determine the problem or the cure.

Such assumptions locate the causes of difficulties experienced by marginal people within the individuals themselves. This reinforces a view of the existing social order as being properly constituted the way it is, and hence as not being in need of (significant) change. Once again, the message is a call to adapt to the given and to be assisted: not to be active, critical, or to seek to know and transform.

Fourth, the development and implementation of adult literacy programs of the APL type must, then, be seen as exercises in anti-dialogue. The APL form is strictly a monologue. Prescriptions and directives are laid down – if not (always) in close detail then certainly in substance. Given that illiterate adults want to be functionally competent – and who would not when the alternative is failure to cope? – there are requirements and procedures which must be followed. The world itself is not negotiable. Neither are the 'recipes' for functioning. These are laid down to be followed. There is no conception whatsoever of print becoming part of a shared project to know and transform modern America (in APL's case) in the interests of expanded human possibilities for all. Dialogue is a non-starter in *Adult Functional Competency*. The world (the United States) has already been named, and the communiqués imposed on illiterate clients proceed from this élite naming. At best, the intellectuals producing such communiqués are (unwitting and well-meaning) accessories to the negation of love, humility, and faith on the part of ruling élites. At worst, they themselves actually practice arrogance, and withhold love and faith. In elaborating a pedagogy of, for, and with the oppressed. Freire challenges us to examine our own pedagogies and consider how far they serve to oppress those we presume to assist.

Fifth, many of the goals and objectives specified by APL as the content of functional literacy have a disquieting affinity with those (typical) myths identified by Freire as being 'indispensable to preserving the status quo' and, as such, characteristic of false communication. Consider, for example, APL's goal 'to develop [among dysfunctional adults] a level of occupational knowledge which will enable them to secure employment in accordance with their individual needs and interests,' and the more specific objective of developing awareness 'of vocational testing and counselling methods which help prospective employees recognize job interests and qualifications'. These harmonize closely with the myth that people are free to work where they wish, and if they do not like their current employment situation they can find another job. Yet we know that in these times increasing numbers of people will take and stick with virtually any job, *if there is a job to get in the first place* (see, e.g. Apple 1986 and Kozol 1985; for an exception, see Garland *et al.* 1988). Similarly, APL's goals and objectives for government and law accord with the myth that the dominant élites (through those who serve them as politicians and senior servants in government departments) promote the advancement of the people, who in turn should accept and conform to the words (formalized as laws and regulations) of the élites. APL's content for government and law generally affirms the belief (myth) that the social order respects human rights, and is therefore worthy of esteem: compare APL's objective to promote understanding of – and, by implication, reverence for and obedience to – society through government and law, and to be aware of government functions, agencies, and regulations which define (and, by implication, uphold) individual rights.

Sixth and finally, APL's approach to making marginal people functional has an air of false generosity about it. The point to be made here is that the privations experienced by marginal groups – including illiteracy itself – should be seen first and foremost as symptoms of oppression. Unemployment, low incomes, inadequate housing, insecure tenancy, disrupted schooling, patterned learning failure, increased susceptibility to certain illnesses, inferior health generally, and minimal access to health care services, reflect the structuring of economic, social, and cultural life around the presumption that some shall have more and others less. For some to have more *necessitates* that others have less, because wealth and (other forms of) power are finite. The social structure institutionalizes this 'necessity.'

In view of this we must accept one or other of two conclusions. Given the very premiss of our society that some – indeed, many – must exist at the bottom of a social hierarchy; and given that under prevailing economic and social conditions life at the bottom is a constant battle for sheer survival; functional literacy as conceived by APL can only help either to redistribute places at the bottom, or to soften (a little) the conditions experienced by subordinated groups. It is possible that some graduands of functional literacy programs may emerge from unemployment into some low-level job slot, or else from a low-level job slot into one slightly higher. But, given a finite and shrunken labor market, movement upwards by some results from/in displacement of others. In this case, functional literacy work resembles the act of rearranging deck chairs on the *Titanic*.

Alternatively, making the dispossessed marginally more functional may help stretch their (meagre) purchasing power a little further, or make movement around the city or locating accommodation a little easier. But the very nature and logic of initiatives like that of APL help maintain the structured routines and material situations wherein oppression is practiced. Absolutely nothing is done to draw attention to the root causes of poverty, distress, and despair. At most there is mild amelioration of symptoms. The risk run by recipients of literacy teaching who accept an imposed view of what is involved in becoming functional, is further and deeper immersion in a debilitating and fatalistic world-view, and a heightened sense of dependence.

Either way we are looking at false generosity, where something is given in order to maintain an existing advantage. As described here, the APL program is best understood as an induction into routines, values, and perceptions of the world which further engage the disadvantaged in a mode of life where most of them will remain disadvantaged (and their children after them), while the few who may achieve some slight advance do so at the expense of others who slide down to replace them. This occurs to the advantage of ruling interest groups and at the expense of the ontological and historical vocation of the oppressed. To this extent, such a model of functional literacy is dehumanizing. The approach represented by APL should, then, be rejected. With what, however, should we seek to replace it?

TOWARD A HUMANIZING MODEL OF FUNCTIONAL LITERACY

Just as Freire's work suggests a critique of dehumanizing models of functional literacy, so does it deliver a model of humanizing functional literacy. Freire shows that literacy work *can* be organized along lines which stimulate illiterate adults into pursuing their ontological vocation within struggle to understand the world, and to transform it in ways which overcome oppressive social–historical structures and relations.

The key to developing an alternative model based on Freire's work is found in the symmetry between his notion that humans have an ontological vocation and Aristotle's argument that the ultimate good for human beings consists in us performing well our human function.

In the *Nicomachean Ethics* Aristotle inquires after the true and final end to be pursued in a human life. He believes it is important to determine this. After all,

> will not the knowledge of it . . . have a great influence on life? Shall we not, like archers who have a mark to aim at, be more likely to hit upon what is right? If so, we must try . . . to determine what it is.
> (Aristotle 1941: 1094a)

Aristotle argues that if there is an ultimate end (or good) for human life it must be something that is always desirable in its own right and never for the sake of something else. Only happiness, he says, meets this criterion. And so happiness is the ultimate end of human living (Aristotle 1941: 1097b).

This on its own does not tell us much. We need to clarify what happiness is. To do this Aristotle begins by trying to identify the function of human beings. His reasoning is that things are good in so far as they perform their function well:

> Just as for a flute-player, a sculptor, or any artist, and in general, for all things that have a function, the good and the 'well' is thought to reside in the function, so it would seem to be for human beings, if they have a function. . . . The function of a lyre-player is to play the lyre, and that of a good lyre-player is to do so well.
> (Aristotle 1941: 1097b–8a)

Given that human beings have a function, the truly good life (seen as an ongoing process or activity) will consist in performing this function well. Since happiness is the ultimate end or good of human living, happiness must be found in performing our function well.

Aristotle associates function with uniqueness or speciality. A's function is something unique to A. Our (human) function, then, must consist in something unique to us as humans. According to Aristotle, it is rationality that is unique to human beings. Consequently, in his view the ideal human life is one based on the best and most noble exercise of reason. 'Human good turns out to be rational activity in accordance with virtue . . . in a complete life' (Aristotle 1941: 1098a).

Having spelled this out, however, we must recognize that it is the *form* rather than the detailed *content* of Aristotle's argument that is most relevant to us here. For in its form it is strikingly similar to Freire's idea that humans have an ontological vocation, and that to live humanly – that is, to live properly, truly, or well – is to pursue this vocation.

In both cases the criterion of 'that which is uniquely human' is used as the basis for an ethic. For Freire, that which is uniquely human consists in our capacity for praxis: our ability to know that we are knowing by the act of transforming reality in accordance with our reflection upon that reality. To live humanly presupposes praxis; dialogue. For Aristotle, it is our rationality that is unique: the capacity to base a life upon the use of reason. These symmetrical views amount to the idea of humans being called upon to live in accordance with what they distinctively are as humans. The details differ a little between the two specifications, but the logic is essentially the same. In saying that living the good life requires us to perform well our human function and laying out what this performance involves, Aristotle in effect lays out a view of what Freire calls our ontological vocation. Conversely, in spelling out our ontological vocation Freire effectively advances an account of what Aristotle would call our function as human beings. In this case, a rose by any other name smells pretty much the same.

Given this symmetry we can re-present Freire's distinction between domesticating and liberating forms of literacy (and, more generally, of education) as the distinction between forms of literacy which impede or enable, respectively, the proper performance of our *function* as human beings. Domesticating literacy contributes to our dehumanization in so far as it thwarts performance of our function. A liberating literacy, on the other hand, fosters this performance. To use the same root word, we may refer to domesticating literacy as 'dysfunctional,' since it undermines our function; and to liberating literacy as 'functional,' since it promotes the expression of our humanity. In other words, by acknowledging the symmetry between the metaphysical and ethical views of Aristotle and Freire, we can generate a conception of functional literacy as a practice of reading and writing integral to living humanly: that is to say, which is integral to pursuing our ontological vocation.

Such a practice of reading and writing is precisely what Freire recounts in his published work. It is described most fully in *Education: The Practice of Freedom* (1976), *Cultural Action for Freedom* (1973), and *Pedagogy of the Oppressed* (1972).

LITERACY, LIBERATION, AND HUMANIZATION

To reclaim their right to live humanly, maginalized groups must confront, in praxis, those institutions, processes, and ideologies that prevent them from naming their world. In this praxis they must address, simultaneously, the reality they inhabit *and* their consciousness of that reality. Drawing on Alvaro Vieira Pinto's idea of consciousness as method,[15] we can say that oppressed groups must adopt a new *method* of relating to the world. Integral to this is the shift from what Freire calls 'naive consciousness' to

109

'critical (active) consciousness.' What this involves is best expressed by Freire himself:

> True dialogue cannot exist unless it involves critical thinking – thinking which discerns an indivisible solidarity between the world and [humans] admitting of no dichotomy between them – thinking which perceives reality as process and transformation, rather than as a static entity – thinking which does not separate itself from action, but constantly immerses itself in temporality without fear of the risks involved. Critical thinking contrasts with naive thinking, which sees 'historical time as a weight, a stratification of the acquisitions and experiences of the past', from which the present should emerge as normalized and 'well behaved'. For the naive thinker, the important thing is accommodation to this normalized 'today'. For the critic the important thing is the continuing humanization of people.
>
> (Freire 1972: 64–5)

The myths and distorted perceptions which hold marginal groups in passivity, or which send them down false (and often destructive or self-destructive) trails, must be exploded. Exploding them can only occur within a praxis of liberation: within dialogue where people's critical transforming action on the world reveals myths and distortions for what they are. One becomes a critical thinker in the *act* of practicing critical thought; in the act of *being conscious* in relation to the world.

Freire's model of problem-posing education is a pedagogy for shifting people from naïve to critical consciousness. It involves two structurally parallel phases: a literacy phase and a post-literacy phase. The former is galvanized around generative *words* and the latter around generative *themes*. Both phases are necessary. This is because, for Freire, the ultimate 'text' to be read and written is the world itself. Learning to read and write words is an important and integral part of coming to 'read' and 'write' – to understand and name – *the world itself*. The full flowering of the literacy phase is achieved only in exploring the generative themes, and by confronting the limit situations revealed in this exploration with limit acts (see Freire 1972: 71–95). Here, however, we must confine ourselves to the literacy phase. Many excellent descriptions of Freire's literacy method exist.[16] This concluding statement seeks only to relate key elements of Freire's method to learning principles implicit in his analysis of domesticating and liberating education.

Six important learning principles are called out by Freire's analysis:

1 The world must be approached as an object to be understood and known by the efforts of the learners themselves. Moreover, their act of knowing is to be stimulated and shaped by their own being, circumstances, needs, and destinies.

110

2 The historical world must be approached as a created, transformable reality which, like humans themselves, is constantly in the process of becoming; of being shaped and made by human deed. Learners are to understand how it has been made into *what it is* by what (other) humans have done, and failed to do.

3 Learners must learn how to connect their own lived conditions and being to the making of reality that has occurred to date.

4 They must consider the possibilities for 'new makings' of reality, and the new possibilities for 'being' that emerge from these new makings, and become committed to shaping a new history. The project aimed at new makings is a collective, shared, social enterprise, in which all participants (must) have a voice.

5 In the literacy phase learners will come to see the role and importance of print/literacy within this shared project. By achieving print competence within the process of becoming committed to remaking history, learners will actually *experience* their own potency in the act of understanding what it means to be(come) a potent historical force.

6 Learners must come to understand how the myths beamed at them *are*, in fact, myths which hold them in oppression.

Freire's literacy method evolved around the centrality of these learning principles. Three features of his pedagogy seem especially important:

1 A distinctive learning environment, called the 'culture circle.'

2 The use of 'codifications' to help focus critical investigation of the world around issues and concerns of direct and primary importance to the illiterate participants themselves.

3 The use of generative words and syllabic families, which allow participants to generate as far as possible the vocabulary with which they learn to read and write – rather than using a donated vocabulary with its attendant ideological perspective (Freire 1976: 49).

The culture circle approach was first used outside of literacy work (Freire 1976: 42). Its success as a setting for encouraging critical inquiry by adult learners about aspects of Brazilian reality encouraged Freire's team to test its feasibility for adult literacy. In a culture circle the role of teacher is replaced by that of co-ordinator; dialogue replaces monologue/lectures; the group comprises participants rather than pupils; and instead of syllabi remote from the experience and vital interest of participants, pressing themes are codified into closely focused learning units. Activity aims 'through group discussion either to clarify situations or to seek action arising from that clarification.' The themes which focused critical discussion within the original culture circles were offered by the groups themselves. Recurring themes included nationalism, profit remittances abroad,

111

the political evolution of Brazil, development, illiteracy, the vote for illiterates, and democracy (Freire 1976: 42).

In the presence of a critically conscious co-ordinator, group discussion of such themes can quickly and easily carry participants at large to a deeper understanding of how their world has been structured, by whom, and in whose interests: by exploring contradictions inherent in participants' own ideas; by considering conflicting evidence; by addressing questions that tap or create dissonance among participants; and so on. Debate – dialogue – addresses elements of participants' everyday life and reality. All members bring their experience, ideas, and prejudices to discussion. Out of this raw material they collectively seek the most coherent and satisfying analysis and explanation of events, situations, and processes which confuse or concern them; which impede or frustrate them. And from these analyses and explanations emerge ideas for action aimed at creative change grounded in popular rather than élite interests. Activity in culture circles emphasizes process rather than specific content. The role of the co-ordinator is not to 'bank' content, since participants generate content of their own out of the process of actively reflecting upon everyday issues and concerns. Rather, the co-ordinator is to assist (other) participants in their efforts to produce a more critical interpretation and understanding of this content, within a discussion setting where each person has an equal voice.

As we have seen, however, the process of promoting critical consciousness assumes a particular orientation or set of epistemological values. Reality must be perceived as constantly evolving rather than as a static entity; as being created rather than given; as transformable rather than immutable; as something to be made rather than accommodated to; etc. Encouraging this orientation among hitherto naïve, fatalistic 'thinkers,' accustomed to receiving 'reality,' calls for special pedagogical techniques. Foremost among those used by Freire are what he calls 'codifications.'

These are pictorial representations – slides, photos, drawings, etc. – of 'typical existential situations of the group with which one is working' (Freire 1976: 51).[17] They are familiar local situations which also have the potential to stimulate critical discussion of regional, national, and global issues. Codifications 'stand in,' as it were, for the world. They capture situations which participants are continually in; but in which they are so immersed that it is difficult otherwise to stand back and view them objectively. Codifications permit participants to step back from the immediate reality which affects them profoundly, and to reflect upon it critically: approaching it as something to be understood, evaluated, and addressed (with a view to beneficial change), rather than as an inescapable 'given' which can only be accepted, suffered, and adapted to.

Of crucial importance here is the value of codifications for enabling participants to arrive at the distinction between nature and culture, and to comprehend their status as cultural agents possessing the ability to make history (Freire 1976: 46–8). By means of discussion focusing on codifications showing elements of reality which have been created by human deed together with others which are truly natural, participants come to see themselves as playing an active role in making the world. They 'discover,' in a way they had not recognized before, the distinction between the world of nature and that of culture – seeing the latter as created by people exactly like themselves, and including themselves:

> From that point of departure, illiterates begin to effect a change in their former attitudes, by discovering themselves to be a maker of the world of culture, by discovering that they, as well as literate persons, have a creative and recreative impulse. They . . . discover that culture is just as much a clay doll made by artists who are their peers as it is the work of a great sculptor . . . that culture is the poetry of lettered poets and also the poetry of their own popular songs – that culture is all human creation.
>
> (Freire 1976: 47)

And, as discussion proceeds, they come to see *society itself* – its institutions, processes, and the effects of these on the lives of different groups – as a human creation. The same (human) powers that make us agents of culture underlie our potency as agents of history. Discovering their fundamental equality with all other agents of culture, marginalized persons can proceed to discover their fundamental equality with those who have hitherto presumed (and usurped) an unequal right to make history in their own interests. In moving to claim and express the right to their voice – to name their world – the oppressed enter the historical struggle for liberation. At this point they are truly acting as agents of their own humanization.

Within the overall discussion of the worlds of culture and nature, and the role humans play in each world, codifications are used to focus attention on more specific aspects of culture. One important facet of this closer discussion is to engender a strong and critically informed commitment among participants to becoming literate. The third and fourth codified situations presented in *Education: The Practice of Freedom* prompt the distinction between lettered and unlettered cultures. In this part of the program participants discuss culture

> as a systematic acquisition of human experience, and discover that in a lettered culture this acquisition is not limited to oral transmission, as is the case in unlettered cultures which lack graphic signs. They conclude by debating the democratization of culture, which opens the perspective of acquiring literacy. . . . These discussions are critical, stimulating, and highly motivating . . . [Illiterate adults] perceive critically that it is necessary to learn to read and write, and prepare [themselves] to become the agent of this learning.
>
> (Freire 1976: 48)

The production of codifications is guided by an important principle: namely, choice of situations which are typical of participants' daily lives. It is *their* reality which they are being invited to examine critically within the process of becoming critical thinkers. The same principle applies in adapting the pedagogy of culture circles and codifications – which is equally valid for use among literate adults – to adult literacy work. The words chosen as the basic materials with which illiterate adults teach themselves to read and write are drawn from research into the vocabulary of the groups being worked with. A minimal vocabulary chosen by the educators from the everyday words of the people is incorporated into a simple, but ingenious technique which ensures maximum activity and creativity on the part of learners during the process of acquiring print skills. Freire speaks of the educator entering into dialogue with learners 'about concrete situations, and simply offering them the instruments with which they can teach themselves to read and write' (Freire 1976: 48).

As already noted, learning to read and write *words* must proceed within the wider agenda of learning to read and write *the world*. For coherence, the process of acquiring literacy must be as active and creative as possible. Freire uses a technique which employs 'generative words' and 'syllabic families.' Languages like Portuguese and Spanish are highly regular, and lend themselves to word-building out of syllables. As few as seventeen or so words in Portuguese provide sufficient syllable combinations for learners to generate almost any word they might wish to use. Drawing on research into the learners' vocabular universe, the literacy team chooses a list of generative words in accordance with the criteria of phonemic richness, phonetic difficulty, and the 'attachment' of a given word to the learners' social, political, and cultural reality (Freire 1976: 50–1). The generative words chosen are then incorporated into the codifications. Following extended critical discussion of the codified situations, learners are directed to the words and they begin to learn to read and write.

Using 'discovery cards' based on syllabic families (Freire 1976: 53–4), learners can begin to generate their own words by combining syllables. These will often be words with *affective* significance for the learners, providing powerful motivation for learning how to read and write them. This whole approach establishes literacy as a medium for expressing one's own intentions, creative potency, and (emerging) critical perspective, rather than serving as a vehicle for absorbing directives and myths imposed from without. And in providing access to wide-ranging information, theory, and other critical perspectives, literacy becomes a means by which learners can continually expand and refine their own critical awareness, and communicate this to others similarly intent on entering history more fully and consciously.

Barbara Bee provides an excellent account of Freire's approach, as employed in Brazil, and its effectiveness (Bee 1980: 40–6). Her work is commended to the reader. She notes that as the generative words were introduced, one by one, learners practiced reading and writing aloud, expressed opinions, wrote them down, explored newspapers, and discussed local issues:

> Those who completed the literacy course could read and write simple tasks, make something of the local newspapers and discuss Brazilian problems. The whole process took between 30–40 hours to complete.
>
> (Bee 1980: 45–6)

We must recall here that this literacy phase is merely the beginning in Freire's scheme. It is to be followed by a post-literacy phase, described at length in *Pedagogy of the Oppressed*. This, however, is another story.

CONCLUSION

Obviously, much more can be said about functional literacy from a Freirean point of view. Indeed, a full appreciation of just how totally the functional literacy championed by Freire differs from that of the mainstream represented by APL can only emerge from a serious reading of Freire's own work. This will also enable us to resist the convenient thought that his approach is appropriate only for deeply impoverished and repressive Third World settings. As Robert Mackie makes plain, however, once we understand Freire's pedagogy we see that it 'focuses on human liberation from oppression not only in Brazil, but everywhere oppression exists. So, while his theory has situated origins, its applications are potentially much wider' (Mackie 1980: 2). Subtleties of technique may have to change across differing linguistic scenes, but the spirit and essence of the pedagogy will remain the same wherever the practice of reading and writing words is seen, ultimately, as an inherent part of reading and writing the world itself.[18]

This chapter has pursued a modest goal: to understand and critique the prevailing approach to functional literacy, and to suggest an alternative. It has not sought to critique the metaphysical, ethical, political, and epistemological bases of Freire's own position. There is a good reason for this. To mount such a critique we must first appreciate what the consequences are, in human terms generally and educational terms in particular, of embracing such bases. For the consequences of a framework must surely enter the evaluation of it. I hope here at least to have shown some of the more important consequences that flow from conceiving functional literacy in Freirean terms. There is a veritable world of difference between his approach and that represented by APL. The nature and effects of that difference merit the attention of all who would call themselves educators. For what is at stake here may be nothing less than the difference between enhancing or violating the humanity of those we are engaged in educating. And *that* must be reckoned with.

NOTES

1 Ira Shor speaks of the literacy 'crisis' as being more of an *invention* than a discovery. He believes that inventing this crisis was a necessary part of the 'conservative restoration' agenda for education in the United States. 'Without a literacy crisis there would have been no cause for launching a traditionalist crusade for the basics' (Shor 1986: 64). Typical figures cited in the 1970s include sixty million functionally illiterate adults in the United States, six to eight million in Britain, and around 10 percent of the adult population in Australia.

2 For the US Office of Education definition of functional literacy, see Nafziger *et al.* 1975. For the British definition, see British Association of Settlements 1974. Both are cited in Levine 1982, p. 256.

3 For typical examples here, see Nafziger *et al.* 1975.

4 See Adult Performance Level Study 1975, p. 2. Reference to 'interpersonal relations skills' indicates how 'functional literacy' does not completely exhaust 'functional competency.' APL's brief includes functional literacy, but goes a little beyond it alone.

5 These ideas reverberate through Freire's many works. For his most detailed statements, see *Education: The Practice of Freedom*, *Pedagogy of the Oppressed*, and *Cultural Action for Freedom*.

6 Compare Freire 1972, p. 21: 'dehumanization, although a concrete historical fact, is *not* a given destiny.'

7 See Freire 1972, Chapter 2 (especially pp. 55–6) and Chapter 3 (especially pp. 70–1). See also Freire 1976, p. 3, and Davis 1980, pp. 58–62.

8 These are Freire's own words, in Davis 1980, p. 59.

9 Ibid., pp. 58–9. Compare also the words of Alvaro Vieira Pinto: 'Consciousness is in essence "a way towards" something apart from itself, outside itself, which surrounds it and which it apprehends by means of its ideational capacity. Consciousness is thus by definition a method, in the most general sense of the word.' Cited in ibid., p. 44.

10 I have used 'humans' here in place of 'men': a practice observed henceforth.

11 This, of course, is to paraphrase Antonio Gramsci's celebrated notion of hegemony. Compare Gramsci 1971, especially the selection entitled 'Notes on Italian History.'

12 These are by no means *all* of the descriptions under which Freire invites us to consider the nature and role of domesticating education. They are, however, sufficient for my purposes here.

13 I have used scare quotes with 'disadvantaged' and 'underprivileged' to signal my unease with such talk. Often these adjectives mask the fact that the groups thus described are systematically oppressed and exploited – and should be described as such.

14 Levine, for example, calls APL's work a major and comprehensive study. Compare Levine 1986, p. 37.

15 Refer to note 9 above.

16 One of the best is the chapter by Barbara Bee (1980). See also Brown 1975 and Sanders 1972.

17 See also Freire 1976, pp. 63–81, for examples of codifications of the type used by Freire's team in Brazil.

18 Kozol provides a First World example of this ideal in operation when he tells of a community-based literacy program with which he was involved in the United States. During the operation of this program, says Kozol,

116

at least 200 persons nightly filled the basement of our church and overflowed into a network of apartments that we rented in the . . . neighbourhood in which we worked. Most of us (teachers and learners both) were also taking action on the words we learned and on the world of anguish and injustice which those words revealed. Literacy sessions that evolved around such words as 'tenant,' 'landlord,' 'lease,' 'eviction,' 'rat,' and 'roach' led to one of the first rent strikes in our city. Words connected to the world, led – not in years but in a matter of days – to the reward of a repainted building, the replacement of illegal exits . . . and the reconstruction of a fire escape that served the tenants of a building of five storeys but could not be used because it had rotted into empty air above the second floor.

(Kozol 1985: pp. 44–5)

Kozol adds that none of the adults he worked with in such programs was prepared to settle in their learning 'for the "functional abilities" of bottom level job slots in available custodial positions,' and many of them became leaders in the struggle for social change – notably, in action to desegregate the Boston schools.

For a fascinating account of an attempt to apply Freirean principles to literary teaching among migrant women in Australia, see Bee (1993).

REFERENCES

Adult Performance Level Study (1975) *Adult Functional Competency: A Summary*, Austin, University of Texas.

Apple, M. (1986) *Teachers and Texts*, London, Routledge & Kegan Paul.

Aristotle (1941) *Nicomachean Ethics*, ed. R. McKeon, New York, Random House.

Bee, B. (1980) 'The politics of literacy,' in R. Mackie (ed.), *Literacy and Revolution: The Pedagogy of Paulo Freire*, London, Pluto Press.

—— (1993) 'Critical literacy and the politics of gender', in C. Lankshear and P. McLaren (eds), *Critical Literacy: Politics, Praxis and the Postmodern*, Albany, State University of New York Press.

British Association of Settlements (1974) *A Right to Read*, London, British Association of Settlements.

Brown, C. (1975) *Literacy in Thirty Hours: Paulo Freire's Process in North East Brazil*, London, Writers & Readers.

Davis, R. (1980) 'Education for awareness: a talk with Paulo Freire,' in R. Mackie (ed.), *Literacy and Revolution: The Pedagogy of Paulo Freire*, London, Pluto Press.

Freire, P. (1972) *Pedagogy of the Oppressed*, Harmondsworth, Penguin.

—— (1973) *Cultural Action for Freedom*, Harmondsworth, Penguin.

—— (1976) *Education: The Practice of Freedom*. London, Writers & Readers.

—— (1978) *Pedagogy in Process: Letters to Guinea-Bissau*, London, Writers & Readers.

—— (1985) *The Politics of Education*, London, Macmillan.

Freire, P. and Macedo, D. (1987) *Literacy: Reading the Word and the World*, South Hadley, Massachusetts, Bergin & Garvey.

Garland, S., Therrien, L. and Hammonds, K. (1988) 'Why the underclass can't get out from under', *Business Week* (international edition), 19 September, New York, McGraw Hill, 60–3.

Giroux, H. (1987) 'Introduction: literacy and the pedagogy of political empowerment', in P. Freire and D. Macedo, *Literacy: Reading the Word and the World*, South Hadley, Massachusetts, Bergin & Garvey.

Gramsci, A. (1971) 'Notes on Italian history,' in Q. Hoare and G. Nowell-Smith (eds), *Selections from the Prison Notebooks of Antonio Gramsci*, London, Lawrence & Wishart.

Hoare, Q. and Nowell-Smith, G. (eds) (1971) *Selections from the Prison Notebooks of Antonio Gramsci*, London, Lawrence & Wishart.

Kozol, J. (1985) *Illiterate America*, New York, Anchor and Doubleday.

Lankshear, C. and Lawler, M. (1987) *Literacy, Schooling and Revolution*, London, Falmer Press.

Levine, K. (1982) 'Functional literacy: fond illusions and false economies,' *Harvard Educational Review* 52 (3), 249–66.

—— (1986) *The Social Context of Literacy*, London, Routledge & Kegan Paul.

McKeon, R. (ed.) (1941) *The Basic Works of Aristotle*, New York, Random House.

Mackie, R. (ed.) (1980) *Literacy and Revolution: The Pedagogy of Paulo Freire*, London, Pluto Press.

McLaren, P. (1988) 'Culture or canon?: Critical pedagogy and the politics of literacy', *Harvard Educational Review* 58 (2), 213–34.

Nafziger, D., Thompson, R. B., Hiscox, M. D. and Owen, T. R. (1975) *Tests of Functional Adult Literacy: An Evaluation of Currently Available Instruments*, Portland, Oregon, North West Regional Educational Laboratory.

Sanders, T. (1972) 'The Paulo Freire method: literacy training and conscientization', in T. J. La Belle (ed.), *Education and Development: Latin America and the Caribbean*, Los Angeles, Latin American Center, 587–602

Shor, I. (1986) *Culture Wars*, London, Routledge & Kegan Paul.

6

FROM THE *PEDAGOGY OF THE OPPRESSED* TO *A LUTA CONTINUA*

The political pedagogy of Paulo Freire[1]

Carlos Alberto Torres

INTRODUCTION

Paulo Freire is perhaps the best-known educationalist of the Third World, whose work has inspired a whole generation of progressive and socialist teachers. His principle of education as cultural action, his method of 'conscientization,' his techniques for literacy teaching have all been adopted and adapted to fit a thousand projects where the learning situation forms part of a social conflict situation. But what is the political background to Freire's theory and practice? What is the political content of the method? How have Freire's ideas evolved over the last three decades? These are the questions this chapter sets out to answer. I trace Freire's development from the beginnings of his work in Brazil and Chile, to his attempts to apply his method in the very different cultural settings of Africa, and then back to the Brazil of the 1980s and early 1990s.

THE LATIN AMERICAN BACKGROUND

Since the publication of *Educacão e Atualidade Brasileira* in Recife, Brazil, in 1959 (afterwards reviewed and published with modifications as *Education as the Practice of Freedom*) the works of Paulo Freire have been influential in pedagogical practice in Latin America as well as in Africa.[2] His main works have been translated into several languages and new generations of educators are looking at Freire as a classic in his field. Notwithstanding this, there has been a theoretical reassessment of Freire's initial works, which emphasizes their connection with the ISEB-developmentalist ideology[3] in Brazil in the early 1960s, and with the sociological theory of Karl Mannheim.[4]

Vanilda Paiva has attempted to show in detail the similarity between

119

Freire's concept of the 'critical consciousness process' with the 'awareness process' proposed by the Hungarian sociologist. Similarly, Mannheim's major themes, such as the whole discussion about liberty, democratic planning, fundamental democratization of society, and the theory of democratic personality, are crucial issues in Freire's early writings. Paiva's 'ex-post' evaluation is risky. It overly emphasizes formal similarities while omitting a substantive analysis of the differences between Mannheim and Freire. It is clear, however, that in his origins the Brazilian educator was ideologically a democratic-liberal thinker strongly influenced by the theory of Christian Personalism (i.e. Tristan de Ataide in Brazil or Emmanuel Mounier in France). Over time, however, his thought and writings have evolved incorporating critical theory, Gramsci's analysis, and concepts from radical Deweyism.[5]

There are several reasons why Freire's work has been so influential. First, Freire's earlier works have philosophical assumptions which reflect an innovative synthesis of most of the main advanced streams of philosophical thought, including Existentialism, Phenomenology, Hegelian dialectics, and historical materialism. This view of Freire as an innovative but firmly grounded philosophical thinker as well as his exceptional talent as a writer in the Spanish and Portuguese languages have given his early works, *Education as the Practice of Freedom* (1967) and *Pedagogy of the Oppressed* (1968), a very large audience among educators, social scientists, theologians, and political militants alike.

Undoubtedly, English readers have to struggle with the translation of his work, rendering its understanding more difficult. However, I will contend that the difficulties that some English readers experience with Freire has less to do with the translation of his work – notwithstanding some serious flaws in some translations – than with the nature of Freire's dialectical thinking and strategy of explanation. This difficulty may be compounded because his most recent books have been 'talked' or 'dialogical' pieces with a distinct oral flavor. Freire's dialectical thinking evolves into a pattern of reasoning and logical analysis different from positivist explanations, thus outside mainstream writing in English-speaking countries.

Second, Freire's initial writings appeared during a period of intense political conflict with substantive phases of class struggle in Latin America; thus, the 'historical moment' is extremely important in understanding Freire's popularity in Latin America. The period extending from the beginning of the 1960s through the early 1970s was marked by several interrelated characteristics: among the most important are the triumph and consolidation of the Cuban Revolution (1959–61) and the installation of the first socialist government in the region (1962); the relative advance and consolidation of the position of popular forces (particularly working-class trade unions and left-wing political parties) under populist regimes;[6] and the project of the Alliance for Progress designed and supported by the

Kennedy administration as the North American response to the radical trends emerging from the Cuban Revolution that brought a sizeable amount of financial support for economic, political, and educational programs in the region. Two aspects of this program of development should be highlighted: first, the support of mild-agrarian reforms of bourgeois origin which were attempting to destabilize the power of the traditional agrarian bourgeoisie and to promote agribusiness in the region; and second, the diversification and expansion of the process of industrialization through import-substitution during this period of consolidation of the penetration of multinational corporations of US origin in the region. The implications that these trends had in altering the original economic and political structures are many.

This was also a period when the first symptoms of a 'crisis of hegemony' amongst the bourgeoisie became clearly perceptible in some countries of the region. In particular, the Bonapartist (populist) experience (that of *Peronismo*, *Vargismo*) appeared only as an interlude between the crisis of the oligarchical state in the 1930s and the attempt to establish a capitalist-industrial bourgeois hegemony in South American societies in the 1960s. The failure of this attempt and the political activation of the masses prompted the bourgeois bloc to appeal for a *coup d'état* and the administrative control of the state by the military, seen as the last chance to restore the bourgeois order.

A major outcome of this process was the rise of the popular-revolutionary movements in Latin America with different expressions and strategies according to each country's historical experience. Therefore, Freire's proposal for education as a practice of freedom – in contrast to the educational positivism and pragmatism then prevailing in educational circles – and his proposal for a *Pedagogy of the Oppressed* were naturally listened to and tried out by progressive educators in the region.

In this period, given the Latin American societies' political and juridical democratic-bourgeois superstructure, these popular movements were able to organize political mass-activities, sometimes confronting the capitalist state. Thus, extensive anti-capitalist and anti-imperialist politics were played out in a context where human rights were moderately well respected, in contrast to the experience of the 1970s and early 1980s.[7] In this sense, the 1960s represents a period during which a political pedagogy like Freire's could arise in Latin America and have an impact upon progressive educational settings worldwide.

Third, and probably one of the main reasons for Freire's success, was the close relation between Freire's early philosophy of education and Catholic thinking. At this time, after the Second Vatican Council (1965) the Catholic Church (as well as some other Christian Churches), underwent a process of ideological transformation and a broadening of their sociocultural policy and strategy toward the civil society.

121

The most important document to support our contention regarding the ideological-political turnabout in the Church may be found in the Final Documents of Medellin, produced at the regional assembly of Bishops in Medellin, Colombia in 1968. The influence of Freire's thought is clearly evidenced in the document on education:

> Without forgetting the existing differences among educational sys-tems in Latin American countries our opinion is that the curriculum, in general, is too abstract and formalistic. The didactic method tries to transmit knowledge rather than, among other values, a critical approach to reality. From a 'social' point of view, the educational system tries to support the social and economic structure rather than its change. When Latin Americans try to find their own being under the banner of rich cultural pluralism, they are confronted with a uniform educational system. Educational systems have an economic orientation toward possession of goods, while youth needs to aug-ment his own being by the enjoyment of self-realization in service and love. Our thinking about this panorama seeks to promote one view of education that agrees with an integral development of our Continent. This education is called education for liberation; that is, education which permits the learner to be the subject of his own development.[8]

This language is similar to that of *Education as the Practice of Freedom* which achieved great resonance as a basic text for Christian educators. In the same way, in 1963, Freire's method of literacy was given official approval by the national Bishop's Conference in Brazil and was adopted by the Movimento de Educação de Base (MEB – Movement of Education from the Bases) as its own method of attaining literacy by means of the teleschool (distance education, using television and monitors).[9]

In summary, the development of Freire's thought reflects the new intellectual horizon in Latin America. Without unfolding a comprehensive history of ideas in Latin America, it may be said that this intellectual atmosphere has several key features: first, the rebirth of Marxist thought after the Stalinist closure. In this sense, the reverberations of the work of Louis Althusser and subsequently Antonio Gramsci in the Latin American scholarly environment, and the emblematic figures of Ernesto 'Che' Guevara and Fidel Castro in the practical and political environment, were symptomatic of the new socialist and progressive groups. In addition to that, the revival of guerrilla and armed struggles whose predominant characteristic was the progressive and massive incorporation of petty-bourgeois militants – many of them from Catholic roots – raised new political issues,[10] and brought about a shift in the main front: from the countryside to the urban centers. In certain cases, these guerrilla move-ments (e.g. Uruguay with the *Frente Amplio* or Argentina with the Montoneros-Peronist experience) were strongly linked with political activation of the masses.

In this connection, the progressive incorporation of Catholic militants was highly significant, especially the symbolic importance of the priest Camilo Torres who died fighting alongside the Colombian guerrillas in the late 1960s. Other indicators of a new era for Catholic and Protestant Churches in the region included the new theology and philosophy of Liberation, the Christian for Socialism Movement, and the widespread new ecumenism supported by the World Council of Churches.[11]

Meanwhile, in the philosophical scholarly environment, there was a renewed interest for national and indigenous issues, as well as a revaluation of the popular content of the national culture, in opposition to past and present emulation of European or North American lifestyles. Finally, in the social sciences, new approaches to the study of the development process such as the so-called Theory of Dependence acquired great relevance, transcending Latin American scholarship and being projected to the United States, the former Soviet Union and even Africa through the writings of Fernando H. Cardoso and Enzo Faletto, André Gunder-Frank, Osvaldo Sunkel and Pedro Paz, Theotonio dos Santos, and others.[12] To this extent, Freire represents and reflects in his writings devoted to pedagogy a particular ideological momentum in Latin American societies.

After the Brazilian *coup d'état* of 1964, Freire left the country and lived and worked in Chile in the Institute for Training in Agrarian Reform (ICIRA), an organ of the Christian Democratic government with responsibility for educational extension within the agrarian reform.[13] There Freire had the opportunity of experiencing his methodology in a new intellectual, political, ideological, and sociological environment; working with the most progressive sectors of the Christian Democratic Party Youth (some of them afterwards incorporated into new parties inside the Unidad Popular coalition) and finding himself in contact with highly stimulating Marxist thought and powerful working-class organizations. This was at the dawn of triumph of the Unidad Popular in Chile which was the first successful electoral experience of transition to socialism in the region, which started in 1970 and ended in 1973 with the *coup d'état* that brought Pinochet to power.

In 1970 Freire left the region after accepting an invitation from the World Council of Churches in Geneva to work as principal consultant for its Department of Education. Meanwhile, the popularity of Freire's method and his problem-posing philosophy of education grew and embraced progressive educators in Latin America, being experienced almost everywhere, on a small scale or incorporated into national experiences of adult education, such as in Uruguay, Argentina, Mexico, Chile, Peru, and Ecuador.[14]

Up to this point, almost without exception each progressive experience in pedagogy advocates to some extent the main Freirean themes and assumptions, and the word *concientizacão* (conscientization or 'critical consciousness') acquires the strength of a political-cultural program for the socialist groups. Its popularity as a new educational perspective grew everywhere. Indeed, Freire had to explicitly warn against the fetishist use of this emblematic word[15] as a front for conservative programs whose educational principles were closer to 'banking education' than to 'problem-posing education' or 'cultural action for freedom.'[16]

Freire's thought can now be clearly perceived as an expression of socialist pedagogy, and the Freirean analysis has been, over time, worked into the historical-materialist framework, redefining to some extent its old existentialist-phenomenological themes without, however, ever adopting an orthodox stance.

This brief introduction leads us in the next section to point out the characterization of the process of education, cultural action, and critical consciousness in Freire's work and consider its contribution to radical social change.

PAULO FREIRE'S POLITICAL PHILOSOPHY

My perspective is dialectical and phenomenological. I believe that from here we have to look to overcome this opposed relationship between theory and praxis: surmounting that should not be done at an idealistic level. From a scientific diagnosis of this phenomenon, we can state the requirement for education as a cultural action. Cultural action for liberation is a process through which the oppressor consciousness 'living' in the oppressed consciousness can be extracted.[17]

Thus, from Freire's perspective, education as a cultural action is related to the process of critical consciousness, and, as problem-posing education, aims to be an instrument of political organization of the oppressed:

The first level of apprehension of reality is the *prise de conscience*. This awareness exists because as human beings are 'placed' and 'dated,' as Gabriel Marcel used to say, men are *with* and *in* the world, looking on. This *prise de conscience*, however, is not yet critical consciousness. There is the deepening of the *prise de conscience*. This is the critical development of the *prise de conscience*. For this reason, critical consciousness implies the surpassing of the spontaneous sphere of apprehension of reality by a criticist position. Through this criticism, reality appears to be a cognoscible objectum within which man assumes an epistemological position: man looking for knowing. Thus, critical consciousness is a test of environment, a test of reality. Inasmuch as we are conscientizing, so much are we unveiling reality, so much are we penetrating the phenomenological essence of the object that we are trying to analyze.

Critical consciousness does not mean to be confronting reality by assuming a falsely intellectual position, that is 'intellectualist.' Critical consciousness cannot exist outside the praxis, that is, outside the action-reflection process. There is no critical consciousness without historical commitment. Thus, critical consciousness means historical consciousness.

In the last analysis, class consciousness is not psychological consciousness. Second, class consciousness does not mean class sensitiveness. Class consciousness does not imply class practice and class knowledge. For this reason the revolution is also an act of knowledge. It is for no other reason that Lenin has emphasized the importance of revolutionary theory without which – he asserted – there would not be a revolution.

Finally, class consciousness has a strong identity with class knowledge. But as it happens, knowledge does not naturally exist as such. If we defined knowledge as a concluded fact in itself, we are losing the dialectical vision that can explain the possibility of knowledge. Knowledge is a process resulting from the permanent praxis of human beings over reality. Indeed, individual existence, even though it will present singular features, is a social existence.[18]

Thus, education implies the act of knowing between knowledgeable subjects, and conscientization is at the same time a logical possibility and a historical process linking theory with praxis in an indissoluble unity. At this point, it is important to summarize some of the major features of Freire's analysis:

1 Freire's global purpose transcends a criticism of the current educative forms, and goes on to virtually become a criticism of culture and the construction of knowledge. In short, the basic assumptions of Freire's works lie in a dialectical epistemology for interpreting the development of human consciousness in its relationships with reality.
2 Nevertheless, for Freire the principal issues and problems of education are not pedagogical issues. Instead, they are political issues. In the last instance, the schooling system does not change society; instead, society can change the schooling system.[19] However, the educational system may play a crucial role in a cultural revolution. For Freire, revolution implies the conscious participation of the masses. Critical pedagogy, as a cultural praxis, contributes to lifting the ideological veil in people's consciousness. Moreover, revolution itself is a meaningful pedagogy for the masses – Freire has spoken of revolutions as a continuing political workshop.

3 But, what can be done before the revolution takes place? Freire's pedagogy of the oppressed is designed as an instrument of pedagogical and political collaboration in the organization of the subordinate social classes. In this sense, it is worthwhile to emphasize the distinction proposed by Freire between 'cultural action' and 'cultural revolution':

> Cultural action is developed in opposition to the elite that controls the power; in contrast, the cultural revolution occurs in complete harmony with the revolutionary regime in spite of the fact that the cultural revolution should not be subordinate to the revolutionary power. The limits of cultural action are determined by the oppressed reality and by the 'silence' imposed by the elite in power. The nature of the oppressed consequently determines the different tactics, necessarily different from the tactics used in the cultural revolution. While cultural action for liberation confronts the 'silence' as an exterior fact and, at the same time, as an internal reality, the cultural revolution confronts the 'silence' only as an internal reality.[20]

4 The specificity of Freire's proposal is the notion of critical consciousness as class knowledge and class praxis. Freire, following Brazilian philosopher Alvaro Viera Pinto, considers the 'heuristic activity of consciousness as the highest possible contribution of the process of thought.'[21] In this sense, he sees his contribution to the process of humanization of social beings as a constant reassessment of the 'subjective' conditions for the revolutionary praxis.

5 It is a pedagogy of consciousness. Thus it emphasizes a fundamental aspect in the process of political organization of the subordinate social classes: the links between revolutionary leadership and mass practices (particularly in *Pedagogy of the Oppressed*). These are mainly expressed in a generic plane, close to a political ethic, without discussing in detail the problems and characteristics of the state and the political revolutionary party – particularly in the early writings before the African experience.

6 Finally, in educational terms, its proposal is an anti-authoritarian though directivist pedagogy, where 'teachers' and 'students' are teaching and learning together. Since education is the act of knowing, 'teacher–student' and 'student–teacher' should engage in a permanent dialogue characterized by its 'horizontal relationship,' which, of course, does not preclude power imbalances or different everyday living experiences and knowledge. This is a process taking place not in a classroom, but in a cultural circle. There is not a 'discursive' knowledge but a knowledge starting from the living everyday and contradictory experience of teachers–students/students–teachers. Certainly this set of notions dismantles the most important framework of authoritarian pedagogy and, to this extent, appears as a 'counter-hegemony' practice and ideology within teacher training institutions.

126

To this extent, the Freirean proposal in the 1960s does not deal with the formal schooling system before the revolution. On the contrary, from its inception this proposal avoided suggesting change within formal schooling which represents a concentration of bureaucratic machinery. Instead, it shifts the concern to the non-formal, less structured system. Another important characteristic of this strategy is that with few exceptions, its representatives have avoided working out this pedagogy within capitalist state institutions and are accustomed to working profession-ally in universities or private institutions, often closely connected with churches.[22]

There are some complementary arguments for this strategy:

1 Freire and Liberation educators had originally developed their approach in this field in Brazil (1960–4), in Chile (1965–70), and in Africa.
2 The political implications of adult education vastly exceed those of formal schooling (e.g. using community needs for designing vocabulary for literacy programs).
3 Adult education programs from the point of view of this educational philosophy are better linked to community needs and more responsive to community pressures than the formal schooling system. Thus, this 'popular education' should be understood more as a form of education developed *by* the oppressed than *for* the oppressed.[23]
4 Also this education has the curricular and organizational flexibility that formal schooling lacks.
5 The results of adult education are more immediate than those of formal schooling. It is not necessary to wait 10–15 years, as in formal training, for the incorporation of the 'graduate' into the labor market or into political activities as in the case of children.
6 The potential demanders of adult education in peripheral capitalist social formations are always the dispossessed. This testifies to their lack of power and, furthermore, shows that illiteracy, far from being a 'social illness,' is an outcome of a hierarchical class structure or violent historical processes such as colonization.
7 Finally, adult education has shown great importance as an instrument for political mobilization and critical consciousness in some processes of transition to socialism, such as in Cuba and Nicaragua.

It is worth adding that, as the Latin American experience shows, this pedagogical approach needs to be used at least in a liberal-democratic institutional and political context. Obviously, this restricts its applicability to some Third World countries under despotic-bourgeois regimes. Similarly, in its full expression, this pedagogy may be carried on by a revolutionary party as part of its educational strategy in a process of social transition, or could be supported by social movements based on non-government organizations.[24]

THE AFRICAN BACKGROUND

Paulo Freire's first contact with Africa came about through his peripheral involvement with the Tanzanian literacy campaign after 1970. He was invited to present his method of literacy teaching at the Institute of Adult Education of the University of Dar es Salaam, and to help in organizing new experimental projects as well as the curriculum in the Adult Education Diploma Course. Unfortunately there are only scattered references in Freire's work on Tanzania, and there is little documentation on experiments with Freire's literacy method, which could help in evaluating his Tanzanian experience.

Nevertheless, Freire's introduction to African reality through the Tanzanian experience was an important step towards his more significant participation in Guinea-Bissau, Cape Verde, and São Tomé e Principe. Moreover, Freire has often expressed his concern with the experiences of Angola and Mozambique in adult education.

At this point, we can roughly summarize some of the more significant contrasts and similarities with the Latin American experience. In Africa educational development has been strongly influenced by the process of decolonization, particularly because the structure of colonial education was distinct from non-colonial education.[25] It was an élitist form of education: for instance, between 1961 and 1965 enrollment in primary education in Guinea-Bissau included only 16.4 percent of the total population in the appropriate age cohort.[26] According to Erick Pessiot,[27] enrollment at school for the year 1974, when the PAIGC came into power in Guinea-Bissau, was as shown in Table 1.

Table 1 School enrollment in Guinea-Bissau, 1974

Level	Number of students
Pre-school	28,500
1st grade Primary Level	23,500
2nd grade	10,500
3rd grade	6,500
4th grade	3,700
1st year Secondary Level	3,000
2nd year	2,000
3rd year	2,000
4th year	600
5th year	300
6th year	350
7th year	80

For the people involved, colonial education was basically a means of cultural 'de-Africanization,' particularly in the more violent colonizing mode (such as the Portuguese style); a means of creating a selected

128

corps of civil servants that usually, after graduating, became government employees in middle positions within the bureaucracy, under the leadership of colonial officials; a means of creating a selected group of the urban élite which would support the colonizers' project: a black-skin, white-mask petty bourgoisie in Frantz Fanon's words. To this extent, Freire has perceived in the Guinea-Bissau case, following Amilcar Cabral's approach, that the petty-bourgeois intellectuals only have this alternative: 'to betray the revolution or to commit class suicide constitutes the real option of the middle class in the general picture of the struggle for national liberation.'[28]

However, Freire argues that the new educational system not only has to help this class suicide of the intellectuals, but also must impede its evolution into an élite in the new society. Thus, to this extent, Freire in the Guinea-Bissau case argues that an important measure should be to link education with productive work, avoiding full-time students and combining study time with working hours in intimate relationship with peasants.

A second important difference is the level of development of the productive forces and social relations of production which has determined the class structure and dynamics of society. The African societies differ from the Latin American in a number of ways. For instance, there is no extensive agrarian bourgeoisie in the rural areas with 'oligarchical' origins – conserving the ownership of the means of production – comparable to the 'coronelismo' in the Brazilian case with its 'patrimonialist' foundations and clientelist practices that have historically affected the configuration of the Brazilian bureaucratic state.[29]

Similarly, there is no extensive industrialization process which to a certain extent can bring about a sort of national-indigenous industrial bourgeoisie with some objective (although secondary) differences in its economic and political interest from those of the agrarian bourgeoisie, multinational corporations, or the state bureaucracy – as might be, for instance, the case of Argentina, Brazil, or Mexico. These differences, expressed in the political struggle, would bring about broadly different political strategies as well as different levels of relative autonomy of the state in Latin America. Likewise, the petty bourgeoisie in African societies, although strongly linked to the postcolonial state, has not developed an extensive educational network as in the post-populist experiments in Latin America.[30] In other words, extended middle classes pushing for an expansion of secondary and higher education institutions are not present. This is compatible with Amilcar Cabral's views that 'in colonial conditions it is the petty bourgeoisie which is the interior of state power.'[31] The military, although having a growing interventionist role in African societies, does not have the same historical importance in the constitution of the nation state as it has had, for instance, in Latin America. Neither has the Catholic Church – another major player in Latin American politics – secured the virtual religious monopoly and cultural influence that it has in Ibero- and Lusoamerica.

These differences notwithstanding, the capitalist social formations in Africa and Latin America share a number of similar characteristics, including the illiteracy of the peasantry. But the African postcolonial governments have already concentrated their educational efforts in the rural areas.[32] In Latin America, by contrast, due to the process of accelerated urbanization, growing internal migrations, and agri-business penetration – in short, the combined effects of uneven capitalist development – a progressive imbalance exists between the rural and the urban areas. The illiterates are concentrated, in equal measure, within the rural areas and within the periphery of metropolitan or major cities. Thus, in Freire's Latin American experience, in addition to the peasantry, there has been an extensive urban marginality (with a recent peasant past, of course) which has represented a central constituency for his problem-posing education. Freire has emphasized the contrast between his Brazilian and Chilean experience and his experience in Guinea-Bissau.[33]

Notwithstanding this, Freire has claimed that adult literacy programs, understood as a political act and as an act of knowledge within the process of national reconstruction,[34] will be successful only under conditions of radical and progressive alteration of the social relations of production in society. Freire argues that:

> As an educator I give much more emphasis to the comprehension of a rigorous method of knowing. . . . My great preoccupation is method as a means to knowledge. Still we must ask ourselves, to know in favor of what and, therefore, against what to know; in whose favor to know?[35]

Freire will argue that the successful conclusion of a literacy campaign and follow-up process (post-literacy) is strongly linked with the progressive attainment of the social transition to socialism in Guinea-Bissau.

To this extent, one of Freire's richest methodological suggestions in Guinea-Bissau and in São Tomé e Principe is to begin adult education programs in those areas in the process of transformation or having experienced key conflict (say, during the war of liberation, or through class tensions and conflicts). Freire would argue that adult education programs would help strengthen the revolutionary consciousness of the people who have been participating in the liberation struggle or are currently committed to the process of transition to socialism and to radical change in the social relations of production. However, there is a claim for linking, in a more coherent and systematic fashion, the process of literacy with the process of production and productive work (this was one of the more recognized theoretical weaknesses in Freire's early writings).

This crucial methodological issue was pointed out by Rosiska and Miguel Darcy de Oliveira in an early evaluation of Freire's (and the IDAC team's) experience in Guinea-Bissau:

> It seems to us that priority areas in the countryside must be chosen in the light of political and technical considerations. Any given population will be more motivated for the literacy program if it has enthusiastically participated in the liberation struggle and accumulated the rich cultural and political experience which the program would hope to bring up to date and develop. However, the criterion of political receptivity growing out of the richness of a group's past experience is not sufficient. If the literacy campaign is to go beyond a celebration of the past and provide an opening towards the future, as mentioned above, the chosen region must be in the process of experiencing a socio-economic transformation. This point seems extremely important to us, for it is questionable whether learning to read and write corresponds to a real need for the peasant in a rural area who continues living and producing in traditional ways. On the other hand, literacy can take on much more meaning if it is related to new production techniques being introduced in a particular area or the creation of new production units, such as, for example, agricultural cooperatives. In other words, within the context of a transformation process, literacy could facilitate the peasant's acquisition of new technical understanding which is necessary to the project being carried out and could also contribute to the political mobilization of the community, enabling the peasant to take charge of the process of change rather than being simply passive 'beneficiaries' of a plan worked out and applied from the outside.[36]

In addition to this 'economic determination,' a third important difference from the Latin American background resides in specific political variables. First, the Tanzanian experience offered Freire the opportunity of working within a socialist experiment, with centralized planning, a revolutionary socialist party, and a substantive concern with adult education as a real methodological alternative to the formal schooling system. Adult education in Tanzania is far from being irrelevant: in a population of seventeen million people, the rate of literacy in 1966-7 (when the functional literacy programs started) was 25-30 percent; when these programs were evaluated in 1975-6, the government claimed that the rate of literacy had grown to 75-80 percent, although other sources have declared that it was 55-60 percent.[37]

These issues were enriched with the PAIGC experience of revolutionary struggle in Guinea-Bissau when the literacy campaign appeared to be an essential step forward in the process of national reconstruction after the war of liberation, an experience comparable to that of Nicaragua during

its own literacy campaign.[38] Adult education was clearly political education that, as Denis Goulet has pointed out,[39] embraced several politicized
themes such as the political unity between Guinea-Bissau and Cape Verde,
the proposal of linking manual and intellectual work, the responsibility of
all citizens to help the PAIGC build a just society, and so forth.

In this respect, Freire has stressed the contrasting results of the first
attempts in Guinea-Bissau: for while the literacy campaign was completely
successful among the militants of the Revolutionary Army in the urban
areas of Guinea-Bissau, adult basic education directed toward society in
general failed in its primary objectives.[40]

Second, another feature of this African period is Freire's enthusiastic
appraisal of the significant role of charismatic leadership or revolutionary
political leaders in the process of social transition to socialism, particularly
in the effects of their writings, speeches, and practice on political mass-
consciousness and political culture (e.g. Amilcar Cabral in Guinea-Bissau,
President Julius Nyerere in Tanzania, or President Pinto de Acosta in São
Tomé e Principe). It is particularly true in the constant references given
by Freire to the writings of Amilcar Cabral as a Marxist revolutionary
theoretician.[41]

Third, Freire has raised the dilemma of choosing a language of teaching
for literacy programs, i.e. should it be in the indigenous language(s) or
should it be done in Portuguese. This issue, even though briefly analyzed,
remains quite relevant – in Freire's approach – to the process of national
identity, particularly when: 'Although precise figures are unavailable,
approximately 80 percent of the Guinea-Bissau total population does not
speak Portuguese. The lingua franca of the country's varied ethnic groups
is Creole, a hybrid of Portuguese and African dialects.'[42] Furthermore,
Creole is spoken by about 45 percent of the population and is not a written
language.

At a personal level, it is very understandable that Freire, a sensitive
intellectual, demonstrates interest in the issues revolving around language,
having re-encountered his own mother language in Guinea-Bissau, not too
far from Brazil, ten years after his exile.

Lastly, and a very different feature in the Freirean African experience,
is the strong emphasis placed on the post-literacy process as indissolubly
linked with the literacy phase. In a letter to co-ordinators of cultural circles
in São Tomé e Principe, Freire has emphasized the following goals for this
post-literacy process:

1 To consolidate the knowledge acquired in the previous phase in the field
of reading, writing, and mathematics.
2 To deepen this knowledge through a systematic introduction of
basic rudiments of grammatic categories and arithmetic (fundamental
operations).

3 To continue, in a more profound manner, 'reading' reality through reading texts with more varied and rich themes.
4 To develop a capability for critical analysis of reality and oral expression of this reality.
5 To prepare the learners for a following stage, in which due to the needs imposed by the national reconstruction process, courses to technical training (never technicist training) have to be created in different sectors. That is to say, these human resource training courses will be developed specifically with a critical view and, through this, with a global view of their own activity, as opposed to a narrow and alienated view.[43]

The work of Paulo Freire in Africa has been the focus of criticism and controversy. What follows is a brief presentation and analysis of literacy training in Guinea-Bissau.

The planning stage of the mass literacy campaign began in 1975, and the first literacy campaign was launched in 1976 with over two hundred literacy animators organizing cultural circles in the villages. Literacy training inspired by Freire's method was held in the rural areas and in the capital city of Bissau. Linda Harasim claims that, by 1980, reports from Guinea-Bissau began to acknowledge that the goals of literacy for national reconstruction had failed to materialize: of the 26,000 students involved in literacy training practically none became functionally literate.[44]

In her study, Harasim claims that the causes for this failure of literacy training are threefold:

1 The underdeveloped material conditions of Guinea-Bissau.
2 The contradictory political conditions of the process of national reconstruction.
3 Some unexamined assumptions of Freire's theory and method, particularly his ideological populism and idealism which seem to have been shared by the ruling revolutionary party (PAIGC) in Guinea-Bissau.

On the one hand, there seems to be an endless list of material conditions undermining any effort of economic or educational development in one of the poorest twenty-five countries in the world. These include a low level of productivity, scattered and isolated self-subsisting villages – Harasim estimates that 88 percent of the total population in Guinea-Bissau is engaged in subsistence farming[45] – cultural, linguistic, tribal, ethnic, and economic differences, and lack of political unity.[46]

On the other hand, exacerbated by the low level of development of productive forces, the effort at national reconstruction in Guinea-Bissau confronted some of the proverbial problems of any transition to socialism in the Third World. Harasim notes as among the key problems of national reconstruction the following: an increasingly bureaucratized, centralized, and inefficient state apparatus; lack of trained cadres, and the need to rely on the colonial bureaucracy who have not supported the struggle of the PAIGC; the centralizing action in the capital city of Bissau, where 83 percent of all the civil servants work, and where 55 percent of total investment was channeled, thus deepening the urban–rural contradiction; the failure of a strategy of development based on establishing state farms and co-operatives; and the need to rely on external financing for literacy training.[47]

Finally, in addition to these contradictions resulting from the poor material conditions and problems of national reconstruction, Freire's theory and practice failed to offer an efficient approach to literacy. Freire is accused of imposing a Westernized world-view in the very different setting of Guinea–Bissau. Harasim claims that this may have led Freire to thinking idealistically that his method has universal validity and appropriateness in any Third World society – a problem which became compounded by his romantic perception of the level of political literacy of the Guinea-Bissau rural population. Due to these misleading assumptions, the planning and organization of the campaign, and the method implemented, did not take into account the lack of well-trained Guinea-Bissau militants capable of understanding and implementing the literacy strategy and method.[48]

According to Harasim, this political criterion was taken at face value:

The fundamental contradiction lay in the fact that Freire's concept of 'the political' was rooted in moral and philosophical notions and contained no implicit practical plan of action.[49]

In Harasim's evaluation, by assuming a Utopian view of social reality and an idealist stance in education, Freire overestimated the ability of literacy animators to implement the process of literacy training, and the need to produce educational material in the appropriate amount, quality, and timing to be effective. Hence:

The introduction of the Freire method into the conditions of the Guinean reality led to mechanical, rote learning, based on memorization – exactly, in fact, what Freire professed to abhor. Students for the most part were unable to progress beyond the first five or six words in the manual; those who did were unable to 'create' new words. Even where there was a high level of participation by the peasants, it was found that after six months the students were able to read and write, but when questioned about what they were reading and writing, the comprehension was found to be nil: they could understand nothing.[50]

Freire has addressed the criticisms of his work in Guinea-Bissau in a number of places, including his conversations with Antonio Faúndez[51] and Donaldo Macedo.[52] Freire does not address the issue of the political economy of Guinea-Bissau, but disputes the charge of ideological populism,[53] emphasizing also the constraints or political conditions imposed upon his practice in a society in social transformation, and how that has affected his work. He makes references to the communalities between his work in Africa and his previous experiences in Chile and Brazil, but the central question that he attributed to the failure of his work in Guinea-Bissau is the selection of language for literacy training.

Revisiting literacy in Guinea-Bissau, Freire argues that, as a militant intellectual, he is not a typical researcher working under the protection of an umbrella of 'academic autonomy' or 'scientific objectivity.' As a militant intellectual, what he could not do in Guinea-Bissau was 'to overstep the political limitations of the moment. As a foreigner, I could not impose my proposals on the reality of Guinea-Bissau and on the needs as perceived by political leaders.'[54]

Freire concludes that he wanted the PAIGC leadership to change their initial decision to conduct the literacy campaign in Portuguese, the language of the colonizers.[55] But, as Freire soon discovered, his suggestion was out of the political boundaries imposed on his work, and he had to accept Portuguese as the language of instruction, even if his own method was not originally designed for second-language acquisition. He defends his experience in literacy training stating that:

> With or without Paulo Freire it was impossible in Guinea-Bissau to conduct a literacy campaign in a language that was not part of the social practice of the people. My method did not fail, as has been claimed. . . . The issue should be analyzed in terms of whether it is linguistically viable to conduct literacy campaigns in Portuguese in any of these countries. My method is secondary to this analysis. If it is not viable to do so, my method or any other method will certainly fail.[56]

THE LAST FREIRE: BRAZIL, 1980–91

After living in exile for sixteen years and following his return to the country in 1980, Freire attempted to 'relearn Brazil,'[57] thus traveling incessantly throughout the country, lecturing, engaging in dialogues with students and teachers, and publishing.

This relearning Brazil was succinctly summarized by Freire himself when he told me in a torrid Californian summer at Stanford University, in July 1983, that he believes in 'reading Gramsci, but also listening to the *popular Gramsci* in the *favelas* [Brazilian shantytowns]. That is the reason why I spend at least two afternoons a week with people in the *favelas*.'

Since 1980 Freire worked as Professor in the Faculty of Education of the

135

Catholic University of São Paulo, and as Professor in the Faculty of Education in the University of Campinas – a research university sponsored by the State of São Paulo, located about 100 kilometers from the City of São Paulo.

In addition to his involvement in higher education, he created the Educational Center 'Vereda' that agglutinates many people who worked in the original projects of popular education in the 1960s. Politically, Freire collaborates with the Commission of Education of the Partido Trabalhista Party or Workers' Party (a socialist democratic party which he joined from Geneva, when it was being formed in 1979), and accepted the honorary position of President of the Workers' University of São Paulo, an institution sponsored by the Workers' Party and mostly concerned with trade union and political education.

Perhaps what has most deeply marked Freire's everyday life experience in the last years has been the loss of his wife, Elza, who died of cardiac failure in October 1986. With Elza's heartbreaking death, Freire not only lost his lifelong companion, friend, and lover, but also his vital optimism and desire. Freire married again in 1988, to a long-time friend of the family and a former student, Ana Maria Araujo.

Most recently, with his appointment in January 1989 as Secretary of Education of the City of São Paulo, Freire took charge of 662 schools with 720,000 students, from K–8 (Kindergarten to grade 8), in addition to heading adult education and literacy training in the City of São Paulo, which, with 11.4 million people, is one of the largest cities in Latin America.

In his capacity as Secretary of Education, Freire found a unique opportunity to implement his educational philosophy in his own country, this time not as an academic adviser but as a policy-maker in a municipality controlled by a socialist party. The socialist goals of the Workers' Party, however, should be considered in the framework of the new democracy and constitutional reform in Brazil. Freire formally resigned on 22 May 1991 as Secretary of Education, but one of his close collaborators has been appointed to replace him. Freire has accepted to remain as a kind of 'Honorary Ambassador' of the Municipal Administration.[58]

Since returning to Brazil in 1980, Freire has produced a number of 'talking' books and articles, which by and large have not been translated into English, including his dialogues with Sérgio Guimarães,[59] Moacir Gadotti and Guimarães,[60] Frei Betto,[61] and Adriano Nogueira and Debora Mazza[62] among others. However, his book with Faúndez has been translated into English.

Paulo Freire's perspective on literacy work becomes relevant for industrial societies. In his book with Donaldo Macedo, Freire calls for a view of literacy as cultural politics. That is, literacy training should not only provide reading, writing, and numeracy but also be considered:

a set of practices that functions to either empower or disempower people. In the larger sense, literacy is analyzed according to whether it serves to reproduce existing social formations or serves as a set of cultural practices that promotes democratic and emancipatory change.[63]

Literacy as cultural politics is also related in Freire's work to emancipatory theory and critical theory of society. Hence, emancipatory literacy

is grounded in a critical reflection on the cultural capital of the oppressed. It becomes a vehicle by which the oppressed are equipped with the necessary tools to reappropriate their history, culture, and language practices.[64]

The reverberation of Freire's work in current pedagogical scholarship is impressive, and cannot be restricted to literacy training. The Freirean approach has been implemented not only in social studies and curriculum studies in adult education, secondary education and higher education, but also in such diverse subjects as the teaching of mathematics and physics, educational planning, feminist studies, romance languages, educational psychology, critical reading and writing, and so forth.[65] Freire's dialogues with Ira Shor[66] attempt to formulate a *Pedagogy of the Oppressed*, taking into account the *problématique* of social reproduction in the context of industrialized societies.

It can be argued that Freire's work has been simultaneously reinterpreted or 'reinvented' as Freire would like to term it[67] in industrially advanced societies by those who attempt to construct a new theoretical synthesis by bringing together Freire, Dewey, and Habermas. A noted representative of this agenda is Henry Giroux and his theory of resistance in pedagogy and curriculum.[68]

In addition, Freire's political philosophy has fared well with socialist democratic perspectives of schooling in the United States. In this respect, the work of Ira Shor is exemplary in trying to understand the reproductive power of schooling in spite of the 'Culture Wars' that prevail in the US mosaic, and the possibilities of linking North American struggles with pedagogy for liberation.[69] Hence, the apparent paradox is that literacy political activism in industrialized societies is nurtured by notions of education and social change developed in the Third World.[70]

ARE THERE ANY DARK CLOUDS IN THE SKY?
FINAL REMARKS

The Latin American and African background in Freire's pedagogy has shown a surprising unity of topics, themes, assumptions, and methodological requirements. This is possibly due to Freire's tendency to discuss his practical experience theoretically. That is, Freire's approach is a systematization of the political-pedagogical practice: 'Without exception, every book that I have written has been a report of some phase of the political-pedagogical activity in which I have been engaged ever since my youth.'[71]

Nevertheless, a pedagogy as controversial as Freire's raises several issues regarding political-pedagogical praxis in peripheral capitalist social formations. In these final remarks, I would like to address myself to only two of the substantive questions: first, is it a pre- or postrevolutionary pedagogy?; second, in Gramscian terms, can the process opened up by critical consciousness be thought of as the process of counter-hegemony in the historical bloc? There are, certainly, many other extremely relevant points that should be treated in a very extensive and theoretical discussion. Nonetheless, I shall confine myself, in this discussion, to offering only some insights in terms of the questioning of, rather than the answering of, both topics.

To begin with, what are the political factors that can give shape to an education for freedom? What are the minimum conditions for starting an education for freedom? Under what functional conditions can we foresee methodological, didactic, curricular, and even organizational or administrative changes that can help in developing this alternative educational proposal?

Moreover, given the strength of the educational bureaucracy – located particularly in the schooling system – and the state ownership of the principal means of production of knowledge, should this political-pedagogical space be abandoned within the schooling system and the concern shifted to the non-formal system? Or, given the priority of political struggle, is pedagogical practice meaningless?

Thus, assuming as Freire does that we cannot change society by changing the school (a liberal Utopia), is it necessary also to abandon altogether educational reforms? In other words, if the schooling system is an arena of struggle in capitalist social formations, which are the real spaces of this struggle? That is, do spaces which will contribute to the process of political organization of the oppressed exist? Or, paradoxically, will they contribute to the process of political legitimation of the capitalist state, through an indulgent state policy sustaining an acceptable and necessary opposition within the schooling system, but systematically obstructing its organic links with the working class and social movements?

By the same token, even assuming the potential utility of this pedagogy in a process of social transition, is it possible to sustain this directivist, non-authoritarian pedagogy in the long haul? Or, instead, is Freire's pedagogy some sort of 'Jacobinism' that should be cleared up after the institutionalization of revolution?

Similarly, considering the strong emphasis placed by this pedagogy on the process of critical consciousness, how can we reconcile the process of political deliberation opened up by this pedagogy with the process of ideological consolidation of a triumphant revolutionary movement?

In the same line of reasoning, emphasizing the importance of critical consciousness, is it possible to underline and in the same way to support 'spontaneist' practices in politics, to the detriment of the process of political organization, co-ordinated struggle, and centralized political leadership needed for a successful revolution?

The second question is of similar importance. Generally speaking, the majority of Marxist authors have been addressing the analysis of education, hierarchical class structure, and ideological domination; that is, focusing on education from the perspective of the hegemonic classes. Freire's works instead, have shown another perspective: the need to redefine education from the perspective of the subordinate classes. To this extent, there is a very wide coincidence with the Gramscian formula of education contributing to the development of a new culture and new *Weltanschauung* (view of the world) of the subaltern classes.

This new culture – Weltanschauung – has to be developed by the oppressed class and, through its organic intellectuals, from the bosom of the capitalist society. In this sense Freire's premises are equally important:

1 It is crucial to study educational process from a dual perspective: using the lens of the hegemonic classes – reproduction of social relations of production – and using the lens of the subordinate classes – education as a means of constructing a new hegemony.
2 Education is important for reconstituting the culture of the oppressed, particularly through the notion of systematic elaboration of popular knowledge: knowledge understood as an instrument of counter-hegemonic struggle.
3 Designing autonomous educational practices within urban–rural poor communities can help in enlarging the organization and power of the oppressed.
4 Finally, Freire's notion of a dialectical relationship between the revolutionary leadership and the masses has in educational practices a rich terrain, indeed – in Gramscian terms – a rich terrain for developing youth workers' leadership. To this extent, the relevance given by Freire to the epistemological and political 'self-vigilance' of the militants' praxis in Guinea–Bissau raises a new important issue for political practice: how should this vigilance be achieved within a revolutionary process?

Nevertheless, some costly experiences of several experiments in popular education in Latin America (e.g. dismantled after a military *coup d'état* and the assassination of certain militants due to their 'public exposure') have led some people to ask themselves: is this pedagogical program a feasible project that can help in the process of building a

139

counter-hegemony or, instead, might it be viewed only as a sympathetic but impossible dream? Or, indeed, should the aforementioned educational process be evaluated in order to discover the political and pedagogical variables that have to be controlled for a better performance of such educational programs? This may include linking educational practices with a revolutionary party, or redefining the importance, scope, and means of the political struggle within the schooling system and within the capitalist state bureaucracy.

To respond to all these questions will demand a comprehensive study well beyond the limits and possibilities of this chapter. However, it is possible to conclude that there are good reasons why, in pedagogy today, we can stay with Freire or against Freire, but not without Freire.

NOTES

1 This is a revised and expanded version of an article originally published in *Education with Production Review*, no. 2 (Spring 1982), pp. 76–97, Gaborone, Botswana. I want to thank Davis Elias, Joel Samoff, Maria Pilar O'Cadiz, and Peter McLaren for their advice in writing this article. A National Academy of Education – Spencer Fellowship, the Graduate School of Education, and the Latin American Center at the University of California at Los Angeles provided the support for my current research on policy-making in São Paulo, Brazil. I am solely responsible, however, for what is being said.

2 There are a number of bibliographies of references on Freire's work. See, for instance, the one prepared by Anne Hartung and John Ohliger in Stanley Grabowski (ed.), *Paulo Freire: A Revolutionary Dilemma for the Adult Educator* (Syracuse University Publications in Continuing Education, 1973). Additional references could be found in the bibliography being prepared by Henry Giroux and Donaldo Macedo (forthcoming).

3 The Higher Institute of Brazilian Studies (ISEB) was the most important experience in Brazil before the *coup d'état* of 1964 for developing a nationalist ideology that should contribute to the process of social modernization supported by the government of João Goulard. Paulo Freire as well as other intellectuals – Helio Jaguaribe, Roland Corbisier, Alvaro Vieira Pinto, Vicente Ferreira da Silva, Guerreiro Ramos, Durmeval Trigueiro Méndez – were participants in the intellectual atmosphere produced within the workshops of ISEB. Among the more influential authors for the *Isebian* theoreticians was Karl Mannheim, but also influential was the German Anthropology of the 30s (J. Spengler, Alfred Weber, Max Scheller), the philosophy of Existence (M. Ortega y Gasset, J. P. Sartre, M. Heidegger, K. Jaspers), and from historical–sociological sources, Max Weber, Alfredo Pareto and Arnold Toynbee. (For an analysis of ISEB, see Caio Navarro de Toledo, *ISEB: Fabrica de Ideologias* (São Paulo, Etica, 1977).) For an analysis of the intellectual traditions underpinning Freire's work, see the polemic work of Vanilda Pereira Paiva.

4 A documented essay on this subject is Vanilda Pereira Paiva, *Paulo Freire e o Nacionalismo-Desenvolvimentista* (Rio de Janeiro, Editora Civilização Brasileira, 1980). The author argues that Freire's perspective was eminently populist, and related to the developmentalist nationalism prevailing in João

Goulart's administration. This argument, which has been considered the first academic criticism of Freire's work in Brazil, overlooked my own more sympathetic criticisms of Freire's work published earlier in Spanish and Portuguese. Paiva's analysis relies heavily on a limited understanding from a fairly orthodox Marxist perspective of the notion of Russian populism, and is coupled with a dissatisfaction with Freire's Christian philosophical and anthropological roots. As an alternative, see Carlos Alberto Torres, *Leitura Crítica de Paulo Freire* (São Paulo, Edições Loyola, 1981) and Carlos Alberto Torres, *Consciencia e História. A Práxis Educativa de Paulo Freire* (São Paulo, Edições Loyola, 1979); and Moacir Gadotti, *Convite a Leitura de Paulo Freire* (São Paulo, Editora Scipione, 1989).

5 See Carlos Alberto Torres, *Paulo Freire: Educación y Concientización* (Salamanca, Sigüeme, 1980).

6 There is an extensive literature on the characterization of the populist or Bonapartist regimes in Latin America. Among the most compelling work is Octavio Ianni, *La Formación del Estado Populista en América Latina* (Mexico, ERA, 1975). Nevertheless, as a very general and descriptive overview, I shall underline the following features of a populist regime:

  i It claims to be a state above the class conflict not representing a particular class, neither the bourgeoisie nor the subordinate classes.
  ii As principal electorate it is supported by the popular sectors and the working class, as well as by broad sectors of the petty bourgeoisie.
  iii Generally it is associated with the figure of a charismatic leader who tries to appear as a 'neutral' referee among the tensions of the multi-class coalition, and claims to rule independently of the internal scheme of forces (e.g. Perón in Argentina, Vargas in Brazil, Ibañez in Chile, Cárdenas in Mexico).
  iv It tends to develop an extensive state bureaucracy.
  v Generally it stimulates the creation of a 'national political movement' instead of a 'classical' liberal-fashioned political party.
  vi Often the proclaimed ideology is nationalist, anti-imperialist, and linked with Western Christianity.

7 For instance, the military dictatorship that ruled Argentina during 1976–83 annihilated the political opposition by kidnapping, torturing, killing, and 'disappearing' thousands of Argentine citizens. See the evidence reported in CONADEP *Nunca Jamás* (Buenos Aires, CONADEP, 1984).

8 See *Documentos Finales de Medellin* (Buenos Aires, Editorial Paulinas, 1971), pp. 70–2 (my translation).

9 See Emmanuel de Kadt, *Catholic Radicals in Brazil* (Oxford University Press, London, 1970); and especially Thomas G. Sanders, 'The Paulo Freire method: literacy training and conscientization,' *South American Series* XV (1) (1968). The most complete study of MEB is Luiz Eduardo W. Wanderley, *Educar para transformar. Educação Popular, Igreja Católica e Politica no Movimento de Educação de Base* (Petrópolis, R.T., Vozes, 1984).

10 Certainly, there is considerable experience of armed struggle in the region during this century such as the Mexican Revolution (1910–17), Sandino's movement in Nicaragua during the 1930s, and the Nicaraguan Revolution in the 1970s leading to the successful overthrow of the Somoza dictatorship in 1979, the popular insurrection in El Salvador (1932), the Bolivian Revolution (1952), the armed struggle in Cuba (1957–9), and the multiple guerrilla experiences in Colombia or Venezuela between 1940 and 1970, to cite only the most relevant cases. But one of the distinct features of the new guerrilla

experience of the 1960s was, particularly the adherence of middle-class members instead of the traditional *campesinos* (peasants) brigades.

11 See Carlos Alberto Torres, *The Church, Society and Hegemony. A Critical Sociology of Religion in Latin America*. Translated by Richard A. Young (New York, Praeger, 1992).

12 Fernando Henrique Cardoso and Enzo Faletto, *Dependency and Development in Latin America* (Los Angeles and Berkeley, University of California Press, 1979); André Gunder-Frank, *Capitalism and Underdevelopment in Latin America* (New York and London, Monthly Review Press, 1969); Osvaldo Sunkel and Pedro Paz, *El Subdesarrollo Latinoamericano y la Teoria del Desarrollo* (Mexico, Siglo XXI, 1979); Theotonio dos Santos, 'La crisis de la teoria del desarrollo y las relaciones de dependencia en America Latina,' in Helio Jaguaribe, Aldo Ferrer, Miguel S. Wionczek, Theotonio dos Santos, *La Dependencia político-económica de América Latina* (Mexico: Siglo XXI Editores, 1970), pp. 147–87. For commentators see Ingolf Vogeler and Anthony de Souza, *Dialectics of Third World Development* (Montclair, New Jersey, Allanheld, Osmun, 1980; and Ronald H. Chilcote, 'Dependency: A critical synthesis of the literature,' *Latin American Perspectives*, I (1) (Spring 1974), pp. 4–29.

13 See John de Witt, *An Exposition and Analysis of Paulo Freire's Radical Psycho-Social Andragogy of Development* (Boston University, School of Education, 1971).

14 See Torres, *Leitura Crítica de Paulo Freire*.

15 See Paulo Freire, 'Pilgrims of the Obvious,' in *Risk* 11 (1) (1975); *Reading the World: Paulo Freire in Conversation with Dr Carlos A. Torres*, videotape (Alberta, Canada, ACCESS Network, 1990).

16 Freire has defined pedagogy as a cultural action, distinguishing two main cultural actions: 'banking education' and 'problem-posing education' – 'The former attempts to maintain the submersion of consciousness; the latter strives for the emergence of consciousness and critical intervention in reality' (*Pedagogy of the Oppressed* (New York, Herder & Herder, 1971), Chapter 2).

17 See Paulo Freire, 'Acción cultural liberadora,' in Carlos A. Torres, *Paulo Freire. Educación y Concientización* (Salamanca, Sigüeme, 1980), p. 85.

18 See Paulo Freire, 'Concientizar para liberar,' in Torres, *Paulo Freire. Educación y Concientización*, pp. 73–4 (my translation); and Paulo Freire, 'Entrevista,' in Torres, *Paulo Freire. Educación y Concientización*, pp. 158–9 (my translation).

19 See Freire in conversation with Chilean philosopher Antonio Faúndez, *Por Uma Pedagogia da Pergunta* (Rio de Janeiro, Paz e Terra, 1985), pp. 139–40.

20 See Paulo Freire, *Cultural Action: A Dialectical Analysis* (Mexico, CIDOC, 1970), notebook 1004, p. 51.

21 See Paulo Freire, 'La concientización desmitificada,' in Torres, *Paulo Freire. Educación y Concientización*, p. 143.

22 It is not surprising that, since Freire returned to Brazil in June 1980, he has worked for the Catholic University of São Paulo (PUC) and the public universities of UNICAMP and the University of São Paulo; while Rosiska and Miguel Darcy de Oliveira – who were members of the Institute for Cultural Action (IDAC), founded in Geneva by Freire, and principal collaborators of Freire in Guinea-Bissau – also worked upon their return to Brazil in São Paulo in a project of popular education supported by the Archdiocese of São Paulo (Brazil). See *Jornal da Educação*, Campinas, April 1980, pp. 3–5, 8–9.

23 Paulo Freire, Rosiska Darcy de Oliveira, Miguel Darcy de Oliveira, and Claudius Ceccon, *Vivendo e Aprendendo – Experiences do IDAC in Educação*

Popular (São Paulo, Livraria Brasilense Editora, 1980), third edition; Carlos A. Torres, *The Politics of Nonformal Education in Latin America* (New York, Praeger, 1990).

24 The experience of the Workers' Party-controlled municipal administration in São Paulo, and the role of Paulo Freire as Secretary of Education of the City of São Paulo, with its new initiatives of a democratic curricular reform, the School Councils, and the Movement of Literacy Training (MOVA–São Paulo), show the limits and possibilities of a progressive state-social movements partnership in public policy.

25 See Philip G. Altbach and Gail P. Kelly, *Education and Colonialism* (New York, Longman, 1978), especially the Introduction, pp. 1–53.

26 See Lars Rudebeck, *Guinea-Bissau: A Study of Political Mobilization* (New York, African Publishing Company, 1974), pp. 27–40.

27 Cited in Rosiska Darcy de Oliveira and Miguel Darcy de Oliveira, *Guinea-Bissau – Reinventing Education*, IDAC Document 11–12 (Geneva, 1976), p. 53.

28 See Paulo Freire, *Pedagogy in Process* (New York, Seabury Press, 1977), p. 16.

29 See Fernando Uricoechea, *The Patrimonial Foundations of the Brazilian Bureaucratic State* (Los Angeles and Berkeley, University of California Press, 1980). In addition, see Luis Roniger, *Hierarchy and Trust in Modern Mexico and Brazil* (New York, Praeger, 1990). For a discussion of patrimonialism and education in Brazil, see Neidson Rodrigues, *Estado, educação e desenvolvimento económico* (São Paulo, Autores Associados e Cortez, 1982).

30 Torres, *The Politics of Nonformal Education in Latin America*, pp. 33–45.

31 See Amilcar Cabral, *Revolution in Guinea* (New York, Monthly Review Press, 1969), p. 69.

32 See, for instance, Martin Carnoy and Joel Samoff, *Education and Social Transition in the Third World* (Princeton, New Jersey, Princeton University Press, 1990), especially the chapters on Tanzania and Mozambique.

33 See Freire, *Pedagogy in Process*, pp. 132–6.

34 See Paulo Freire, 'Quatro cartas aos animadores de circulos de cultura de São Tomé e Principe,' in Carlos Rodrigues Brandão (ed.), *A Questão Política da Educação Popular* (São Paulo, Livraria Brasiliense Editora, 1980), pp. 136–97.

35 See Paulo Freire, 'Educação O sonho possivel,' in Carlos Rodrigues Brandão (onganizador), *O Educador: Vida e Morte* (Rio de Janeiro, Edições Graal, 1986), p. 97 (my translation).

36 Darcy de Oliveira and Darcy de Oliveira, *Guinea-Bissau – Reinventing Education*, p. 49.

37 See Carlos Alberto Torres et al., Comparative adult education in Canada, Tanzania and Mexico: final report, Edmonton, Canada, University of Alberta, mimeographed, 800 pages.

38 See Robert Arnove, *Education and Revolution in Nicaragua* (New York, Praeger, 1986); and Martin Carnoy and Carlos Alberto Torres, 'Education and Social Transformation in Nicaragua,' in Carnoy and Samoff, *Education and Social Transition in the Third World*.

39 See Denis Goulet, *Looking at Guinea-Bissau: A New Nation's Development Strategy*, Occasional Papers N., 9 March 1978 (New York, Overseas Development Council).

40 See Freire et al., *Vivendo e Aprendendo*; and Freire, 'Quatro cartas.'

41 See Amilcar Cabral, *L'Arme de la Theorie* (Paris, Maspero, 1975).

42 See Goulet, *Looking at Guinea-Bissau*, p. 31. See also Paulo Freire and Donaldo Macedo, *Literacy, Reading the Word and the World* (Amherst, Massachusetts, Bergin & Garvey, 1987), especially pp. 108–19.

43 See Freire, 'Quatro cartas,' p. 177 (my translation).
44 See Linda M. Harasim, 'Literacy and national reconstruction in Guinea-Bissau: a critique of the Freirean literacy campaign,' Ph.D. dissertation, OISE–University of Toronto, 1983, p. 6.
45 Harasim, 'Literacy and national reconstruction in Guinea-Bissau,' p. 139.
46 Harasim, 'Literacy and national reconstruction in Guinea-Bissau,' p. 107.
47 Harasim, 'Literacy and national reconstruction in Guinea-Bissau,' pp. 148–52.
48 Harasim, 'Literacy and national reconstruction in Guinea-Bissau,' pp. 197–9.
49 Harasim, 'Literacy and national reconstruction in Guinea-Bissau,' p. 345.
50 Harasim, 'Literacy and national reconstruction in Guinea-Bissau,' pp. 377–8.
51 See note 19.
52 See note 42.
53 See Freire and Macedo, *Literacy. Reading the Word and the World*, pp. 100–2. See also criticisms of Freire in Rosiska Darcy de Oliveira and Pierre Dominice, 'Pedagogía dos oprimidos. Opressão de Pedagogía. O Debate Pedagógico,' in Torres, *Leitura Crítica de Paulo Freire*, pp. 134–8.
54 See Freire and Macedo, *Literacy. Reading the Word and the World*, p. 103.
55 See Freire and Faúndez, *Por Uma Pedagogía da Pergunta*, p. 124.
56 See Freire and Macedo, *Literacy. Reading the Word and the World*, pp. 112–13. It is well known that Amilcar Cabral dismissed as cultural opportunism any criticisms of his strong suggestion of adopting Portuguese as the official language. For Cabral, Portuguese was the only truly universal gift that the colonizers gave to Guinea-Bissau; see Amilcar Cabral, *Analise de Alguns Tipos de Resistencia* (Guinea-Bissau: Edição do PAIGC, 1979), pp. 102–5. Freire disagrees; see Freire and Faúndez, *Por uma Pedagogia da Pergunta*, p. 126.
57 Paulo Freire, 'Os planos de Paulo Freire,' *Jornal da Educação*, CEDES, Campinas, Year 1, no. 0 (April 1982), pp. 3–5.
58 See Carlos Alberto Torres, 'Educational Policy and Social Change in Brazil. The Work of Paulo Freire as Secretary of Education in the Municipality of São Paulo,' paper presented at the Symposium on Educational Policy and Social Change in Brazil: The Work of Paulo Freire as Secretary of Education in São Paulo, Brazil, American Educational Research Association (AERA), Chicago, 4–7 April 1991.
59 Paulo Freire and Sérgio Guimarães, *Sobre Educação: Diálogos* (Rio de Janeiro, Paz e Terra, 1982), 2 vols.
60 Moacir Gadotti, Paulo Freire, and Sérgio Guimarães, *Pedagogia: Diálogo e Conflito* (São Paulo, Cortez Editora–Editora Autores Associados, 1986).
61 Paulo Freire and Frei Betto, *E Esta Escola da Vida* (São Paulo, Atica, 1985).
62 Paulo Freire, Adriano Nogueira, and Debora Mazza, *Fazer Escola Conhecendo a Vida* (Campinas, Papirus, 1986).
63 See Freire and Macedo, *Literacy. Reading the Word and the World*, p. viii.
64 See Freire and Macedo, *Literacy. Reading the Word and the World*, p. 157.
65 See, for instance, Ira Shor (ed.), *Freire for the Classroom: A Sourcebook for Liberatory Teaching* (Portsmouth, New Hampshire, Boynton/Cook Publishers, 1987); Peter McLaren, 'Postmodernity and the death of politics: a Brazilian reprieve,' *Educational Theory* 36 (4) (1986), pp. 389–401; Peter McLaren, Review of Freire for the classroom: 'A Sourcebook for Liberatory Teaching' by Ira Shor (ed.), Portsmouth, New Hampshire, Boynton/Cook Publishers (mimeographed, 1987).
66 Paulo Freire and Ira Shor, *A Pedagogy for Liberation, Dialogues on Transforming Education* (Amherst, Massachusetts, Bergin & Garvey, 1987).

67 See Paulo Freire's Foreword in this volume.
68 See, for instance, Henry Giroux, *Theory and Resistance in Education: A Pedagogy for the Opposition* (South Hadley, Massachusetts: Bergin & Garvey, 1983); Henry Giroux, 'Introduction,' in Paulo Freire, *The Politics of Education, Culture, Power, and Liberation* (Amherst, Massachusetts, Bergin & Garvey Publishers, 1984).
69 See the analysis of Shor in Ira Shor, *Culture Wars: School and Society in the Conservative Restoration, 1969–1984* (Boston, Routledge & Kegan Paul, 1986); and Freire and Shor, *A Pedagogy for Liberation. Dialogues on Transforming Education.*
70 See Daniel Wagner, 'Literacy campaigns: past, present, and future,' *Comparative Education Review*, 33 (2) (1989), pp. 256–60.
71 See Freire, *Pedagogy in Progress*, p. 176.

7

BELL HOOKS SPEAKING ABOUT PAULO FREIRE – THE MAN, HIS WORK

bell hooks

This is a playful dialogue with myself. Gloria Watkins talking with bell hooks – my writing voice. I wanted to speak about Paulo and his work in this way for it afforded me an intimacy – a familiarity – I do not find it possible to achieve in the essay. And here I have found a way to share the sweetness – the solidarity I talk about.

Watkins: Reading your books *Ain't I a Woman: Black Women and Feminism, Feminist Theory: from Margin to Center*, and *Talking Back*, it is clear that your development as a critical thinker has been greatly influenced by the work of Paulo Freire. Can you speak about why his work has touched your life so deeply?

hooks: Years before I met Paulo Freire, I had learned so much from his work – learned new ways of thinking about social reality that were liberatory. Often when university students and professors read Freire, they approach his work from a voyeuristic standpoint, where as they read they see two locations in the work, the subject position of Freire the educator (whom they are often more interested in than the ideas or subjects he speaks about) and the oppressed/marginalized groups he speaks about. In relation to these two subject positions, they position themselves as observers – as outsiders. When I came to Freire's work, just at that moment in my life when I was beginning to question deeply and profoundly the politics of domination, the impact of racism, sexism, class exploitation, and the kind of domestic colonization that takes place in the United States, I felt myself to be deeply identified with the marginalized peasants he speaks about, or with my black brothers and sisters, my comrades in Guinea-Bissau. You see, I was coming from a rural southern black experience, into the university. And I had lived through the struggle for racial desegregation and was in resistance without having a political language to articulate that process. Paulo was one of the thinkers whose work gave me a language. He made me think deeply about the construction of an identity in resistance. There was this one sentence of Freire's that became a revolutionary mantra for me: 'We cannot enter the struggle as objects in order later to become subjects.' Really, it is difficult to find words adequate to explain how this statement was like a locked door – and I struggled within myself to find the key – and that struggle engaged me in a process of critical thought that was transformative. This experience positioned Freire in my mind and heart as a challenging teacher whose work furthered my own struggle against the colonizing process – the colonizing mind-set.

Watkins: In your work, you indicate an ongoing concern with the process of decolonization particularly as it affects African-Americans living within the white supremacist culture of the United States. Do you see a link between the process of decolonization and Freire's focus on 'conscientization?'

hooks: Oh, absolutely. Because the colonizing forces are so powerful in this white supremacist capitalist patriarchy it seems that black people are always having to renew a commitment to a decolonizing political process that should be fundamental to our lives and is not. And so Freire's work, in its global understanding of liberation struggles, always emphasizes that this is the important initial stage of transformation – that historical moment when one begins to think critically about the self and identity in relation to one's political circumstance. Again, this is one of the concepts in Freire's work and in my own work that is frequently misunderstood by readers in the United States. Many times people will say to me that I seem to be suggesting that it is enough for individuals to change how they think. And you see, even their use of the *enough* tells us something about the attitude they bring to this question. It has a patronizing sound, one that does not convey any heartfelt understanding of how a change in attitude (though not a completion of any transformative process) can be significant for colonized/oppressed people. Again and again Freire has had to remind readers that he never spoke of conscientization as an end itself but always as it is joined by meaningful praxis. In many different ways Freire articulates this. I like when he talks about the necessity of verifying in praxis what we know in consciousness: 'That means, and let us emphasize it, that human beings do not get beyond the concrete situation, the condition in which they find themselves, only by their consciousness or their intentions – however good those intentions may be. The possibilities that I had for transcending the narrow limits of a five-by-two foot cell in which I was locked after the April 1964 coup d'etat, were not sufficient to change my condition as a prisoner. I was always in the cell deprived of freedom, even if I could imagine the outside world. But on the other hand, the praxis is not blind action, deprived of intention or of finality. It is action

147

and reflection. Men and women are human beings because they are historically constituted as beings of praxis, and in the process they have become capable of transforming the world – of giving it meaning'. I think that so many progressive political movements fail to have lasting impact in the United States precisely because there is not enough understanding of 'praxis.' This is what touches me about Antonio Faundez asserting in *Learning to Question*: '. . . one of the things we learned in Chile in our early reflection on everyday life was that abstract political, religious or moral statements did not take concrete shape in acts by individuals. We were revolutionaries in the abstract, not in our daily lives. I believe that revolution begins precisely with revolution in our daily lives. It seems to me essential that in our individual lives we should day to day live out what we affirm.' It always astounds me when progressive people act as though it is somehow a naïve moral position to believe that our lives must be a living example of our politics.

Watkins: There are many readers of Freire who feel that the sexist language in his work, which went unchanged even after the challenge of the contemporary feminist movement and feminist critique, is a negative example. When you first read Freire what was your response to the sexism of his language?

hooks: There has never been a moment when reading Freire that I have not remained aware of not only the sexism of the language but the way he (like other progressive Third World political leaders, intellectuals, critical thinkers such as Fanon, Memmi, etc.) constructs a phallocentric paradigm of liberation – wherein freedom and the experience of patriarchal manhood are always linked as though they are one and the same. For me this is always a source of anguish for it represents a blind spot in the vision of men who have profound insight. And yet, I never wish to see a critique of this blind spot overshadow anyone's (and feminists in particular) capacity to learn from the insights. This is why it is difficult for me to speak about sexism in Freire's work; it is difficult to find a language that offers a way to frame critique and yet maintain the recognition of all that is valued and respected in the work. It seems to me that the binary opposition that is so much embedded into Western thought and language makes it nearly impossible to project a complex response. Freire's sexism is indicated by the language in his early works notwithstanding that there is so much that remains liberatory. There is no need to apologize for the sexism. Freire's own model of critical pedagogy invites a critical interrogation of this flaw in the work. But critical interrogation is not the same as dismissal.

Watkins: So you see no contradiction in your valuing of Freire's work and your commitment to feminist scholarship?

148

hooks: It is feminist thinking that empowers me to engage in a constructive critique of Freire's work (which I needed so that as a young reader of his work I did not passively absorb the world-view presented) and yet there are many other standpoints from which I approach his work that enable me to experience its value, that make it possible for that work to touch me at the very core of my being. In talking with academic feminists (usually white women) who feel they must either dismiss or devalue the work of Freire because of sexism, I see clearly how our different responses are shaped by the standpoint that we bring to the work. I came to Freire thirsty, dying of thirst (in that way that the colonized, marginalized subject who is still unsure of how to break the hold of the status quo, who longs for change, is needy – is thirsty), and I found in his work (and the work of Malcolm X, Fanon, etc.) a way to quench that thirst. To have work that promotes one's liberation is such a powerful gift – that it does not matter so much if the gift is flawed. Think of the work as water that contains some dirt. Because you are thirsty you are not too proud to extract the dirt and be nourished by the water. For me this is an experience that corresponds very much to the way individuals of privilege respond to the use of water in the First World context. When you are privileged, living in one of the richest countries in the world, you can waste resources. And you can especially justify your disposal of something that you consider impure, unclean, etc. Look at what most people do with water in this country. Many people purchase special water because they consider tap water unclean and of course this purchasing is a luxury. Even our ability to see the water that comes through the tap as unclean is itself informed by an imperialist consumer perspective. It is an expression of luxury and not just simply a response to the condition of water. If we approach the drinking of water that comes from the tap from a global perspective we would have to talk about it differently. We would have to consider what the vast majority of the people in the world who are thirsty must do to obtain water. Paulo's work has been living water for me.

Watkins: To what extent do you think your experience as an African-American has made it possible for you to relate to Freire's work?

hooks: As I already suggested, growing up in a rural area in the agrarian south, among black people who worked the land, I felt intimately linked to the discussion of peasant life in Freire's work and its relation to literacy. You know there are no history books that really tell the story of how difficult the politics of everyday life was for black people in the racially segregated south when so many folks did not read and were so often dependent on racist white people to explain, to read, to write. And I was among a generation learning those skills, with an accessibility to education that was still new. The emphasis on education as necessary for liberation that black people made in slavery and then on into reconstruction informed our lives. And so Freire's emphasis on education as the practice of freedom made such immediate sense to me. Conscious of the need for literacy from girlhood, I took with me to the university memories of reading to folks, of writing for folks. I took with me memories of black teachers in the segregated school system who had been critical pedagogues providing us liberatory paradigms. It was this early experience of a liberatory education in Booker T. Washington and Crispus Attucks, the black schools of my formative years, that made me forever dissatisfied with the education I received in predominantly white settings. And it was educators like Freire who affirmed that the difficulties I had with the banking system of education, with an education that in no way addressed my social reality, was an important critique. Returning to the discussion of feminism and sexism, I want to say that I felt myself included in *Pedagogy of the Oppressed*, which was one of the first Freire books I read, in a way that I never felt myself – my experience as a rural black person – included in the first feminist books I read, works like *The Feminist Mystique, Born Female*, etc. In the United States we do not talk enough about the way in which class shapes our perspective on reality. Since so many of the early feminist books really reflected a certain type of white bourgeois sensibility, this work did not touch many black women deeply, not because we did not recognize the common experiences women shared but because those commonalities were mediated by profound differences in our realities created by the politics of race and class.

Watkins: Can you speak about the relationship between Freire's work and the development of your work as feminist theorist and social critic?

hooks: Unlike feminist thinkers who make a clear separation between the work of feminist pedagogy and Freire's work and thought, for me these two experiences converge. Deeply committed to feminist pedagogy, I find that, much like weaving a tapestry, I have taken threads of Paulo's work and woven it into that version of feminist pedagogy I believe my work as writer and teacher embodies. Again, I want to assert that it was the intersection of Paulo's thought and the lived pedagogy of the many black teachers of my girlhood (most of them women) who saw themselves as having a liberatory mission to educate us in a manner that would prepare us to effectively resist racism and white supremacy, that has had a profound impact on my thinking about the art and practice of teaching. And though these black women did not openly advocate feminism (if they even knew the word) the very fact that they insisted on academic excellence and open critical thought for young black females was an anti-sexist practice.

Watkins: Be more specific about the work you have done that has been influenced by Freire.

hooks: Let me say that I wrote *Ain't I a Woman: Black Women and Feminism* when I was an undergraduate (though it was not published until years later). This book was the concrete manifestation of my struggle with the question of moving from object to subject – the very question Paulo had posed. And it is so easy now that many, if not most, feminist scholars are willing to recognize the impact of race and class as factors that shape female identity, for everyone to forget that early on the feminist movement was not a location that welcomed the radical struggle of black women to theorize our subjectivity. Freire's work (and that of many other teachers) affirmed my right as a subject in resistance to define my reality. His writing gave me a way to place the politics of racism in the United States in a global context wherein I could see my fate linked with that of colonized black people everywhere struggling to decolonize, to transform society. More than in the work of many white bourgeois feminist thinkers, there was always in Paulo's work recognition of the subject position of those most disenfranchised, those who suffer the gravest weight of oppressive forces (with the exception of his not acknowledging always the specific gendered realities of oppression and exploitation). This was a standpoint which affirmed my own desire to work from a lived understanding of the lives of poor black women. There has been only in recent years a body of scholarship in the United States that does not look at the lives of black people through a bourgeois lens, a fundamentally radical scholarship that suggests that indeed the experience of black people, black females, might tell us more about the experience of women in general than simply an analysis that looks first, foremost, and always at those women who reside in privileged locations. One of the reasons that Paulo's book, *Pedagogy in Process: the Letters to Guinea-Bissau*, has been important for my work is that it is a crucial example of how a privileged critical thinker approaches sharing knowledge and resources with those who are in need. Here is Paulo at one of those insightful moments. He writes: 'Authentic help means that all who are involved help each other mutually, growing together in the common effort to understand the reality which they seek to transform. Only through such praxis – in which those who help and those who are being helped help each other simultaneously – can the act of helping become free from the distortion in which the helper dominates the helped.' In American society where the intellectual, and specifically the black intellectual, has often assimilated and betrayed revolutionary concerns in the interest of maintaining class power, it is crucial and necessary for insurgent black intellectuals to have an ethics of struggle that informs our relationship to those black people who have not had access to ways of knowing shared in locations of privilege.

Watkins: Comment if you will on Freire's willingness to be critiqued, especially by feminist thinkers.

151

hooks: In so much of Paulo's work there is a generous spirit, a quality of open-mindedness that I feel is often missing from intellectual and academic arenas in US society, and feminist circles have not been an exception. Of course, Paulo seems to grow more open as he ages. I, too, feel myself more strongly committed to a practice of open-mindedness, a willingness to engage critique as I age, and I think the way we experience more profoundly the growing fascism in the world, even in so called 'liberal' circles, reminds us that our lives, our work, must be an example. In Freire's work in the last few years there are many responses to the critiques made of his writing. And there is that lovely critical exchange between him and Antonio Faundez in *Learning to Question* on the question of language, on Paulo's work in Guinea-Bissau. I learn from this example, from seeing his willingness to struggle non-defensively in print, naming shortcomings of insight, changes in thought, new critical reflections.

Watkins: What was it like for you to interact personally with Paulo Freire?

hooks: For me our meeting was incredible; it made me a devoted student and comrade of Paulo's for life. Let me tell you this story. Some years ago now, Paulo was invited to the University of Santa Cruz, where I was then a student and teacher. He came to do workshops with Third World students and faculty and to give a public lecture. I had not heard even a whisper that he was coming, though many folks knew how much his work meant to me. Then somehow I found out that he was coming only to be told that all slots were filled for participants in the workshop. I protested. And in the ensuing dialogue, I was told that I had not been invited to the various meetings for fear that I would disrupt the discussion of more important issues by raising feminist critiques. Even though I was allowed to participate when someone dropped out at the last minute, my heart was heavy because already I felt that there had been this sexist attempt to control my voice, to control the encounter. So, of course, this created an inner war within myself because indeed I did want to interrogate Paulo Freire personally about the sexism in his work. And so with courtesy, I forged ahead at the meeting. Immediately individuals spoke against me raising these questions and devalued their importance, Paulo intervened to say that these questions were crucial and he addressed them. Truthfully, I loved him at this moment for exemplifying by his actions the principles of his work. So much would have changed for me had he tried to silence or belittle a feminist critique. And it was not enough for me that he owned his 'sexism,' I want to know why he had not seen that this aspect of earlier work be changed, be responded to in writing by him. And he spoke then about making more of a public effort to speak and write on these issues – this has been evident in his later work.

Watkins: Were you more affected by his presence than his work?

hooks: Another great teacher of mine (even though we have not met) is the Vietnamese Buddhist monk Thich Nhat Hanh. And he says in *The Raft is Not the Shore* that 'great humans bring with them something like a hallowed atmosphere, and when we seek them out, then we feel peace, we feel love, we feel courage.' His words appropriately define what it was like for me to be in the presence of Paulo. I spend hours alone with him, talking, listening to music, eating ice cream at my favorite café. Seriously, Nhat Hanh teaches that a certain milieu is born at the same time as a great teacher. And he says: 'When you [the teacher] come and stay one hour with us, you bring that milieu. . . . It is as though you bring a candle into the room. The candle is there; there is kind of light-zone you bring in. When a sage is there and you sit near him, you feel light, you feel peace.' The lesson I learned from witnessing Paulo embody the practice he describes in theory was profound. It entered me in a way that writing can never touch one and it gave me courage. It has not been easy for me to do the work I do and reside in the academy (lately I think it has become almost impossible) but one is inspired to persevere by the witness of others. Freire's presence inspired me. And it was not that I did not see sexist behavior on his part, only that these contradictions are embraced as part of the learning process, part of what one struggles to change – and that struggle is often protracted.

Watkins: Have you anything more to say about Freire's response to feminist critique?

hooks: I think it important and significant that despite feminist critiques of his work, which are often harsh, Paulo recognizes that he must play a role in feminist movements. This he declares in *Learning to Question.* 'If the women are critical, they have to accept our contribution as men, as well as the workers have to accept our contribution as intellectuals, because it is a duty and a right that I have to participate in the transformation of society. Then, if the women must have the main responsibility in their struggle, they have to know that their struggle also belongs to us, that is, to those men who don't accept the machista position in the world. The same is true of racism. As an apparent white man, because I always say that I am not quite sure of my whiteness, the question is to know if I am really against racism in a radical way. If I am, then I have a duty and a right to fight with black people against racism.'

Watkins: Does Freire continue to influence your work? There is not the constant mention of him in your latest work as was the case with the first books.

hooks: Though I may not quote Freire as much, he still teaches me. When

I read *Learning to Question* just at a time when I had begun to engage in critical reflections on black people and exile, there was so much there about the experience of exile that helped me. And I was thrilled with the book. It had a quality of that dialogue that is a true gesture of love that Paulo speaks about in other work. So it was from reading this book that I decided that it would be useful to do a dialogical work with the philosopher Cornel West. We have what Paulo calls 'a talking book' that will soon be published. Of course my great wish is to do such a book with Paulo. And then for some time I have been working on essays on death and dying, particularly African-American ways of dying. Then just quite serendipitously I was searching for an epigraph for this work, and came across these lovely passages from Paulo that echo so intimately my own world-view that it was as though, to use an old southern phrase, 'My tongue was in my friend's mouth.' He writes: 'I like to live, to live my life intensely. I am the type of person who loves his life passionately. Of course, someday, I will die, but I have the impression that when I die, I will die intensely as well. I will die experimenting with myself intensely. For this reason I am going to die with an immense longing for life, since this is the way I have been living'.

Watkins: Yes! I can hear you saying those very words. Any last comments?

hooks: Only that words seem to not be good enough to evoke all that I have learned from Paulo. Our meeting had that quality of sweetness that lingers, that lasts for a lifetime, even if you never speak to the person again, see their face, you can always return in your heart to that moment when you were together and be renewed – that is a profound solidarity.

154

8

CRITICAL PEDAGOGY AND STATE WELFARE

Intellectual encounters with Freire and Gramsci, 1974–86

Peter Leonard

INTRODUCTION

To understand the impact of a text requires historical specificity, an account of the text's relationship to the reader situated within a defined configuration of material and ideological circumstances. What preceded the encounter with the text, what accompanied it, and what followed?

The historical circumstances which are subjected to investigation in this chapter are those which I experienced in the attempt to establish an alternative, critical form of social work education in Britain during the period from 1974 to 1986. It was an educational venture which aimed at encouraging socialist practice within the heart of the state welfare apparatus. It was intended as a contribution to understanding and working with the contradictions of state welfare in order to develop practice 'in and against the State' (London–Edinburgh Weekend Return Group 1980).

In examining this particular historical specificity, I shall be rendering an account not of a relationship with one text, but of an encounter with the work of two writers – Paulo Freire and Antonio Gramsci – though specific texts were crucial to this encounter. The intellectual influences which structure a person's practice are, of course, multiple. In this instance, however, it is possible to identify two sources of influence which, in interaction with each other, formed a major set of ideas experienced as profoundly relevant to the struggle for a socialist pedagogy within an advanced capitalist state during a particular historical period. Although this chapter is a contribution to a critical examination of the work of Paulo Freire, his influence cannot easily, or even legitimately, be treated separately from that of other progressive theorists and activists who have had an impact on recent left political struggles.

In evaluating my intellectual encounters with Freire and Gramsci in the

155

context of a particular educational program and practice, I shall attempt two kinds of analytic accounts. The first will identify the positives, problems, and limitations of these encounters as experienced during the period from 1974 to 1986. The second account will analyze the educational struggles of that period from the vantage point of the present, drawing upon the work of Freire and Gramsci as a means of understanding their successes and failures.

My approach in this chapter will be to contextualize these intellectual encounters not only within the ideological conditions of a specific educational institution at a particular point in time, but also in relation to relevant parts of my own biography. I will, in other words, endeavor to relate the political to the personal, to render an account of myself not simply as an external observer but as a social actor. Taking account of my own subjectivity is necessary to an understanding of the 'lived experience' of the period I am describing, especially the struggle against the 'pessimism of the intellect' and the attempt to practice an 'optimism of the will' (Gramsci 1971). Furthermore, my approach stands, alongside Freire and Gramsci, against the objectification of mechanical Marxism, preferring that focus on subjectivity and its social construction which reflects the tradition of critical theory and, more recently, feminist politics and scholarship. Taking account of subjective experience is necessary in order to demystify the intellectual and practical labor involved in any kind of politics.

THE WELFARE STATE APPARATUS: AN ARENA OF STRUGGLE?

The context of intellectual encounters with Freire and Gramsci during 1974–86 can be understood, in the first instance, against a background of intensive discussion and dispute amongst those socialists engaged in the teaching and practice of social work as to whether a non-oppressive, socialist form of social work practice was possible within a capitalist social order. The year 1974 marked the beginning of my appointment at the University of Warwick to establish a School of Social Work; more importantly, it signals in Britain a decisive turning-point in the attempt to establish a social democratic welfare state begun in 1945. In 1974, under the pressures of its own contradictions and the external conditions laid down by the International Monetary Fund, a Labour government began the process of massive public expenditure cuts and an emphasis on the needs of the market economy, which prepared the way for the neo-conservative electoral triumph of 1979 and the ideological and material shifts which followed. The debate about the possibility of socialist struggle within the welfare state apparatus became most intensive precisely during a period when social democratic hegemony was losing ground to increasing ideological assaults from the new radical right.

By the early 1970s, the left critique of the social democratic welfare state, based primarily on an orthodox Marxist class analysis, but accompanied to a small extent by an emerging feminist analysis of gender relations in welfare, formed the background of most 'radical' arguments against social work. The dominant orthodox Marxist position maintained that as the welfare state was primarily a means of exploiting and controlling the working class, then social work practice must necessarily perform the same ideological and material function. The state in advanced capitalism was monolithically oppressive, and the role of social work was to contribute to the reproduction of certain ideological and material conditions within the working class. In order to function as control agents for the state, social workers focused on the control of working-class deviance and the 'appropriate' socialization of children, including the maintenance of women's subordination as mothers, and men's subordination as workers.

This entirely negative view of social work was especially problematic for socialist social workers because it contained a clear understanding that a *different* form of social work practice – liberating and resistant to the social order – was impossible. The monolithic view of the state and society as oppressive provided no space for an optimistic view of the progressive possibilities of social work. Social workers were simply 'agents of social control' and could not be otherwise.

Amongst social workers of the left, the monolithic and pessimistic view of the possibilities of social work practice were represented in two institutional forms: the magazine *Case Con* and the National Deviancy Conference. *Case Con* was a rallying-point for socialists disillusioned with the bureaucratic and controlling functions of the organizations within which they worked, especially as represented by the new, powerful local social-service departments established in 1970. In this magazine and in the meetings organized around it, social workers were able to vent their rage and disappointment at the failure of social work to confront the structural conditions which lay at the root of the problems they met in their daily practice – poverty, unemployment, child neglect and abuse, delinquency. The political analysis predominantly presented in *Case Con* was that *as social workers* its readers could not do anything progressive about the problems they confronted. Only as union activists and members of revolutionary political parties could they play any positive role in contributing to establishing the preconditions for revolutionary change – the central ideological task. Practicing social work was no different from other forms of labor undertaken in the interests of capital and the state – a means of maintaining one's material existence but not, in the labor process itself, a means of challenging the social order.

The National Deviancy Conference (NDC) was the academic forum for debate and discussion on the new sociology of deviance, the 'new criminology' (see Cohen 1971; Taylor and Taylor 1973). With its left critique of

157

existing institutional responses to deviance and crime founded on a mixture of labelling theory, symbolic interactionism, and Marxism, it directed its attention to state welfare as one means of controlling deviance. Although primarily a meeting place for 'radical' sociologists, it also attracted many social workers who were there frequently subjected to a detailed theoretical analysis of their oppressive social control functions as part of the state apparatus. The pessimistic and debilitating message that was often transmitted to social workers at these conferences and elsewhere was rarely applied to the roles of the sociologists themselves within the state apparatus of education, roles that involved the reproduction of an appropriately prepared sector of the labor force. From their own experience of state education sociologists believed that they could act progressively, even though within severe constraints, although they often lacked the theoretical analysis of contradictions which would have enabled them to understand this experience intellectually. Similarly, social workers and some of their NDC sociological allies knew that *some* possibilities of a progressive practice existed, that they tried to be socialists in their social work practice even though they could not easily understand this experience politically.

An emphasis on the critical analysis of social work as oppressive and generally pernicious was a feature at this time also, within the minority of social work education programs where left academics had established a foothold. This critique was predominantly provided by sociologists firing from the flanks, whilst the social work practice teachers usually maintained a traditional positive social democratic perspective on social work. The students were thereby provided with a critical analysis which was unaccompanied by prescriptions for a critical practice, together with a mainstream analysis which was accompanied by detailed prescriptions for traditional practice. Inevitably, therefore, the social democratic perspective was generally experienced as more useful and relevant. At the same time, where at the extreme a Leninist view of revolutionary struggle confronted the complacency of social democratic social-work education, the resulting educational process was characterized by authoritarian dogmatism on one side and defensive disengagement on the other.

In the late 1960s and early 1970s then, the predominant left answers to the question whether the welfare state apparatus was an arena of class struggle and whether social workers could contribute to this struggle, was a negative one. For socialist social work educators dissatisfied with this answer, the way forward was clear – a critical, radical *practice* had to be established as one way of confronting a monolithic and economistic analysis. If orthodox Marxism seemed unproductive at this point, within what intellectual terrain should the enterprise of constructing a critical education and practice of social work be undertaken? A later section of this chapter will show that in one such enterprise the terrain was developed in the context of encounters with the work of Freire and Gramsci. Before we move to this account, however, it is necessary to locate myself historically within the left debate about the welfare state and the progressive possibilities for social work. The brief autobiographical element at this point serves to focus attention on a particular reader within particular material and ideological circumstances encountering specific texts.

READER, WRITER, CONTEXT, TEXT

With an academic background in the British Fabian tradition of social administration at the London School of Economics, and a training in psychoanalytic psychiatric social work, my practice during the 1950s and 1960s was located ideologically within a left social democratic perspective. My writing during this period (see, for example, Leonard 1964; Leonard 1966a; Leonard 1966b) attempted to construct a critique and a practice which linked to the more 'critical' Mertonian wing of the dominant structural–functional sociology of that time, and which was reformist within the social democratic tradition. Gradually, I became convinced of the impossibility of developing a truly critical approach within the reformist tradition in which I had been socialized. Membership of a British government committee (1966–8) which proposed the reorganization and unification of personal social services proved to be my last intimate involvement in the Fabian reformist element of the British Labour movement. Experience of that committee and the implementation of its plans in legislation in 1970 marked, for me, a watershed.

Whilst working in a quintessential Fabian institution, the National Institute for Social Work in London, I became increasingly immersed in the Marxist perspective on social science theorization (published later in Leonard 1975) and began an encounter with Paulo Freire's work, particularly *Pedagogy of the Oppressed*. My Marxism at this point was of an idealist, philosophical form, not yet linked to revolutionary politics, and it seemed to connect well with Freire's critique of 'banking' education, a form of dogmatic instruction characteristic of both mainstream social work education and its left authoritarian critics.

By the early 1970s, whilst still at the National Institute for Social Work, I began to turn to Freire in order to explore his possible contribution to a critical social work practice. The result was a chapter, 'Towards a paradigm for radical practice,' which was published in a book of articles on radical social work (Bailey and Brake 1975). This chapter was an awkward mixture of Marxist theory, Freire's ideas, systems theory, and US 'model making' quite contrary to British and European traditions, both empirical and theoretical. It represented my personal intellectual terrain immediately prior to an opportunity to establish a new Department of Applied Social Studies in the University of Warwick, thereafter referred in this chapter as *the Warwick School*, the location of the encounters with Freire and Gramsci which are my focus here.

With this brief autobiographical note completed, we can now move to an examination of the ideas of Freire and Gramsci as they resonated with the left debate on welfare and social work in the 1970s and early 1980s, and which was the wider intellectual context of developments at the Warwick School.

FREIRE, GRAMSCI, AND THE SEARCH FOR A CRITICAL SOCIAL WORK

In an attempt to move forward from a monolithic and pessimistic view of the possibilities of social work practice under capitalism, engagement with the work of Freire and Gramsci played a significant part, for it promised a path which was neither reformist nor mechanically Marx:st. The central problem, as we shall see, was to interrogate and render relevant to the tasks at hand ideas which had their origins in different sociocultural contexts and, in the case of Gramsci, in a different historical period.

Paperback translations of Freire's *Cultural Action for Freedom* and *Pedagogy of the Oppressed* appeared in Britain in 1970. At the same time, the most significant of Gramsci's work on politics and philosophy appeared in English as *Selections from the Prison Notebooks* (Gramsci 1971). The impact of both writers on the attempt to construct a critical social work practice in the early 1970s and onwards was profound. What was especially interesting was the extent to which the texts, in interaction with each other, were able to address major intellectual and political issues in a way which, at the time, appeared to give hope to those concerned to use state welfare as an arena of struggle.

The work of both Freire and Gramsci appeared, during the 1970s, to enable this reader to begin to construct some answers to a number of central questions. What alternatives were there to a determinist and pessimistic account of social work and state welfare? What was the possible role of a left, critical social worker? What kinds of objectives and processes might be involved in developing a critical social work practice? How should social workers be educated for critical practice? To each of these questions Freire and Gramsci, *especially when considered together*, seemed to provide possible answers. Furthermore, in a political climate which was increasingly encouraging broad left alliances, the conjunction of ideas originating from both Marxism and the social gospel of the Church seemed especially interesting.

The arguments against a left determinism, which is a central feature of Freire's and Gramsci's perspective, was fundamental to the struggle to establish a critical social work practice. Freire's account of peasant fatalism and how it can be overturned by conscientization resonated with an

160

understanding of a form of fatalism often experienced by social workers and welfare bureaucrats. Their experience of relative powerlessness in the face of massive structures and seemingly irreducible problems showed the split between their private and public lives. As part of an intellectual stratum, they felt they were 'in charge' of their private lives and careers, they could 'make choices.' In their public lives, however, they experienced subordinancy to dominant ideas and practices *more directly*. Here their individualism was no longer of much use to them in making their intentions count for something. The experience of social workers as powerless in their daily work did much to encourage left determinism as an influential view, and countering this view with the voluntarist politics of Freire and Gramsci became an important stratgy. Freire's focus on cultural action showed that human intention, organized collectively, could count, and in reading Gramsci one found a similar emphasis. Gramsci supported the voluntarist side of Marxism rather than the fatalistic, determinist side, arguing that revolution comes not primarily from the breakdown of the capitalist economy in accordance with objective laws, but as a result of struggle.

To argue for the possibility of a critical social work practice against a deterministic and monolithic picture of the state and civil society required an understanding of deterministic fatalism as *ideological*. For Freire, such understanding emerged from an analysis of the structures of domination in Latin American countries and the ways that these structures were incorporated into the fatalistic passivity which must be struggled against. Reading Gramsci enabled a focus to be placed on the concept of hegemony. For Gramsci, hegemony was a world-view that is diffused by agencies of ideological control and socialization into every area of daily life. Opposing it is problematic because hegemonic ideas become part of 'common sense' and encourage fatalism and passivity. For both Freire and Gramsci the subjectivity of the oppressed is of great importance because they tend to consent to their own oppression through the internalization of dominant ideology. In a famous passage Gramsci writes:

> To the extent that ideologies are historically necessary they have a validity which is 'psychological'; they 'organize' human masses and create the terrain on which men move, acquire consciousness of their position, struggle, etc.
>
> (Gramsci 1971: 377)

Given the historical emphasis within social work on the importance of subjectivity, the connection made between individual consciousness and subordination to dominant ideology by both Freire and Gramsci was used to show that the struggle against fatalism, including amongst social workers, was likely to be a significant part of a critical social work practice.

To counter a determinist view of the dynamics of the state and civil society was the first step in laying the groundwork for the possibility of a

161

critical social work practice. The emphasis in Freire and Gramsci on the central significance of cultural revolution indicated further that the crucial objective of a critical social work would be to contribute to ideological struggle. An important issue to be considered here was whether, in the present historical period, ruling classes were experiencing a crisis which made them especially vulnerable to assault from the oppressed, a crisis which might be variously described as a 'hegemonic crisis' or, to use Habermas's phrase, a 'legitimation crisis' (Habermas 1976). Writing in the 1930s, Gramsci saw the capitalist crisis as consisting of the undermining of traditional social relations in terms of cultural patterns and beliefs, where the ruling class moves from leading a consensus to being simply dominant. In the 1970s, in Britain, social democratic ideology was certainly experienced as being in crisis, and later with the triumph of Thatcherism and the defeat of the Labour movement, severe capitalist crises seemed to have been once again averted. There was a great deal of *discussion* about crisis, for example, in a politically significant book called *Policing the Crisis* (Hall *et al.* 1978), but whether this discussion was a form of intellectual whistling in the dark in the face of defeat and retreat was less than clear.

Although in the mid and late 1970s the prospects for the left in Britain looked increasingly gloomy in terms of a mass socialist politics, for socialist social work educators encounters with the work of Freire and Gramsci enabled them, as we have seen, to move from a determinist and monolithic view of state welfare to one which emphasized struggle and contradiction. From this basis, it was possible to move on to develop a critical social work practice aimed at contributing to the ideological struggle of social service users and communities against a state apparatus which we argued, had to contend with its own contradictions and problems of control. The role of the critical social worker was to be committed to conscientization, to enabling service users and others experiencing oppression to develop their consciousness of the structural forces which shaped their lives and their deprivations. No longer would the social worker reinforce the official state definitions of social problems which focused on individual, family, or community pathology, but would resist them and help others to do the same, individually and collectively.

But to pursue socialist objectives in social work practice required the development of new kinds of social work relationships, ones which did not reproduce the class, gender, and ethnic hierarchies of the dominant social order. Here, the work of Freire had, perhaps, its greatest impact and relevance. If conscientization was to be achieved through dialogical relations rather than through interactions characterized by 'banking,' by the imposition of definitions and solutions, as Freire argues, then a critical social work practice must explore the ways in which such dialogue with the oppressed can be established. As an alternative to the dogmatism of the authoritarian left, an approach through dialogue was especially attractive.

Finally, the development of a critical social work practice required, it seemed, a critical social work *education* which was congruent with it in terms of objectives and processes. Reading Freire and attempting to translate his work, however critically, into the realities of British university education was an extremely difficult task, one which preoccupied me during the years I was part of the Warwick School

THE WARWICK SCHOOL AND THE PROBLEM OF 'DOING SOMETHING'

What precedes this section indicates the intellectual discourse within which the Warwick School was established and developed during the years from 1974 to 1986. The purpose of this section is to identify briefly some of the specific problems, failures, and successes encountered in the Warwick School during this period, preparatory to a concluding section which will reflect on intellectual encounters with Freire and Gramsci from the perspective of the present.

The starting-point in the establishment of the Warwick School did not lie in the articulation of prescriptions for action, in specifying what precisely should be done to develop a critical practice and a critical form of education. We had no detailed alternative models available to us. For myself, all my previous experience of education had been within institutions reflecting liberal and social democratic ideologies. The Warwick School was to be itself the location of a new model – a critical, socialist model of education in the welfare field, one for which there was no precedent in Britain. Like the social movements and political parties to which its participants became attached at various times, the Warwick enterprise was, at its establishment, as strong on critique as it was weak on prescription. It began with a negation, with what was wrong with social work practice and social work education from a critical, socialist point of view. Emphasis on critique enabled us to see our educational project as always unfinished, always uncertain and experimental. Sometimes our lack of certainty, of dogmatism even, enraged some of our orthodox revolutionary students because they knew the answers or wanted us to provide them in a banking fashion.

The problem in starting with critique was that the critical analysis could lead to paralysis when it came to actually 'doing something,' because the structural determinants of a particular social problem – the needs of international capital, or the nature of patriarchal social relations – appeared so distant from social work practice. When we understood that the economic and social fate of a local working-class community depended not on the politics of the city in which it was located, not on the policies of the British government, but on decisions made by the senior management of a motor-manufacturing corporation in Detroit, then the feeling of powerlessness, of not being able to do something, was, at least for a while, overwhelming.

The Warwick School searched continuously for dialogical ways of developing models of critical practice in interaction with its graduate students, all of whom were experienced in some area of social service or community provision before coming to Warwick. In the mid-1970s, in the belief that a critical framework could be derived from a radicalized systems theory (see Leonard 1975), a systems approach to social work practice was tested out. It proved, predictably, incapable of carrying the class analysis, and later the gender and ethnic analyses, which were the political corner-stones of the Warwick School. The approach to critical practice was gradually built up piecemeal through reflection and action. No complete alternative single *model* of social work practice was established, rather the school became an arena in which various critical perspectives – feminist, socialist, anti-racist – could be tried out and argued. In this way, the educational process was able to maintain its dialogical character, for no single orthodoxy ruled and no single banking system could be established.

The search to overcome, in Freire's words, 'the student–teacher contra-diction' led to considerable instability and tension. The curriculum was continually revised as a result of discussions with students. The notion that the teachers had a 'body of knowledge' to impart had no place in the scheme of things. Student input, *their* teaching, had such a high ideological priority that in one particular year students began with a blank page on which to inscribe, collectively, their own educational objectives, content, and processes. No curriculum existed in advance, but was created by students and teachers in educational workshops which, in the first two weeks, planned the rest of the academic year. That this occurred only once is unsurprising, for it placed intolerable anxiety and strain on both students and teachers. Gradually, as teachers we had to learn what a non-oppressive, non-banking form of educational leadership meant, one which demanded of students a critical attitude to the educational process, but which allowed knowledge to be transmitted and shared. The struggle to establish dialogical relationships between students and teachers was always problematic, always needing renewed commitment; in times of extreme uncertainty both students and teachers tended to yearn for safer, more familiar banking forms of relationships where the teacher teaches and the student is taught, where the teacher speaks and acts, and the student listens and is acted upon.

Whilst the Warwick School struggled with making operational Freire's conception of dialogical education, it also confronted the challenge of newer critical perspectives which inserted themselves as a practice into the School. Primary amongst these was the impact of both radical and socialist feminism. It confronted what was seen as the 'male Marxism' of many teachers and students, accusing it of objectification, economism, workerism, and commitment to monolithic party organizations as the vehicles for revolutionary change. The emphasis in the feminist critique on consciousness-raising and its attack on 'fatalism' resonated with Freire's work, as did its humanism and its emphasis on the role of ideology in social change. The separatist radical tendency within feminism which was also represented amongst students at the same time served to provide a continuous critique of the socialist enterprise of the School.

Following closely the impact of feminist critique on the discourse at Warwick was that presented by the anti-racist perspective which was critical of both Marxism and feminism. At the same time, the connection of Freire with the Third World struggle, with liberation theology, and with Marxism were all elements in the dialogue which took place within the critical pluralism of the Warwick School. It enabled, eventually, the recognition of the similarity and 'equality' of the various oppressions resulting from the social divisions of race, gender, and class, and so formed the basis of discourse concerning the interconnection between the various social divisions and their implications for social work practice.

CRITICAL DISCOURSE WITHIN WELFARE AND THE ROLE OF INTELLECTUAL DEFECTORS

Reflection on past intellectual encounters with Freire and Gramsci is possibly instructive, but certainly painful. The attempt to use ideas generated in different cultural contexts or different historical periods is always fraught with dangers: dangers of over-simplification, vulgarization, distortion. Drawing on the work of 'authorities' is always in danger of becoming authoritarian, dogmatic. In the name of the 'authority' – God, Marx, or others – great oppressions have been established, great dogmas promulgated. The continued vitality of a triumphal, nature-destroying capitalism shows us that the critical perspectives of Freire and Gramsci are having little impact on mass politics. From the viewpoint of the beginning of the 1990s, after over ten years of neo-conservatism in most Western countries, and the accompanying dismantling of the 'Welfare State,' the prospects for socialism look bleak. East European countries, in turning to a democratic structure, are abandoning socialism of any kind and embracing market capitalism and nationalism.

To look back at an experiment in the possibilities of a socialist education within a bourgeois university system is painful, not least because of the contrast between the hopes that existed then and the defeats that have been suffered since. But Freire shows us continuously the importance of hope in defeating present fatalisms. Revolutionary optimism is an essential element in the process of establishing socialism, and this optimism can emerge in part through reflection on the lessons to be learned from any particular episode of struggle.

I am too close, too personally involved, to be able to reflect with much confidence on the attempt to develop a critical social work practice in Britain from 1974 to 1986 in one particular place. I can, however, point to three issues which I believe deserve attention in understanding the processes involved in working towards a critical, socialist, practice: the role of the intellectual, the development of critical pluralism, and the place of subjectivity.

In the heyday of the experiment at the Warwick School, the influence of Gramsci could be detected in the very frequent references to the role of 'organic intellectuals' in relation to classes. For Gramsci, intellectual activity was not that which was the exclusive domain of a particular kind of individual, such as an academic, but rather a set of activities that serve to either advance or undermine various world-views (see Boggs 1976: 75, 76). The idea which was grasped most fiercely at Warwick was that of ideological struggle, the ongoing 'war of position.' Gramsci argued that to be effective, intellectuals must be 'organic,' that is, part of the class they serve, working and living within the class. Because Gramsci saw the Party as a 'collective intellectual' representing an alternative, proletarian world-view, those of us who were then members of the British Communist Party and other socialist parties were able to believe that we could, in fact, fulfill that organic intellectual role. But I, for one, was not by that time any longer very close to the working class into which I was born. The situation in Britain was not a revolutionary one and the working class turned out to be relatively easily defeated by the new right. The role we played, in fact, was that of 'intellectual defectors,' in Gramsci's phrase, left-wing traditional academics who have an initial role to play in the interregnum between the old order and the establishment of new developed class forces which can push revolutionary activity forward.

As intellectual defectors we faced, but never fully escaped from, the dangers inherent in traditional bourgeois intellectual activity – élitism, the cult of the expert, the belief in the superiority of mental over manual labor. To grasp the role of a critical intellectual, and through the development of dialogical relationships engage in a critical *process*, enabled us, however, to avoid some of the dogmatic and authoritarian excesses which were always dangerously close.

If, as intellectual defectors, we were able to avoid dogma, and engage in dialogue, the reason for this lay also in the pluralist nature of discourse at the Warwick School. Despite the preponderant influence of numbers of 'authorities' – Marx, Gramsci, Freire, and several feminist scholars – we were unable to establish a 'line.' In spite of their humanism, Freire and Gramsci present us always with the dangers of charisma, the certainty, the dominance of ideas over practice, the compelling belief system. Sometimes the discord and dispute amongst us in the Warwick School produced in me a feeling of defeat and despair. How could she or he be so blind to reality, so sexist, so lacking in revolutionary commitment and courage, so *wrong*? We all shared the same feelings about each other and we all struggled to overcome them. Collectivity is so hard to achieve, and for intellectual defectors individualism and competitiveness so hard to avoid. Despite the argument and dispute, in fact, *because* of it, we were able to establish a state of critical pluralism which enabled us to achieve the small gains we made, including substantial contributions to a critical, alternative literature on social work and the welfare state.[1] The example of recent revolutionary changes in European socialist states shows us the importance of a *critical* pluralism as the basis of socialist advance. Without it, socialism as a material reality loses its progressive nature and is ultimately discredited and defeated.

The third issue which emerges as a lesson to be learned from encounters with Freire and Gramsci is the limitations which follow from the absence of a well-developed theory of the individual. With their emphasis on subjectivity, on cultural transformation, on ideology, they show us the necessity for a theory of the social construction of individuality without actually articulating one themselves. Feminists have since been in the forefront in beginning to sketch out a feminist psychology (see Eichenbaum and Orbach 1982), whilst a psychology based upon an orthodox Marxist perspective (see Séve 1978) has proved interesting but limited. From the Warwick School, a theory of the production of a gendered class subject (Leonard 1984) does not avoid the over-determinism and failure to give sufficient attention to social divisions other than class and gender, which may be said to characterize perspectives which develop from critical Marxism. It is clear, at this point, that a critical social work practice and education must be based on an adequate critical psychology which has still to be developed but which should draw a number of critical perspectives, including the work of Freire and Gramsci.

NOTE

1 One vehicle for this alternative literature was provided by the series of volumes published by Macmillan Press under the general title of Critical Texts in Social Work and the Welfare State. The series was edited by Peter Leonard, and the majority of the authors were either members of the Warwick School (staff or students) or associated with the School and its work. The volumes include: Alcock, P. and Harris, P. (1982) *Welfare Law and Order*; Banton, R., Clifford, P., Frosh, S., Lousada, J. and Rosenthall, J. (1985) *The Politics of Mental Health*; Bolger, S., Corrigan, P., Docking, J., and Frost, N. (1981) *Towards Socialist Welfare Work*; Corrigan, P. and Leonard, P. (1978) *Social Work Practice Under Capitalism: A Marxist Approach*; Dominelli, L. and McLeod, E. (1989) *Feminist Social Work*; Ginsburg, N. (1980) *Class, Capital and Social Policy*; Gough, I. (1979) *The Political Economy of the Welfare State*; Jones, C. (1983) *State Social Work and the Working Class*; Joyce, P., Corrigan, P., and Hayes, M. (1988) *Striking Out: Trade Unionism in Social Work*; Leonard, P.

(1984) *Personality and Ideology*; Phillipson, C. (1982) *Capitalism and the Construction of Old Age*.

REFERENCES

Bailey, R. and Brake, M. (eds) (1975) *Radical Social Work*, London, Edward Arnold.

Boggs, C. (1976) *Gramsci's Marxism*, London, Pluto Press.

Cohen, S. (ed.) (1971) *Images of Deviance*, Harmondsworth, Penguin.

Eichenbaum, L. and Orbach, S. (1982) *Outside In Inside Out: Women's Pscyhology. A Feminist Psychoanalytic Approach*, Harmondsworth, Penguin.

Freire, P. (1970a) *Pedagogy of the Oppressed*, Harmondsworth, Penguin.

Freire, P. (1970b) *Cultural Action for Freedom*, Harmondsworth, Penguin.

Gramsci, A. (1971) *Selections from the Prison Notebooks*, London, Lawrence & Wishart.

Habermas, J. (1976) *Legitimation Crisis*, London, Heinemann.

Hall, S., Critcher, C., Clarke, J., and Roberts, B. (1978) *Policing the Crisis: Mugging, the State and Law and Order*, London, Macmillan.

Leonard, P. (1964) 'Depression and family failure,' *British Journal of Psychiatric Social Work*, VII(4), 191–7.

Leonard, P. (1966a) 'The place of scientific method in social work education,' *Case Conference* (UK) 13(5), 163–8.

Leonard, P. (1966b) *Sociology in Social Work*, London, Routledge & Kegan Paul.

Leonard, P. (1975) 'Towards a paradigm of radical practice,' pp. 46–61 in Bailey, R. and Brake, M. (eds) *Radical Social Work*, London, Edward Arnold.

Leonard, P. (1984) *Personality and Ideology*, London, Macmillan Press.

London–Edinburgh Weekend Return Group (1980) *In and Against the State*, London, Pluto Press.

Séve, L. (1978) *Man in Marxist Theory and the Psychology of Personality*, Brighton, Harvester Press.

Taylor, I. and Taylor, L. (eds) (1973) *Politics and Deviance*, Harmondsworth, Penguin.

9

A DIALOGUE WITH PAULO FREIRE

Paulo Freire and Donaldo Macedo

The contributing authors in this volume have all raised important and pertinent issues that need to be addressed rigorously and reflectively. To do so, however, would mean writing one or two more books in order to do justice to the complexity of the problems delineated by these authors. Obviously we will not be able to undertake such an ambitious task due to both time and space constraints. What we would like to do is to address a recurring challenge of Freirean pedagogy concerning its treatment of gender.

Macedo: Some educators, particularly North American feminists, argue that your work tends to universalize oppression while ignoring the historical specificities of diverse and contradictory positions that characterize subordinate groups along the lines of culture, ethnicity, language, race and gender. In particular, some feminists point out that your failure to address these historical specificities reveals 'the shortcomings that emerge in the attempt to enact a pedagogy that assumes a universal experience and abstract goals' (Weiler in press, p. 11). Weiler argues that 'like Freirean pedagogy, feminist pedagogy is grounded in a vision of social change. And, like Freirean pedagogy, feminist pedagogy rests on truth claims of the primacy of experience and consciousness that are grounded in historically situated social change movements' (p. xx). She further contends that some feminist critics feel, for instance, that you have failed 'to address the various forms of power held by teachers depending on their race, gender, and the historical and institutional settings in which they work' (p. 18).

Paulo, you have shared with me in various conversations that since the publication of *Pedagogy of the Oppressed* you periodically receive letters from some feminists who contend that, although your books and your theories deal with oppression and the need for social transformation so as to end all forms of domination, you tend to relegate the issue of gender to a minor position. Some of these feminists point out that not only do you not give primacy to the issue of gender, but the very language that you use, particularly in *Pedagogy of the Oppressed*, is sexist in nature. They also point out that your goals for liberation and social and political transformation are embedded in universals that, at some level, negate both your own position of privilege as an intellectual man and the specificity of experiences which characterize conflicts among oppressed groups in general. That is to say, in theorizing about oppression as universal truth you fail to appreciate the different historical locations of oppression. For example, a black man, although oppressed, still enjoys a privileged position *vis-à-vis* a black female. For this reason you need to take into consideration that these different levels of oppression necessitate a specific analysis with a different focus that calls for a different pedagogy. An emancipatory feminist pedagogy must also, as Gary Olson argues

> reject the kind of popular feminism championed principally by 'Western white women' – the kind that posits patriarchy as the principal form of domination while ignoring race and class, the kind that frames gender relations in a simplistic us/them binary. Such a modernist, totalizing conception of gender power relations is not in keeping with the type of poststructuralist feminism championed expecially by women of color, lesbians, and poor and working-class women and that attempts to challenge the essentialism, separatism, and ethnocentricism that have been expressed in feminist theorizing over the last several decades.
>
> (Olson 1992)

Can you comment on these issues?

Freire: I believe that the question feminists in the United States raise concerning my treatment of gender in *Pedagogy of the Oppressed* is not only valid but very timely. Given the seriousness and the complexity of the gender issue, it merits reflection in conjunction with a rigorous analysis regarding the phenomenon of oppression. It also requires new pedagogical practices so as to achieve the dream of the struggle for liberation and the victory over all forms of oppression.

Early in my youth I began to feel the pain of oppression in my country. I felt all forms of discriminatory expression ranging from the most vulgar racial oppression to the criminal theft that characterizes the unconscious appropriation of the national resources from the dispossessed class by the ruling élite to gender discrimination. Ever since the time when I was touched by the discriminatory practices that were part and parcel of the social landscape in which I was socialized, I felt angry. For example, when a black servant was verbally abused by the white ruling-class discourse – a discourse that often reflected psychological violence while profiling blacks as subhumans, almost animal-like creatures. In fact, it is safe to say that, in some cases, domestic pets received better treatment by the society than the unprotected, subordinated blacks.

It was during my twenties that the verbal violence against blacks alerted my consciousness to the degree that I began not only to understand that the Brazilian society was profoundly racist and unjust but this injustice provoked in me a sense of revolt and disgust. This awareness that began to take root, as I said during my twenties, radicalized me to take a very critical position against all forms of discrimination and expressions of oppression, including the oppressive position to which Brazilian women, particularly women of color, were relegated. But to be honest, at that time I was first and foremost struck by class and racial oppression. Being a product of the Brazilian Northeast region, a highly patriarchal and *machista* society, I became also, in my early developmental years, a victim of a cultural context that systematically discriminated against women. I say victim because within this framework of sexism, my sensitivities against oppression were most predominant along the lines of class and race. It is precisely through the anger which class and race oppression produce in me that I began to open my eyes more sharply towards the total subordination of women in this highly patriarchial cultural milieu which is Northeast Brazil.

It is with great satisfaction that I admit that my engagement with the feminist movements led me to take a sharper focus on the issues of gender. For this, I am indebted to the North American feminists who called gender discrimination to my attention on numerous occasions. It was during the 1970s, after the publication of *Pedagogy of the Oppressed*, that I began to reflect more profoundly and learn more systematically from the work of the feminists. After the publication of *Pedagogy of the Oppressed* I received a few letters criticizing my sexist language from some North American feminists. In fact, I received not long ago a letter from a young woman who recently came across *Pedagogy of the Oppressed* for the first time, criticizing my *machista* language. This letter was very insulting and somewhat vulgar but I was not upset by it. I was not upset by her letter because, most certainly, she has only read *Pedagogy of the Oppressed* and evaluated my language as if this book were written last year. That is, she did not contextualize *Pedagogy of the Oppressed* in its historical context. But do not misunderstand me: I am not making any excuse for the sexist language of this book. I am just pointing out that during my formative years I did not escape the enveloping powers of a highly sexist culture in my country. However, since the publication of *Pedagogy of the Oppressed* I have attempted to rid my language of all those features that are demeaning to women. I have insisted that my English translators pay close attention and present my work in a non-sexist English. If this young woman were to read, for example, *The Politics of Education* which you, Donaldo, translated – you remember my insistence about the avoidance of sexist language – and *Literacy: Reading the Word and the World*, which we co-authored, she would see a marked difference in language use.

Let us now turn to the central issue of sexism. During the 1970s when

I began to learn with the feminists, particularly North American feminists, I must say that I was, at that time, mostly influenced by Marxist analysis, particularly the analysis of class. When I wrote *Pedagogy of the Oppressed* I was so influenced by Marx's class analysis, and given the incredibly cruel class oppression that characterized my developing years in Northeast Brazil, my major preoccupation was, therefore, class oppression. It is ironic that some Marxists even criticised me for not paying enough attention to social class analysis. In *Pedagogy of the Oppressed*, if my memory serves me correctly, I made approximately thirty-three references to social class analysis.

It was exactly because of my preoccupation with the process of transformation of the world which included obviously the struggle of women, the *reivindicação das muheres*, that led me to focus on what I believed to be mainly a class issue. I believed that this word *transformation* implied a bit of interest in class more so than individual or sex interest. In other words, liberation should take place for both men and women and not just for men or for women or along color and ethnic lines.

Macedo: Paulo, but here lies the problem of overgeneralizing oppression and liberation. In other words, one would have to identify the specificity and location of oppression within an historical moment. You need to appreciate that both black women and black men are oppressed by the white class but within this oppressive structure the position of the black man differs somewhat from that of the black woman. That is, the black woman experiences not only white racism but also male domination.

Freire: But I do not disagree with that position.

Macedo: Yes, but the criticism leveled against your work, particularly your position concerning gender in *Pedagogy of the Oppressed* raises the issue that you universalize oppression without appreciating the multiplicity of oppressive experiences that characterized the lived histories of individuals along race, gender, ethnic, and religious lines. For this reason, a critical pedagogy must address these specificities of oppression so as to create the necessary pedagogical structures for liberation. You cannot assume that by eradicating racism, black women will automatically or magically cease to experience male oppression. The sad fact remains that the asymmetrical power position to which a black woman is relegated by her male counterpart is not at all affected by the erasure of racist structures.

Freire: Without avoiding the issue of gender I must say that readers have some responsibility to place my work within its historical and cultural context. That is, the person reading *Pedagogy of the Oppressed* as if it were written yesterday, somehow denies its historicity. What I find absurd is to read a book like *Pedagogy of the Oppressed* and criticize it because the author did not treat all of the potential oppressive themes equally. I believe that what one needs to do is to appreciate the contribution of the work within its historical context. That I was not as acutely aware of issues of gender as I wrote *Pedagogy of the Oppressed* is an absolute fact. It is equally an absolute fact that the knowledge base with respect to gender oppression we have today, thanks to the great and comprehensive works of feminists, was not available to me then nor was it available to many women. I feel that, if I were to write *Pedagogy of the Oppressed* today and ignore the immense world of information regarding sex discrimination and the level of awareness concerning sexism that both men and women have today, some of the criticism leveled against *Pedagogy of the Oppressed* would not only be valid but would be most necessary. What I would like to think is that, without wanting to universalize oppression, I did make some positive contributions to the understanding of oppressive structures and that this understanding did also contribute to the struggle of all women in their rightful quest for equality and liberation.

I believe that there are specificities in oppression without a doubt. It is interesting. For example, the other day I was making references to the mayor of São Paulo, an extraordinary woman who is also from Northeast Brazil. In a television interview she gave recently she said: 'To be a woman in Brazil is very difficult – To be a woman mayor of São Paulo is something even more difficult, particularly if this woman is from the Northeast region of Brazil.' That is, she is first discriminated against in her condition as woman and second in her position as a woman from the Northeast. She then added: 'My difficulty as a woman mayor would be correspondingly worse if I were black and a peasant.'

Macedo: This example you just cited captures the spirit of the criticism leveled against your work. That is to say, there exists a hierarchical structure of oppression that ranges from being a white middle-class woman to an underclass black woman who may also be a peasant.

Freire: Exactly, I do not disagree.

Macedo: You need to appreciate the fact that as a man from Northeast Brazil you would experience less discrimination than the present mayor is experiencing in her capacity as a woman from your region. Your male position privileges you to certain social acceptances which are denied her.

Freire: As I said, I do not disagree with this position. However, let me ask the following question: In what ways do these specificities alter the analysis of oppression and its relations in *Pedagogy of the Oppressed*?

Macedo: I am not sure that these criticisms claim that the specificities of oppression alter your analysis of oppression and its relations. What we need to do is to understand the fact that the different historical locations of oppression necessitate a specific analysis with a different and unique focus that calls also for a different pedagogy.

173

Freire: If you consider both men and women from Northeast Brazil, it is evident that they are more discriminated against than men and women from São Paulo. A woman from São Paulo has a more privileged condition than a woman from the Northeast. For me, one of the fundamental tactical problems in the struggle for transformation is to see how, even in view of the differences, the oppressed assume their position as such and join their forces to effectively and successfully confront a greater enemy. What I want to say is that we need to create structures of collective struggle in which the women from the Northeast who are the most discriminated against begin to learn to join forces with the less-discriminated-against women from São Paulo in a collective struggle against a greater oppression perpetrated against all women. We need to understand the extent to which the oppressed men in the Northeast will also learn to join forces with the women from the same region to struggle towards the eradication of those sociopolitical structures that have relegated both of them to a highly discriminated position.

Macedo: The joining of forces could only take place when the women from the Northeast cease to experience subordination with respect to the men of their social and cultural milieu.

Freire: For me the correct pedagogical practice is for feminists to understand the different levels of male oppression, while at the same time creating pedagogical structures in which men will have to confront their oppressive position. I believe that it is not enough for women to liberate themselves from the oppression of men who are in turn oppressed by the society as a whole, but that together they simultaneously move toward cutting the chains of oppression. Obviously, both these oppressed men and women need to understand their different positions in the oppressive structures so that together they can develop effective strategies and cease to be oppressed.

It may be the case that some will accuse me of being naïve. I do not believe that I am being naïve. I think that, whenever possible, the pessimists need to rectify the sexist behavior of men who are also oppressed by making them assume their position as oppressed so that, in the process, these men will also recognize their role as oppressors of women as well. And in turn, these oppressed men, by maintaining certain coherence in their struggle of liberation, will have to renounce their role as oppressors of women. I believe that through this process the struggle for liberation would envelop a collective war against all oppression. If the oppressed women choose to fight exclusively against the oppressed men when they are both in the category of oppressed, they may rupture the oppressor–oppressed relations specific to both women and men. If this is done, the struggle will only be partial and perhaps tactically incorrect.

It is for this reason that one day while at the University of London during

174

the 1970s, a person raised the issue of gender in a debate to which I gave a shocking answer. I repeated this same answer years later in Brazil where I shocked incredibly the macho egos that predominate in my country. I said: 'I am too a woman.' That is to say, this affirmation was not sexual but was an eminently political statement. What I would like to make very clear, even if my feminist friends do not agree, is that the concept of the gender struggle is political and not sexual. I do not want to have an antagonistic relationship with women. But it is possible that I may need to be reprimanded by women. If that is the case, I deserve it and I accept it. I do recognize the sexual differences which positions both men and women in different oppressive locations, but for me, the fundamental issue is the political vision of sex, and not the sexist vision of sex. What is at stake is liberation and the creation of liberatory structures which is the overriding issue for both men and women.

Macedo: But, Paulo, you must recognize that there are various levels of liberation.

Freire: Exactly. These levels require different tactics. In life you will not be able to accomplish much without establishing tactics with an eye towards strategies. For me the problem is the following: What is the strategy of the struggle of the oppressed? It is the Utopia of liberty that severs the chains of oppression. This should be the dream of the struggle for liberation that never reaches a plenitude. In other words, when you achieve some freedom you discover, in the process, that you need more liberation. Then, my basic strategy would have to be this Utopia of freedom, that involves creativity, risks, compassion, political commitment, etc.

Macedo: But Utopia should not undervalue the specificities of oppression.

Freire: Obviously. In fact, in certain moments these differences will have to decree tactics that may even appear as not too liberating. For example, let me tell you how I recognize these differences. I remember that in the 1970s, I was discussing in a seminar about the right that women have, in their initial struggle, of not accepting the presence of men during their debates. And why this tactic? It is precisely because of these specificities. That is, in the initial struggle of a group of women to coalesce as a movement, the presence of men should not be permitted precisely because of the *machista* ideology that characterizes most societies, and gives men, at the very minimum, a sarcastic and ironic air with respect to the position of women.

Macedo: Don't forget the power privilege that men enjoy.

Freire: Yes. Precisely. For this reason, they should prohibit the presence of men in their initial debates. However, as their movement takes hold and, in the process of a critical reflection, they should also incorporate men in their struggle. This is the undeniable process of the maturing of the struggle.

You see, during the 1970s the feminist movements did not criticize the treatment of gender in my work. But the feminist movements of the 1990s are being very critical. Why? Because the feminists of the 1990s are now seeing what in the 1970s they were, perhaps, not yet aware of. I think what is wrong is to criticize an author using tools that history had not given him or her. I wrote *Pedagogy of the Oppressed* twenty years ago.

REFERENCES

Freire, P. (1970) *Pedagogy of the Oppressed*, New York, Seabury Press.
—— (1985) *The Politics of Education*, South Hadley, Massachusetts, Bergin & Garvey.
Freire, P. and Macedo, D. (1987) *Literacy: Reading the Word and the World*, South Hadley, Massachusetts, Bergin & Garvey.
Olson, G. (1992) 'Postcolonial discourse and the border intellectual: Henry Giroux and the politics of hope', *Journal of Urban and Cultural Studies* 3.
Weiler, K. (in press) 'Freire and a feminist pedagogy of difference', in P. McLaren and C. Lankshear (eds), *Conscientization and Resistance*, London and New York: Routledge.

10

PAULO FREIRE AND THE POLITICS OF POSTCOLONIALISM[1]

Henry A. Giroux

> Yet we have different privileges and different compensations for our
> positions in the field of power relations. My caution is against a form
> of theoretical tourism on the part of the first world critic, where the
> margin becomes a linguistic or critical vacation, a new poetics of the
> exotic.[2]

The work of Paulo Freire continues to exercise a strong influence on
a variety of liberal and radical educators. In some quarters his name
has become synonymous with the very concept and practice of critical
pedagogy. Increasingly, Freire's work has become the standard reference
for engaging in what is often referred to as teaching for critical thinking,
dialogical pedagogy, or critical literacy. As Freire's work has passed from
the origins of its production in Brazil, through Latin America and Africa
to the hybrid borderlands of North America, it has been frequently
appropriated by academics, adult educators, and others who inhabit the
ideology of the West in ways that often reduce it to a pedagogical
technique or method. Of course, the requisite descriptions generally
invoke terms like 'politically charged,' 'problem-posing,' or the mandatory
'education for critical consciousness' and often contradict the use of
Freire's work as a revolutionary pedagogical practice.[3] But in such a
context, these are terms that speak less to a political project constructed
amidst concrete struggles than they do to the insipid and dreary demands
for pedagogical recipes dressed up in the jargon of abstracted progressive
labels. What has been increasingly lost in the North American and Western
appropriation of Freire's work is the profound and radical nature of its
theory and practice as an anti-colonial and postcolonial discourse. More
specifically, Freire's work is often appropriated and taught 'without any
consideration of imperialism and it cultural representation. This lacuna
suggests the continuing ideological dissimulation of imperialism today.'[4]
This suggests that Freire's work has been appropriated in ways that denude
it of some of its most important political insights. Similarly, it testifies to

how a politics of location works in the interest of privilege and power to cross cultural, political, and textual borders so as to deny the specificity of the other and to reimpose the discourse and practice of colonial hegemony.

I want to argue that Paulo Freire's work must be read as a postcolonial text and that North Americans, in particular, must engage in a radical form of border-crossing in order to reconstruct Freire's work in the specificity of its historical and political construction. Specifically, this means making problematic a politics of location situated in the privilege and power of the West and how engaging the question of the ideological weight of such a position constructs one's specific reading of Freire's work. At the same time, becoming a border-crosser engaged in a productive dialogue with others means producing a space in which those dominant social relations, ideologies, and practices that erase the specificity of the voice of the other must be challenged and overcome.

In order to understand the work of Paulo Freire in terms of its historical and political importance, cultural workers have to become border-crossers. This means that teachers and other intellectuals have to take leave of the cultural, theoretical, and ideological borders that enclose him or her within the safety of 'those places and spaces we inherit and occupy, which frame our lives in very specific and concrete ways.'[5] Being a border-crosser suggests that one has to reinvent traditions not within the discourse of submission, reverence, and repetition, but 'as transformation and critique. [That is] . . . one must construct one's discourse as difference in relation to that tradition and this implies at the same time continuities and discontinuities.'[6] At the same time, border-crossing engages intellectual work not only in its specificity and partiality, but also in terms of the intellectual function itself as part of the discourse of invention and construction, rather than a discourse of recognition whose aim is reduced to revealing and transmitting universal truths. In this case, it is important to highlight intellectual work as being forged in the intersection of contingency and history arising not from the 'exclusive hunting grounds of an elite [but] from all points of the social fabric.'[7]

This task becomes all the more difficult with Paulo Freire because the borders that define his work have shifted over time in ways that parallel his own exile and movement from Brazil to Chile, Mexico, the United States, Geneva, and back to Brazil. Freire's work not only draws heavily upon European discourses, but also upon the thought and language of theorists in Latin America, Africa, and North America. Freire's ongoing political project raises enormous difficulties for educators who situate Freire's work in the reified language of methodologies and in empty calls that enshrine the practical at the expense of the theoretical and political.

Freire is an exile for whom being home is often tantamount to being 'homeless' and for whom his own identity and the identities of Others are viewed as sites of struggle over the politics of representation, the exercise of power, and the function of social memory.[8] It is important to note that the concept of 'home' being used here does not refer exclusively to those places in which one sleeps, eats, raises children, and sustains a certain level of comfort. For some, this particular notion of 'home' is too mythic, especially for those who literally have no home in this sense; it also becomes a reification when it signifies a place of safety which excludes the lives, identities, and experiences of the Other, that is, when it becomes synonymous with the cultural capital of white, middle-class subjects.

'Home', in the sense I am using it, refers to the cultural, social, and political boundaries that demarcate varying spaces of comfort, suffering, abuse, and security that define an individual or group's location and positionality. To move away from 'home' is to question in historical, semiotic, and structural terms how the boundaries and meanings of 'home' are constructed in self-evident ways often outside of criticism. 'Home' is about those cultural spaces and social formations which work hegemonically and as sites of resistance. In the first instance, 'home' is safe by virtue of its repressive exclusions and hegemonic location of individuals and groups outside of history. In the second case, home becomes a form of 'homelessness,' a shifting site of identity, resistance, and opposition that enables conditions of self and social formation. Abdul JanMohammed captures this distinction quite lucidly:

> 'Home' comes to be associated with 'culture' as an environment, process, and hegemony that determine individuals through complicated mechanisms. Culture is productive of the necessary sense of belonging, of 'home;' it attempts to suture . . . collective and individual subjectivity. But culture is also divisive, producing boundaries that distinguish the collectivity and what lies outside it and that define hierarchic organizations within the collectivity. 'Homelessness,' on the other hand, is . . . an enabling concept . . . associated with . . . the civil and political space that hegemony cannot suture, a space in which 'alternative acts and alternative intentions' which are not yet articulated as a social institution or even project can survive. 'Homelessness,' then, is a situation where utopian potentiality can endure.[9]

For Freire, the task of being an intellectual has always been forged within the trope of homelessness: between different zones of theoretical and cultural differences; between the borders of non-European and European cultures. In effect, Freire is a border intellectual,[10] whose allegiance has not been to a specific class and culture as in Gramsci's notion of the organic intellectual; instead, Freire's writings embody a mode of discursive struggle and opposition that not only challenges the oppressive machinery of the state but is also sympathetic to the formation of new cultural subjects and movements engaged in the struggle over the modernist values of freedom, equality, and justice. In part, this explains Freire's interest for educators, feminists, and revolutionaries in Africa, Latin America, and South Africa.

As a border intellectual, Freire ruptures the relationship between individual identity and collective subjectivity. He makes visible a politics that links human suffering with a project of hope, not as a static plunge into a textuality disembodied from human struggles, but as a politics of literacy forged in the political and material dislocations of regimes that exploit, oppress, expel, maim, and ruin human life. As a border intellectual, Freire occupies a terrain of 'homelessness' in the postmodern sense that suggests there is little possibility of ideological and hegemonic closure, no relief from the incessant tensions and contradictions that inform one's own identity, ideological struggles, and project of possibility. It is this sense of 'homelessness,' this constant crossing over into terrains of Otherness, which characterizes both Freire's life and work. It is as an exile, a border being, an intellectual posed between different cultural, epistemological, and spatial borders that Freire has undertaken to situate his own politics of location as a border-crosser.

It is to Freire's credit as a critical educator and cultural worker that he has always been extremely conscious about the intentions, goals, and effects of crossing borders and how such movements offer the opportunity for new subject positions, identities, and social relations that can produce resistance to and relief from the structures of domination and inequality. While such an insight has continously invested his work with a healthy 'restlessness,' it has not meant that Freire's work has developed unproblematically. For example, in his earlier work, Freire attempted to reconcile an emancipatory politics of literacy and a struggle over identity and difference, with certain problematic elements of modernism. Freire's incessant attempts to construct a new language, produce new spaces of resistance, imagine new ends and opportunities to reach them were sometimes constrained in totalizing narratives and binarisms that de-emphasized the mutually contradictory and multiple character of domination and struggle. In this sense, Freire's earlier reliance on emancipation as one and the same with class struggle sometimes erased how women were subjected differently to patriarchal structures; similarly, his call for members of the dominating groups to commit class suicide downplayed the complex, multiple, and contradictory nature of human subjectivity. Finally, Freire's reference to the 'masses' or oppressed as being inscribed in a culture of silence appeared to be at odds with both the varied forms of domination these groups labored under and Freire's own belief in the diverse ways in which the oppressed struggle and manifest elements of practical and political agency. While it is crucial to acknowledge the theoretical and political brilliance that informed much of this work, it is also necessary to recognize that it bore slight traces of vanguardism. This is evident not only in the binarism that informs *Pedagogy of the Oppressed* but also in *Pedagogy in Process: The Letters to Guinea-Bissau*, particularly in those sections where Freire argues that the culture of the masses must develop on the basis of science and that emancipatory pedagogy must be aligned with the struggle for national reconstruction.

Without adequately addressing the contradictions these issues raise between the objectives of the state, the discourse of everyday life, and the potential for pedagogical violence being done in the name of political correctness, Friere's work is open to the charge made by some leftist theorists of being overly totalizing. But this can be read less as a reductive critique of Freire's work than as an indication of the need to subject it and all forms of social criticism to analyses that engage its strengths and limitations as part of a wider dialogue in the service of an emancipatory politics. The contradictions raised in Freire's work offer a number of questions that need to be addressed by critical educators about not only Freire's earlier work but also their own. For instance, what happens when the language of the educator is not the same as that of the oppressed? How is it possible to be vigilant against taking up a notion of language, politics, and rationality that undermines recognizing one's own partiality and the voices and experiences of Others? How does one explore the contradiction between validating certain forms of 'correct' thinking and the pedagogical task of helping students assume rather than simply follow the dictates of authority, regardless of how radical the project informed by such authority? Of course, it cannot be forgotten that the strength of Freire's early discourse rests, in part, with its making visible not merely the ideological struggle against domination and colonialism but also the material substance of human suffering, pain, and imperialism. Forged in the heat of life and death struggles, Freire's recourse to binarisms such as the oppressed vs. the oppressor, problem-solving vs. problem-posing, science vs. magic, raged bravely against dominant languages and configurations of power that refused to address their own politics by appealing to the imperatives of politeness, objectivity, and neutrality. Here Freire strides the boundary between modernist and anti-colonialist discourse; he struggles against colonialism, but in doing so he often reverses rather than ruptures its basic problematic. Benita Parry locates a similar problem in the work of Frantz Fanon: 'What happens is that heterogeneity is repressed in the monolithic figures and stereotypes of colonialist representations. . . . [But] the founding concepts of the problemlatic must be refused.'[11]

In his later work, particularly in his work with Donaldo Macedo, in his numerous interviews, and in his talking books with authors such as Ira Shor, Antonio Faundez, and Myles Horton, Freire undertakes a form of social criticism and cultural politics that pushes against those boundaries that invoke the discourse of the unified, humanist subject, universal historical agents, and Enlightenment rationality.[12] Refusing the privilege of home as a border intellectual situated in the shifting and ever-changing universe of struggle, Freire invokes and constructs elements of a social criticism that shares an affinity with emancipatory strands of postmodern discourse. That is, in his refusal of a transcendent ethics, epistemological foundationalism, and political teleology, he further develops a provisional ethical and political discourse subject to the play of history, culture, and power. As a border intellectual, he constantly re-examines and raises questions about what kind of borders are being crossed and revisited, what kind of identities are being remade and refigured within new historical, social, and political borderlands, and what effects such crossings have for redefining pedagogical practice. For Freire, pedagogy is seen as a cultural practice and politics that takes place not only in schools but in all cultural spheres. In this instance, all cultural work is pedagogical and cultural workers inhabit a number of sites that include but are not limited to schools. Most recently in a dialogue with Antonio Faundez, Freire talks about his own self-formation as an exile and border-crosser. He writes:

> It was by travelling all over the world, it was by travelling through Africa, it was by travelling through Asia, through Australia and New Zealand, and through the islands of the South Pacific, it was by travelling through the whole of Latin America, the Caribbean, North America and Europe – it was by passing through all these different parts of the world as an exile that I came to understand my own country better. It was by seeing it from a distance, it was by standing back from it, that I came to understand myself better. It was by being confronted with another self that I discovered more easily my own identity. And thus I overcame the risk which exiles sometimes run of being too remote in their work as intellectuals from the most real, most concrete experiences, and of being somewhat lost, and even somewhat contented, because they are lost in a game of words, what I usually rather humorously call 'specializing in the ballet of concepts.'[13]

It is here that we get further indications of some of the principles that inform Freire as a revolutionary. It is in this work and his work with Donaldo Macedo, Ira Shor, and others that we see traces, images, and representations of a political project that are inextricably linked to Freire's own self-formation. It is here that Freire is at his most prescient in unraveling and dismantling ideologies and structures of domination as they emerge in his confrontation with the ongoing exigencies of daily life as manifested differently in the tensions, suffering, and hope between the diverse margins and centers of power that have come to characterize a postmodern/postcolonial world.

Reading Freire's work for the last fifteen years has drawn me closer to Adorno's insight that, 'It is part of mortality not to be at home in one's home.'[14] Adorno was also an exile, raging against the horror and evil of another era, but he was also insistent that it was the role of intellectuals, in part, to challenge those places bounded by terror, exploitation, and human suffering. He also called for intellectuals to refuse and transgress those systems of standardization, commodification, and administration pressed into the service of an ideology and language of 'home' that occupied or were complicitous with oppressive centers of power. Freire differs from Adorno in that there is a more profound sense of rupture, transgression, and hope, intellectually and politically, in his work. This is evident in his call for educators, social critics, and cultural workers to fashion a notion of politics and pedagogy outside of established disciplinary borders; outside of the division between high and popular culture; outside of 'stable notions of self and identity . . . based on exclusion and secured by terror;'[15] outside of homogeneous public spheres; and outside of boundaries that separate desire from rationality, the body from the mind.

Of course, this is not to suggest that intellectuals have to go into exile to take up Freire's work, but it does suggest that in becoming border-crossers, it is not uncommon for many of them to engage his work as an act of bad faith. Refusing to negotiate or deconstruct the borders that define their own politics of location, they have little sense of moving into an 'imagined space,' a positionality, from which they can unsettle, disrupt, and 'illuminate that which is no longer home-like, *heimlich*, about one's home.'[16] From the comforting perspective of the colonizing gaze, such theorists often appropriate Freire's work without engaging its historical specificity and ongoing political project. The gaze in this case becomes self-serving and self-referential, its principles shaped by technical and methodological considerations. Its perspective, in spite of itself, is largely 'panoptic and thus dominating.'[17] To be sure, such intellectuals cross borders less as exiles than as colonialists. Hence, they often refuse to hold up to critical scrutiny their own complicity in producing and maintaining specific injustices, practices, and forms of oppression that deeply inscribe the legacy and heritage of colonialism. Edward Said captures the tension between exile and critic, home and 'homelessness' in his comment on Adorno, though it is just as applicable to Paulo Freire:

To follow Adorno is to stand away from 'home' in order to look at it with the exile's detachment. For there is considerable merit in the practice of noting the discrepancies between various concepts and ideas and what they actually produce. We take home and language for granted; they become nature and their underlying assumptions recede into dogma and orthodoxy. The exile knows that in a secular and contingent world, homes are always provisional. Borders and barriers, which enclose us within the safety of familiar territory can also become prisons, and are often defended beyond reason or necessity. Exiles cross borders, break barriers of thought and experience.[18]

Of course, intellectuals from the First World, especially white academics, run the risk of acting in bad faith when they appropriate the work of a Third World intellectual such as Paulo Freire without 'mapping the politics of their forays into other cultures,'[19] theoretical discourses, and historical experiences. It is truly disconcerting that First World educators rarely articulate the politics and privileges of their own location, in this case, so at the very least to be self-conscious about not repeating the type of appropriations that inform the legacy of what Edward Said calls 'Orientalist' scholarship.[20]

I want to conclude by raising some issues regarding what it might mean for cultural workers to resist the recuperation of Freire's work as an academic commodity, a recipe for all times and places. Similarly, I want to offer some broad considerations for reinventing the radicality of Freire's work within the emergence of a postcolonial discourse informed by what Cornel West terms the 'decolonization of the Third World, [and characterized by] the exercise of . . . agency and the [production of] new . . . subjectivities and identities put forward by those persons who had been degraded, devalued, hunted, and harassed, exploited and oppressed by the European maritime empires.'[21] The challenge presented by Freire and other postcolonial critics offers new theoretical possibilities to address the authority and discourses of those practices wedded to the legacy of a colonialism that either directly constructs or is implicated in social relations that keep privilege and oppression alive as active constituting forces of daily life within the centers and margins of power.

Postcolonial discourses have made clear that the old legacies of the political left, center, and right can no longer be so easily defined. Indeed, postcolonial critics have gone further and provided important theoretical insights into how such discourses either actively construct colonial relations or are implicated in their construction. From this perspective, Robert Young argues that postcolonialism is a dislocating discourse that raises theoretical questions regarding how dominant and radical theories

> have themselves been implicated in the long history of European colonialism – and, above all, the extent to which [they] continue to determine both the institutional conditions of knowledge as well as the terms of contemporary institutional practices – practices which extend beyond the limits of the academic institution.[22]

This is especially true for many of the theorists in a variety of social movements who have taken up the language of difference and a concern for the politics of the Other. In many instances, theorists within these new social movements have addressed political and pedagogical issues through the construction of binary oppositions that not only contain traces of racism and theoretical vanguardism but also fall into the trap of simply reversing the old colonial legacy and problematic of oppressed vs. oppressor. In doing so, they have often unwittingly imitated the colonial model of erasing the complexity, complicity, diverse agents, and multiple situations that constitute the enclaves of colonial/hegemonic discourse and practice.[23]

Postcolonial discourses have both extended and moved beyond the parameters of this debate in a number of ways. First, postcolonial critics have argued that the history and politics of difference is often informed by a legacy of colonialism that warrants analyzing the exclusions and repressions that allow specific forms of privilege to remain unacknowledged in the language of Western educators and cultural workers. At stake here is the task of demystifying and deconstructing forms of privilege that benefit maleness, whiteness, and property as well as those conditions that have disabled others to speak in places where those who are privileged by virtue of the legacy of colonial power assume authority and the conditions for human agency. This suggests, as Gayatri Spivak has pointed out, that more is at stake than problematizing discourse. More importantly, educators and cultural workers must be engaged in 'the unlearning of one's own privilege. So that, not only does one become able to listen to that other constituency, but one learns to speak in such a way that one will be taken seriously by that other constituency.'[24] In this instance, postcolonial discourse extends the radical implications of difference and location by making such concepts attentive to providing the grounds for forms of self-representation and collective knowledge in which the subject *and* object of European culture are problematized.[25]

Second, postcolonial discourse rewrites the relationship between the margin and the center by deconstructing the colonialist and imperialist ideologies that structure Western knowledge, texts, and social practices. In this case, there is an attempt to demonstrate how European culture and colonialism 'are deeply implicated in each other.'[26] This suggests more than rewriting or recovering the repressed stories and social memories of the Other: it means understanding and rendering visible how Western knowledge is encased in historical and institutional structures that both privilege and exclude particular readings, particular voices, certain aesthetics, forms of authority, specific representations, and modes of sociality. The West and Otherness relate not as polarities or binarisms in postcolonial discourse but in ways in which both are complicitous and resistant, victim and accomplice. In this instance, criticism of the dominating Other returns as a form of self-criticism. Linda Hutcheon captures the importance of this issue with her question: 'How do we construct a discourse which displaces the effects of the colonizing gaze while we are still under its influence?'[27] While it cannot be forgotten that the legacy of colonialism has meant large-scale death and destruction as well as cultural imperialism for the Other, the Other is not merely the opposite of Western colonialism, nor is the West a homogeneous trope of imperialism. This suggests a third rupture provided by postcolonial discourses. The current concern with the 'death of the subject' cannot be confused with the necessity of affirming the complex and contradictory character of human agency. Postcolonial discourse reminds us that it is ideologically convenient and politically suspect of Western intellectuals to talk about the disappearance of the speaking subject from with institutions of privilege and power. This is not to suggest that postcolonial theorists accept the humanist notion of the subject as a unified and static identity. On the contrary, postcolonial discourse agrees that the speaking subject must be decentered but this does not mean that all notions of human agency and social change must be dismissed. Understood in these terms, the postmodernist notion of the subject must be accepted and modified in order to extend rather than erase the possibility for creating the enabling conditions for human agency. At the very least, this would mean coming to understand the strengths and limits of practical reason, the importance of affective investments, the discourse of ethics as a resource for social vision, and the availability of multiple discourses and cultural resources that provide the very grounds and necessity for agency.[28]

Of course, while the burden of engaging these postcolonial concerns must be taken up by those who appropriate Freire's work, it is also necessary for Freire to be more specific about the politics of his own location and what the emerging discourses of postmodernism and post-colonialism mean for self-reflectively engaging both his own work and his current location as an intellectual aligned with the state (Brazil). If Freire has the right to draw upon his own experiences, how do these get reinvented so as to prevent their incorporation by First World theorists within colonialist rather than decolonizing terms and practices? But in raising that question, I want to emphasize that what makes Freire's work important is that it does not stand still. It is not a text for but against cultural monumentalism, one that offers itself up to different readings, audiences, and contexts. Moreover, Freire's work has to be read in its totality to gain a sense of how it has engaged the postcolonial age. Freire's work cannot be separated from either its history or its author, but it also cannot be reduced to the specificity of intentions or historical location. Maybe the power and forcefulness of Freire's works are to be found here in the tension, poetry, and politics that make it a project for border-crossers, those who read history as a way of reclaiming power and identity by rewriting that space and practice of cultural and political resistance. Freire's work represents a textual borderland where poetry slips into politics, and solidarity becomes a song for the present begun in the past while waiting to be heard in the future.

NOTES

1 This chapter draws from a chapter in Henry A. Giroux and Donaldo Macedo, *Paulo Freire: History, Pedagogy, and Struggle* (University of Minnesota Press, forthcoming).
2 Caren Kaplan, 'Deterritorializations: the rewriting of home and exile in Western feminist discourse,' *Cultural Critique* 6 (Spring 1987), p. 191.
3 An excellent analysis of this problem among Freire's followers can be found in Gail Stygall, 'Teaching Freire in North America,' *Journal of Teaching Writing* (1988), pp. 113–25.
4 Robert Young, *White Mythologies: Writing History and the West* (New York: Routledge, 1990), p. 158.
5 Joan Borsa, 'Towards a politics of location,' *Canadian Women Studies* (Spring 1990), p. 36.
6 Ernesto Laclau quoted in: *Strategies* Collective, 'Building a new left: an interview with Ernesto Laclau,' *Strategies*, no. 1 (1988), p. 12.
7 *Strategies* Collective, 'Building a new left,' p. 27.
8 My use of the terms exile and 'homelessness' have been deeply influenced by the following essays: Carol Becker, 'Imaginative geography,' School of the Art Institute of Chicago, unpublished paper, 1991, 12 pp.; Abdul JanMohammed, 'Worldliness-without world, homelessness-as-home: toward a definition of border intellectual,' University of California, Berkeley, unpublished paper, 34 pp.; Edward Said, 'Reflections on exile,' in Russell Ferguson, Martha Gever, Trinh T. Minh-ha and Cornel West (eds) *Out There: Marginalization and Contemporary Cultures* (New York, New Museum of Contemporary Art and MIT Press, 1990); Biddy Martin and Chandra Talpade Mohanty, 'Feminist politics: what's home got to do with it?' in Teresa de Lauretis (ed.) *Feminist Studies/Critical Studies* (Bloomington, Indiana University Press, 1986); Kaplan, 'Deterritorializations,' pp. 187–98; see also selected essays in bell hooks, *Talking Back* (Boston, South End Press, 1989), and bell hooks, *Yearning* (Boston, South End Press, 1990).
9 JanMohammed, 'Worldliness-without world, homelessness-as-home,' p. 27.
10 I have taken this term from JanMohamed, 'Worldliness–without world, homelessness-as-home,' p. 27.
11 Benita Parry, 'Problems in current theories of colonial discourse,' *The Oxford Literary Review*, 9 (1987), p. 28.
12 See, for example, Paulo Freire, *The Politics of Education* (New York: Bergin & Garvey, 1985); Paulo Freire and Donaldo Macedo, *Literacy: Reading the Word and the World* (New York: Bergin & Garvey, 1987); Paulo Freire and Ira Shor, *A Pedagogy for Liberation* (London, Macmillan, 1987); Myles Horton and Paulo Freire, *We Make the Road by Walking: Conversations in Education and Social Change*, eds Brenda Bell, John Gaventa, and John Peters (Philadelphia, Temple University Press, 1990).
13 Paulo Freire quoted in Paulo Freire and Antonio Faundez, *Learning to Question: A Pedagogy of Liberation* (New York, Continuum, 1989), p. 13.
14 Adorno cited in Said, 'Reflections on exile,' p. 365.
15 Martin and Mohanty, 'Feminist politics,' p. 197.
16 Becker, 'Imaginative geography,' p. 1.
17 JanMohamed, 'Worldliness-without world, homelessness-as-home,' p. 10.
18 Said, 'Reflections on exile,' p. 365.
19 JanMohamed, 'Worldliness-without world, homelessness-as-home,' p. 3.
20 Edward W. Said, *Orientalism* (New York, Vantage Books, 1979).

21 Cornel West, 'Decentring Europe: a memorial lecture for James Snead,' *Critical Inquiry* 33(1) (1991), p. 4.
22 Robert Young, *White Mythologies: Writing History and the West* (New York, Routledge, 1990), p. viii.
23 For an excellent discussion of these issues as they specifically relate to postcolonial theory, see Parry, 'Problems in current theories of colonial discourse,' pp. 27–58; Abdul JanMohamed, *Manichean Aesthetics: The Politics of Literature in Colonial Africa* (Amherst, University of Massachusetts Press, 1983): Gayatri C. Spivak, *The Post-Colonial Critic: Interviews, Strategies, Dialogues*, ed. Sarah Harasym (New York, Routledge, 1990). The ways in which binary oppositions can trap a particular author into the most superficial arguments can be seen in a recent work by Patti Lather. What is so unusual about this text is that its call for openness, partiality, and multiple perspectives is badly undermined by the binarisms which structure its arguments. See Patti Lather, *Getting Smart* (New York, Routledge, 1991).
24 Spivak, *The Post-Colonial Critic*, p. 42.
25 This position is explored in Helen Tiffin, 'Post-Colonialism, Post-Modernism, and the Rehabilitation of Post-Colonial History,' *Journal of Commonwealth Literature* 23(1) (1988), pp. 169–81; Helen Tiffin, 'Post-Colonial Literatures and Counter-Discourse,' *Kunapipi* 9(1) (1987), pp. 17–34.
26 Young, *White Mythologies*, p. 119.
27 Linda Hutcheon, 'Circling the downspout of empire,' in Ian Adam and Helen Tiffin (eds) *Past the Last Post* (Calgary, Canada, University of Calgary Press, 1990), p. 176.
28 I explore this issue in Henry A. Giroux, *Border Crossings: Cultural Workers and the Politics of Education* (New York, Routledge, 1992).

NAME INDEX

189

SUBJECT INDEX